The Age of Charlemagne

General Editor: D. A. BULLOUGH, M.A., F.S.A.(SCOT.),
Professor of Medieval History, Nottingham University

The Age
of Charlemagne

Donald Bullough

Photographs by Edwin Smith

Exeter Books

NEW YORK

Publishers' Note

Where sizes of manuscripts are given in captions, they refer to the sizes of whole pages, except where otherwise stated.

The maps in this volume were drawn specially by Mr. T. Stalker Miller and the ground-plans and sketches by Mr. Godfrey Rubens.

The Publishers would like to express their gratitude for the considerable help provided in the collecting of the illustrations by the Directors and staff of the museums, libraries and photographic agencies which they approached. They would like to acknowledge the following sources: *Plates:* Alberto Luisa, Brescia (1); Giraudon, Paris (4, 76, 80, 84, 85, 86, inside back cover); Hessischen Landesmuseum, Darmstadt (5); Foto Attilio Brisighelli, Udine (7); Atelier Niko Haas, Trier (8); Fotohaus, Westmüller, Linz (9); Trustees of the British Museum, London (12, 23, 54, 55, 63); Bibliothèque Royale de Belgique, Brussels (16, 34); Bibliothèque Nationale, Paris (back of jacket, 18, 20, 38, 53); Gino Mendico, Rome (19); Biblioteca Apostolica Vaticana (22, 61, 64); Valerio Gramignazzi-Serrone, Benevento (24, 25); Carl Pospesch, Kremsmünster (26); Réunion Musée Nat., Versailles (28); Bildarchiv Foto Marburg, Marburg (31, 72, 77); Bulloz, Paris (32, 87); Deutsche Fotothek, Dresden (33); Bodleian Library, Oxford (35); Mr. F. E. de Wilde, Oegstgeest (36, 46); Ann Bredol-Lepper, Aachen (37); Board of Trinity College, Dublin, and photographed by the Green Studio, Dublin (41); Luc Joubert, Paris (inside front cover, 42); Universitetets Oldsaksamling, Oslo (43); Yan, Toulouse (47, 82, 83); Scala, Milan (48); Bayerische Staatsbibliothek, Munich (50); Österreichische Nationalbibliothek, Vienna (58); Radio Times Hulton Picture Library (60); Bibliotheek der Rijksuniversiteit te Utrecht (62); Würtembergische Landesbibliothek, Stuttgart (65); Syndics of the Fitzwilliam Museum, Cambridge (66); Pierpont Morgan Library, New York (67); Photohaus Gebr. Zumbühl, St. Gallen (74); Staatliche Museen, Berlin (78). *Text Illustrations:* Serge Martin, Orléans (1, 2); Österreichische Nationalbibliothek, Vienna (3, 29, 32, 36, 47, 54); Ashmolean Museum, Oxford (4); Cleveland Museum of Art, Cleveland (5); Römische-Germanische Zentralmuseum, Mainz (7, 44, 48); Aartsbisschoppelijk Museum, Utrecht (10); Biblioteca Apostolica Vaticana (11, 13, 30); Bildarchiv Foto Marburg, Marburg (12, 20); André Vergnol, Soissons (14); Bibliothèque Nationale, Paris (15, 27); Giraudon, Paris (16); Staatliche Museen, Berlin (17); Dr. K. Schwarz, Munich (18a, 18b); Fot. G. Chiolini, Pavia, by courtesy of Prof. Adriano Peroni (19); Stiftsbibliothek, St. Gallen (21, 23); Dr. A. Herrnbrodt, Rheinisches Landesmuseum, Bonn (22); Dombibliothek, Cologne (24); Bodleian Library, Oxford (25); Bibliothèque Municipale, Cambrai (26); Bayerische Staatsbibliothek, Munich (28, 31); Trustees of the British Museum, London (33, 35); Ed. Alinari, Rome (39); Luc Joubert, Paris (42); E. Houvet, Chartres (51, 52); Sammlungen Schloss-Ambras, Innsbruck (53).

Finally, Edwin Smith took all the photographs not mentioned above and the Publishers would like to thank Prof. Mutinelli, Director of the Museo, Cividale, Piero Gazzola of the Belle Arti, Verona, and Dr. Falkenstein of the Cathedral, Aachen, for the courtesy and help which they gave him.

Copyright © Paul Elek Productions Ltd 1965

This edition published in USA 1980
by Exeter Books
Distributed by Bookthrift, Inc
New York, New York

ISBN 0-89673-045-X
LC 79-92322

Printed in Hong Kong
by South China Printing Co.

Contents

Preface

Book-titles, like the contents of books, are subject to the dictates of fashion. A title that includes the words ' Life and Times ' is unacceptable today: which is a pity, because ' The Life and Times of Charles the Great ' would probably most accurately indicate the scope and emphasis of this book. The justification for its semi-biographical form and its concentration on (western) Europe will, I hope, emerge sufficiently from the text.

The picture of Charlemagne and his age that is here presented is the result of a number of years' thinking about particular aspects of the period and of trying to make it intelligible and interesting to a succession of undergraduate students. My ideas have been greatly influenced by the teaching and writing of three outstanding scholars: Mr. J. M. Wallace-Hadrill, Professor F. L. Ganshof and Professor Richard Krautheimer, although they will not necessarily find the results of their guidance acceptable. This book would, however, never have been written without an invitation from Mr. Paul Elek and perhaps never finished without his insistence on an early completion-date.

The illustrations are intended as an integral part of the book and not as mere decoration. Wherever possible they show monuments, manuscripts and other objects that have an historical as well as an artistic interest and, with a few exceptions accounted for in the text, they belong to the period covered by the volume. Occasionally it would have been possible to include more appropriate or instructive examples. This defect is not the fault of Miss Moira Johnston who was responsible for gathering the photographs, often under great difficulties, but to the regrettable unco-operativeness of one or two libraries. This makes it the more pleasurable to thank those librarians who went to great trouble to provide photographs of the quality required and of items that could not always be precisely specified; and to thank Mr. Edwin Smith, whose architectural and other photos are as beautiful as they are instructive.

Mr. J. M. Wallace-Hadrill and Mr. Alan Harding generously read the work in manuscript and made a number of pointed and helpful suggestions: I have adopted many of them and would probably have done better to adopt many more. Miss Isabel Geddie re-typed the original manuscript.

I dedicate the book jointly:
to Belinda, who drove me through Carolingian Germany;
to Paul Meyvaert, whose friendship Alcuin would have appreciated.

Edinburgh, *die natali SS. Marcellini et Petri.*

D. A. BULLOUGH

Preface to second edition

Revision and correction of the original (1965) text for the present edition have necessarily been restricted almost entirely to the elimination of misprints and of simple factual errors—the latter mostly pointed out by the excellent copy-editor of F. A. Brockhaus who published a German edition in 1967. At three places, however, more substantial changes which were already made for the German edition have been introduced into the text. Other points on which I would modify my earlier views—without, however, seriously altering my overall interpretation—can be gathered from my '*Europae Pater*: Charlemagne and his achievement in the light of recent scholarship', *English Historical Review*, vol. lxxv (1970), pages 59-105. This same article provides much fuller references to the scholarly literature since 1965 than will be found in the revised 'Bibliography and Notes'.

Nottingham, *die natali S. Birini*

D. A. BULLOUGH

Plates

9

Inside front cover: From ' Chasse of Mumma ' (Saint-Benoit-sur-Loire).
Inside back cover: Detail of diploma relating to the gift of the Forest of Kirnsheim, near Schlettstadt (Alsace), by Charles, dated 14th September 774.
Binding Brass: Monogram of Charles.
Jacket Illustrations:
Front: Statue of Charles, east end of the Church of St. Johann, Münstair in Grisons (Switzerland).
Back: Manuscript page: The Adoration of the Lamb from the Gospels of Saint-Medard-de-Soissons: Paris, Bibliothèque Nationale Lat. 8850, fol 1.

Introductory: modern interpretation and early sources

In 1804, in the aftermath of a revolution that had been dedicated to the 'abolition of feudalism' and the sweeping-away of all that was medieval in French life, Napoleon Bonaparte was proclaimed 'Emperor of the French'. Writers hailed him as 'a reborn Charlemagne', a rôle in which the new Emperor had already cast himself: although as if to emphasize that Charles the Great was only a link in an even longer chain of French history, the design on Napoleon's Imperial robe was based on jewellery found in the tomb of the fifth-century Merovingian king Chilperic. Four decades earlier the German critic and philosopher of history, J. G. von Herder, had lamented Charles' success in imposing upon the Germans an entirely alien culture.

In the later nineteenth century, after the re-unification of Germany under a monarch who himself assumed the Imperial title, Charles' *Germanentum* and warlike spirit were rediscovered and enthusiastically displayed; and even British scholars discussed whether *Karl* ought not to replace *Charles* as the name of a man whose spiritual forbears were Scyld and Beowulf. Nationalist German historians of the 1930s insisted even more strongly on the essential 'German-ness' of *Karl der Grosse* and saw in the Holy Roman Empire that had been brought to an end only in 1806 the precursor of their own 'Thousand-year *Reich*'. Since the Second World War a 'Charles the Great Prize' has been established to be awarded 'for outstanding services to the cause of European unity' and in 1965 Aachen (Aix-la-Chapelle) is the setting of an exhibition arranged under the auspices of the Council of Europe to commemorate Charles and his period, in the eighth-centenary year of his 'canonisation'.

An American writer in recent years has claimed Charles as 'a profound theologian and one of the foremost intellectuals of his age'; a British historian has blamed his Court for 'saddling us with a stilted literary tradition of derivative book-learning which hangs today, in an age of technology, like a millstone around the neck of our educational system'. A Belgian scholar, Professor F. L. Ganshof, whose knowledge of the later eighth and early ninth centuries is unrivalled, believes that he can discern Charles' 'personality as a statesman' behind the recorded events of his reign; Mr. Wallace-Hadrill, an English scholar who is hardly less well qualified to speak, asserts bluntly that 'his personality as a statesman does not and probably never did exist'.

Eleven centuries after his death, then, Charles the Great, *Charlemagne*, *Karl der Grosse*, *Carlomagno* is still capable of arousing passionate feelings and can be claimed as the precursor of and a suitable hero for political and cultural movements of very different kinds. And among professional historians who are not spurred on by propagandist fervour, there is fundamental disagreement over what can be known about the man and his achievement. Why is this? Is it not possible to derive from the contemporary and near-contemporary evidence for his life and age—on which generations of scholars have lavished so much labour and critical acumen—a more or less agreed picture that will survive shifts in the political spectrum and changes in intellectual fashions?

The straight answer to the second question is ' No '. The very fact that Charles is thought to have influenced the development of Western Europe in so many different ways (and subsequently, therefore, of those other regions to which Western Europe sought to export its way of life) means that re-interpretation of his achievement will be natural and inevitable so long as the study of the past is regarded as a mainspring of action in the present and not merely as a dry academic exercise. As Western Europe's place in the world is seen to diminish, Charles too may suffer a diminution in stature—a process that Professor Barraclough for one regards as considerably overdue. But the attempt to place him convincingly in the context of his society and his age will still appeal to those who believe in the autonomy of historical inquiry.

A biography in the modern sense, in which motives, influences and the relation of idea and action are analysed and judged, will never be possible. As Mr. Wallace-Hadrill sternly reminds us: ' We must admit that most of what we want to know for a full picture is missing '. There are no personal documents connected with the man. Even if he had been skilled in expressing himself through the written word (and one of the more obviously trustworthy early statements about him is that he never learnt to write properly), it is unlikely that he would ever have felt impelled to record his private thoughts or reflections on the events of the day: self-revelation and self-analysis are widely indulged in only at a much later date in the West, although St. Augustine's ' Confessions ', which would have been known to the better-educated men who visited Charles' court, offered some sort of model to those struggling with the problem of personal holiness. The twenty-odd surviving letters sent in Charles' name clearly do not preserve his own words and few scholars would be tempted to suppose that any one of them accurately reflects his own ideas rather than those of the writer of the letter and other courtiers. There are not even any well-authenticated early anecdotes (of the kind we have for many late medieval figures) that reveal something of the private as distinct from the public man. Charles is known, if at all, from the picture of his actions and aspirations given by men more or less closely associated with him or who at any rate were familiar with some of the consequences of his actions, and from the individual concessions and injunctions and the general commands that issued from his Court.

With unimportant exceptions, the sources for the history of Charles and of the territories he ruled are in Latin, as indeed they continue to be, within the same region, for many centuries more: in the early part of his life the language of some of them was very close to the popular spoken ' Romance ' of the period (below, p. 41); long before his death it was closer to the standard literary Latin used by, for example, Christian writers of the fourth and fifth centuries and was only the language of a small educated class. Most of the writers, compilers and copyists of these Latin texts were monks or secular clergy, although less exclusively so than was to be the case from the later ninth to the later eleventh century: the consequences of this for the written record of the period are, however, as we shall see, less marked than is commonly imagined.

The essential starting-point of any account of the reigns of Charles and his immediate successors is to be found in the Annals of the period. These are, as the word suggests, consecutive year-by-year summaries of events that seemed of significance to the writer or to the person who had an interest in seeing that a record was kept, with the minimum of comment and no literary pretensions. Natural phenomena and sumptuary displays are noted side-by-side with the ruler's movements or the course of a military expedition, as may be seen from the following

Fig. 1   Stucco work from Germigny-des-Prés.
Musée Historique d'Orléans.

abbreviated translation of an account of the year 798:

A legate came [to the Frankish royal court] from King Alfonso of Galicia and Asturia, Froia by name, who handed over a tent of marvellous beauty. But at Easter-time the *Nordliudi* across the Elbe rose in rebellion and seized the royal legates who at that time were residing among them to dispense justice . . . The king collected an army and defeated them in battle and took hostages. And proceeding to his palace at Aachen, he received a Greek legation sent from Constantinople . . . In this year the star called Mars was not to be seen anywhere in the Heavens (from July in the previous year) until July. The Balearic Islands were plundered by Moors and Saracens. King Alfonso, who had plundered Lisbon, sent his legates Froia and Basiliscus in winter-time to the Lord King with breastplates, mules and Moorish prisoners as evidence of his victory. Then Christmas and Easter were celebrated in this place by the king.

This particular extract comes from the so-called 'Royal Annals', the most elaborate and informative of the whole group. It is now agreed that the earlier sections, from 741 to 793 or shortly before, were a compilation from various sources: these were in particular the briefer entries, or subsequent copies of them, made more or less contemporaneously in the tables used to calculate the date of Easter in some of the major monasteries and churches of the area under Frankish rule. There is also fairly general agreement that the later entries, including the one quoted, were made not long after the year they record. Unlike the unique annals illustrated on page 14 which, exceptionally, are preserved in the form in which they were first written down, the Royal Annals are known only from later, and often altered or incomplete, copies: for this reason among others, there is no agreement about where or under whose guidance they were produced, although the central place given to the monarch and the often detailed account of his activities points to the clergy of the royal court or to some religious community in very close contact with it. The relationship between this comparatively full record and the briefer factual statements that continued to be set down after 793 in various religious communities (and were then often passed on to and copied by others, with or without the introduction of new material of local interest) is much discussed: fortunately, there are only a few occasions—although these admittedly concern some of the most crucial moments in Charles' reign—when the evidence of these so-called 'minor annals' is seriously at variance with that of the Royal Annals or where it is of primary importance to the scholar to decide the degree of authority to be given to a statement not to be found in the more 'official' source. Of greater importance is some of the additional material incorporated in a revised text of the Royal Annals, written shortly after Charles' death; for although the unknown reviser was primarily concerned to improve their literary quality, even if this involved falsifying the original, and to suggest that the king and later Emperor had clearly-formed ambitions in the very early years of his reign, he was not afraid to record in much greater detail some of its less happy moments; and in at least one instance and possibly more he seems to have used a first-hand account supplied by one of the participants.

No contemporary or near-contemporary of Charles, so far as we know, attempted to leave a record of the age in a continuous chronicle written in a more polished style than that used for annals, although the notion of 'history as the reconstruction of the past in literary form' was familiar to some of the scholars at

Fig. 2 Stucco work from
Germigny-des-Prés.
Musée Historique d'Orléans.

his court. The desire to have a record of the 'doings' (*gesta*) of the successive bishops or abbots of an episcopal church or monastery occasionally allows us to see in some detail the involvement of a particular place or community in some of the events of the reign: but this was local and not general history. The work of this kind that has most to tell us about some of the most significant events in Charles' reign comes from outside his dominions proper: the Roman *Liber Pontificalis* or 'Book of the Popes' gives a comparatively detailed account—written shortly after their deaths with the help of records made in their lifetimes—of the careers of the three bishops of the see of Rome during Charles' reign. A number of churchmen of the period, and in particular several who brought Christianity to hitherto un-evangelized regions, were the subject of individual 'Lives'. The authors' purpose was to put them forward as men whose sanctity showed the working of God's grace and who therefore offered examples to others: the influence of the recently-established English tradition of hagiography that had given to them a more factual, narrative and biographic, cast than their traditional counterpart on the Continent is, however, very apparent, and a number of the 'Lives' are by no means negligible as historical sources.

The influence of writings of this kind on the composition of the first 'Life' of Charles, which is also 'the first secular biography of the Middle Ages', is perhaps no more than incidental. When its author Einhard, a layman and a former courtier, began it about the year 830, Charles had already been dead nearly two decades and the Empire that he had created and passed on to his son was already in serious

Fig. 3   Part of a page from the Annals, wrongly called 'of Lorsch', showing the end of the entry for 788 and the beginning of the entry for 799; *Vienna, Österreichische Nationalbibliothek* Cod. 515, fol 3. (*Actual size*)

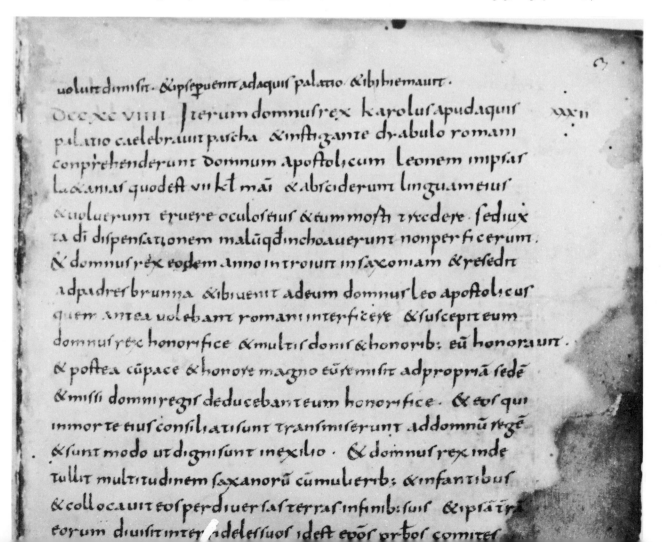

trouble. He accordingly produced a picture of the old Emperor as contemporaries, who were unhappy about the new trends in Frankish affairs, liked or wanted to remember him; and he did so by combining a highly-selective record of his origin and actions—usually based, not very accurately, on the Royal Annals—with an account of the man closely modelled on the ' Lives of the Twelve Caesars ' by the second-century writer Suetonius. The result is none the less a very remarkable and justifiably influential piece of historiography; and because Einhard adapts earlier texts for the description of his hero, it does not follow that Charles had none of the qualities and characteristics attributed to him by his biographer: it means simply that we should beware of regarding Einhard's words as accurate reflections of personal observation. And if the *Vita Karoli* gives us the educated layman's ideal of the great leader, whose outstanding qualities are *magnanimitas* and *constantia* rather than piety and spiritual fervour, this at least may caution us against accepting too easily the more clerical portrait of Charles drawn by other authors.

Only slightly affected by Einhard's method and style are two biographies of Charles' son and successor Louis: the second, written c. 843 by an unnamed writer who was more than usually interested in comets and stars, contains much valuable information about the relations of father and son and about events in the south-western regions of Francia. Nearly half a century later a monk of St. Gallen, probably the schoolmaster and poet Notker, wrote the puzzling *Gesta Karoli Magni* at the request of another Charles (' the Fat ') who, for a short time before his abdication and death in 887/8, managed to reunite almost the whole of Charles the Great's one-time Empire under his nominal authority. The ' doings ' attributed to the earlier Charles seem particularly to have been intended to illustrate how a great monarch handled his clergy and how clergy should behave towards their ruler if he was to serve his people effectively, although an incidental purpose may have been to associate the memory of the Emperor more closely with the monastery. To disregard Notker's gossipy and anecdotal work entirely is as unsound as treating it as a first-hand source for the late eighth century: some of his stories may contain more than a grain of truth as well as a moral. But in general it tells us more about how Charles was remembered than about the man he had been.

We are brought nearer to the events and ideas of Charles' reign, although not necessarily to the personality of the monarch, through the various collections of letters of the period. In 791, to avoid further loss and damage, the texts of the Papal letters still to be found at the Frankish court, in originals or copies, were transcribed into a single volume, the so-called *Codex Carolinus*. This irreplaceable source for the political and ecclesiastical history of the previous half-century survives in a single, ninth-century, copy—a reminder of the tenuous thread on which our knowledge of the period depends. Hardly less important although very different in character are the letters of Alcuin whom Einhard referred to as Charles' teacher (*praeceptor*) and described—in a phrase that goes back to late Antiquity—as ' a man who in any place would have been thought most learned '. A few of the letters are purely personal, conveying the sentiments that may be found in any exchange of correspondence between men who have found friendship in living and working in the same place or share similar interests. A majority have some reference to the conditions of the day as seen by men closely associated with the court and person of Charles. It was not, however, because of the factual information they contained that they were transmitted to posterity. Alcuin observes in one place that he does not blush when using a second time what he has written before and repeating what he has said previously, and it was as models of epistolary style that they were read and copied: one collection (fig. 54) was made by Salzburg clergy as early as 798/9. Letters of several of the correspondents of Alcuin and of other writers of the period are doubtless preserved for the same reason: many of them are of interest to the literary rather than the political historian, but occasionally they throw a graphic light on the problems facing the monarch and the means available for their solution.

The most important sources of information on these topics, however, are to be found in the miscellaneous texts that record administrative commands or acts of legislation or are preliminary to or derived from these and are known collectively as 'capitularies'. In the eighth and early ninth century, the word *capitulare* seems to have been used in a narrower sense, of the edict in which the monarch made known his commands or decisions after discussion with whomsoever he had thought fit to consult. It might cover a limited range of matters or a very wide one; it was likely to combine 'once-for-all' injunctions, relating to particular persons or particular places with general rules affecting all or a large number of the monarch's subjects. A capitulary of the beginning of the year 802 opens with the statement that:

> The most serene and most Christian lord Emperor Charles has chosen from his magnates the wisest and most prudent men, archbishops and some of the other bishops also, together with venerable abbots and pious laymen, and has sent them throughout his whole kingdom; through them he would have all the various classes of persons mentioned in the following sections live strictly in accordance with the law. Moreover, where anything established by law seems to be other than right and just, he has ordered them to seek this out most zealously and let him know about it: he desires, God willing, to reform it.

The remaining thirty-nine clauses vary from:

> (c.2) Concerning the fidelity to be promised to the lord Emperor: he has ordered that every man in his whole kingdom, whether ecclesiastic or layman, each according to his vow and pursuit, shall now promise to him as Emperor the fidelity which he has previously promised to him as king . . .

and (c.39) In our forests no one shall dare to steal our game, which has already been forbidden many times. And once again we firmly order by virtue of the authority that we possess, that no one shall do this . . .

to (c.10) Let bishops and priests live according to the canons and teach others likewise;

and (c.32) We enjoin absolutely that wilful killing—through which many Christian men perish—be given up and prevented . . .

Texts of this kind have nothing in common either with modern Acts of Parliament or with Government *White Papers*, although there are recognizable similarities with ministerial exhortations. In fact the decisions and instructions of the monarch were usually made known verbally to the magnates and others who were present at the court. It was 'the word of the king' (*verbum regis*) that gave these instructions their authority; and it is neither necessary nor wise to assume that Charles or his representative spoke Latin. Only exceptionally (mostly perhaps where the intended recipients were exclusively clergy) was a standard version of a capitulary made by someone connected with the court and multiple copies sent out. The precise form in which other capitularies were carried away from court and were subsequently

16

Fig. 4 Coins of Charles the Great; left hand page: before 791/4, minted Melle (*size* 17 mm.); top: 791/800, minted Quentovic (*size* 16 mm.); bottom: Coin of Louis the Pious, mint unknown. (*Size* 20 mm.). *Oxford, Ashmolean Museum.*

entered in one or other of the manuscript collections through which, usually in much later copies, they alone have come down to us, seems to be very largely a matter of chance—as indeed is their survival at all. It is unlikely that the modern editions of the capitularies are anything near a complete record of all that were published; they are none the less far more comprehensive than anything that was available to the ordinary royal servant of the period.

The official records of grants made by the monarch to an individual church, monastery or private person of such assets as lands, tolls and exemption from the interference of the regular royal officials—what contemporary texts generally call *praecepta* or *praeceptiones* and historians call diplomas—make a striking contrast with the capitularies. They were prepared by specially-trained persons at court; they were distinctive and impressive in appearance (inside back cover); their wording obeys certain definite rules and makes use of fixed formulae. Like other similar documents of the early Middle Ages, their formal part generally includes some pious sentiment such as that the grant ' will bring us perpetual recompense and help to ensure the stability of our realm '. The core of the diploma was the passage, often at this period quite brief and therefore imprecise, which defined the scope of the grant. Diplomas of Charles' son and successor Louis, but not of Charles himself, normally specify the fearful monetary penalty that will be laid on any one who dares to flout its terms; and they all have an elaborate conclusion to establish that the document is an authentic and lawful record of what it purports to convey—including, until shortly after 800, a tiny section in which the monarch literally ' made his mark '. To their recipients they were unimpeachable evidence of the lawful possession of some right or the source of income and they were therefore carefully treasured, either in the original or through some later copy. Even so, the total number of genuine diplomas that survives from the forty-three and a half years of Charles' reign, including several in which, as scholars have been able to show, additions have been made to the wording of the original text, usually for reasons that are not difficult to imagine, is less than 165; and these are very unevenly distributed over the period and still more unevenly distributed over the geographical area of Charles' dominions. Apart from the light which their method of preparation helps to throw on the organization and personnel of part of the royal court, the diplomas are obviously a major source for the history of the period: the recording of the place where they were issued provides most of the detailed evidence for Charles' itinerary (map p. 50); the names of the recipients tell us much about the men or the churches who were closely associated with the ruler and his policies; and the substance of the grants throws light on both the sources of authority and resources of the monarch and, at least incidentally, on local conditions and persistent differences in various parts of his dominions.

One other type of document of an official or semi-official kind—a classification which need not and must not be defined too closely—which deserves individual mention has been strangly neglected by all but a few historians of the period. This is the class of records of judicial proceedings or ' pleas ', in contemporary parlance *iudicata*, *notitiae iudicati* or simply *notitiae*. They have many defects as source-material: they are even more unevenly distributed chronologically and geographically than the diplomas; almost without exception they are the records of disputes over land in which the successful party was a major church, since only an institution of this kind had the means of preserving such documents through political upheaval and many centuries; and the combination of set formulae, of course in Latin, and the reporting of particular happenings, the background of which is generally totally unknown to us, makes their interpretation often extremely difficult. Nevertheless they are among the very few documents of the period that enable us to see the public law and royal administration of the period, as it were, 'in action' and not through the filter of royal expectation and aspiration; they are almost the only means of determining how far Charles' rule gave a unified character to the administration of justice to all his free-born subjects and the safeguarding of the royal resources in his wide-flung territories; and they help us to fill out—only very slightly, it is true—our knowledge of the activities of various royal servants.

A complete picture of Charles the Great's Europe, or more strictly as complete a picture as the historian can ever hope to draw, must take account of many other kinds of material. 'Private' charters, the records of gifts, sales and exchanges of land and the like by persons other than the king provide vital information about magnates and their families and are the primary source of our knowledge of the economic life of the period. They also tell us about the organization and life of the church at the ordinary, parish, level and supplement the generalities of records of church synods. The texts used in the worship, or liturgy, of the church throw sometimes unexpected light on current ideas of royal authority and on intellectual contacts between different regions. The different scripts used for the writing of manuscript-books of all sorts can be made to yield valuable information. Light can be thrown on several different aspects of the period from coins.

Even though the total amount of material is small by comparison with that for most later centuries in the same areas of Europe, no scholar can be expected to be equally at home with all types of source or even to be equally familiar with the documents coming from widely-separated parts of Charles' dominions. Moreover, their satisfactory interpretation may depend on a knowledge of material of a similar kind or of other kinds of material from the same region both earlier and later in date than that with which the scholar is primarily concerned; and since the written material is, as we have seen, often known only through the activities of later copyists who altered or re-handled what they had in front of them, a new critical examination of the manuscripts may sometimes alter the foundation on which previous scholars have built. Finally, the kind of conclusions that an historian draws from his raw material, from his sources, will depend very much on the problems that he poses because they seem to him interesting or significant. For all these reasons, and for several others, there can be no final picture of 'The Age of Charlemagne' any more than there can be a final and universally-acceptable account of, say, the French Revolution or of Stalinist Russia. What can perhaps be asked of any account of the period is that it should make clear what the sources do *not* permit us to say, and that its author should avoid, in so far as he may, imposing on it concepts and prejudices that are peculiar to his own time and society. It may then give a plausible, but still personal, answer to the questions: in what ways did eighth century and early ninth century Europe differ from what had gone before? What did it hand on to later ages? And to what extent can these changes and achievements be credited to Charles himself?

Fig. 5 A late Merovingian medallion, cloisonné enamel on copper, showing the figure of Christ with other Christian symbols. *Cleveland Museum of Art, Cleveland.* (*Diameter* 5 cm.)

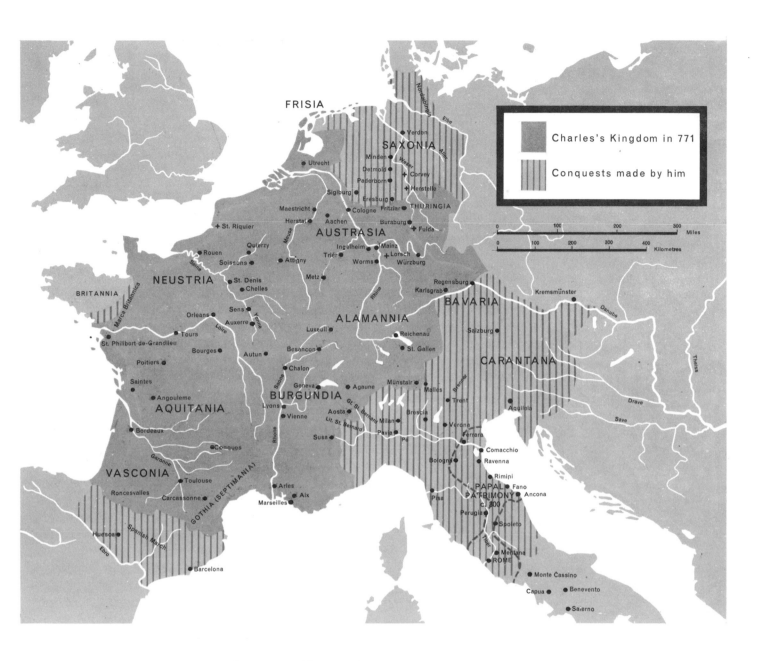

General map of Europe and the Mediterranean

Europe before Charlemagne

1

In 695 the Christian inhabitants of Carthage, subjects of the Roman Emperor, surrendered to the forces of Islam; and in the next three years, in spite of being constantly harassed by the Berbers, Arab armies succeeded in eliminating the last Imperial garrisons in Africa—in the very region in which republican Rome had begun its conquest of the southern shores of the Mediterranean. In the same decade the Caliph Abd al-Malik established a single, distinctive, gold and silver coinage for all Muslim territories. For half a century historians have been debating how far the economic and cultural unity of the Mediterranean shores and hinterland—in the three anciently-recognised continents of Europe, Asia and Africa—can be said to have persisted up to this time and how sharp the break was at the end of the seventh century. What is undeniable is that the one-time political and religious unity of this vast region, already threatened several centuries earlier when men coined the word *Romania* to describe what they wanted to save, had been finally destroyed without hope of recall. The Emperor, whose rule was thought of as the earthly counterpart of the Divine Ruler of the universe, was effective sovereign now only of present day Asia Minor, parts of Greece and the Balkans—predominantly coastal areas—south, central and a small part of north Italy, Sardinia and Corsica.

Yet in spite of the immense losses that the Empire had suffered in little over half a century, its ruler still had a prestige and authority unique among the Christian monarchs of the period. He was the heir of Augustus and of Constantine; his title was shared with no one and it had no territorial qualification because his authority was assumed to be without territorial restriction. Admission to the family of the Emperor was itself a jealously-guarded privilege. The only monarch to have been accorded the title of ' brother of the Emperor ' was the Persian ruler, in the early seventh century; and the circle from which spouses were sought for sons and daughters of the Emperor did not normally include the families of kings of Germanic origin.

Alliances were not between equals but in the spirit of the earlier Roman practice of securing federates or hired warriors by payment. Heraclius (610-41) was the last monarch for a century to treat with the Franks in this way and it is clearly no accident that after 629 Byzantine coinage is not found in Gaul until the late eighth century. The Imperial capital, Constantinople, was unrivalled in size, population and the luxury of its buildings: nowhere else could a man live his whole life without a sight of fields or open country or gaze at visitors from so many distant places. Asia Minor, on which fell the main burden of supplying the capital and providing recruits for the army, was still immensely rich in men and resources. A radically remodelled administrative hierarchy kept even the most distant provinces under the close surveillance of the Imperial court, whose bureaucratic departments were staffed by educated and salaried laymen. The Imperial ' sacred ' palace and its associated buildings, which occupied as much ground as the inhabited area of many cities farther west, was the setting of an elaborately

1. Nave of S. Salvatore, Brescia (Italy); early ninth century, showing excavations of the late Lombard church.

thought-out court ceremonial, through which, in the words of a tenth-century scholar-Emperor, ' the imperial power is displayed in greater beauty and magnificence, thus filling with admiration both foreign nations and our citizens '. Most of the rulers of the foreign nations that had settled in western Romania in the centuries before the Arab advance continued to show a perhaps surprising respect for imperial prerogatives: thus, the coins that were minted in their territories were at first imitations of existing imperial coins, and the change to new types bearing the name of a king instead of the emperor was recognised as a novel assertion of sovereignty.

At the same time the Roman Empire at the beginning of the eighth century was Greek rather than Latin. Latin had never had more than a tenuous footing in the eastern Mediterranean. Greek had inevitably remained the language of the liturgy in Asia Minor and the Balkan peninsula when the western provinces changed to Latin; and the churches of these regions naturally looked for leadership to the patriarchal see of Constantinople which had been decreed to be ' second only to Rome '. The contents of the Emperor Justinian's great corpus of law were increasingly inaccessible even to the educated in the east, a fact that was recognised by the publication of the first code in Greek in 726. Greek was the normal language of administration. In the western provinces it remained, however, an alien one, fully understood by few laymen or clergy, except for those who had fled from east Mediterranean lands to escape a zealously orthodox emperor or Arab domination.

Rome had long ceased to be a political capital. But as the see of St. Peter, whose reputed burial place was an object of exceptional veneration, it was the primatial see of a professedly universal Christian Church. It was also in a special sense supreme among but not over the churches of western Latin Romania. Through its activities, a region that was now politically divided and partly barbarized continued to be made aware both of the cultural heritage of the recent past and, however vaguely, of a greater unity on earth as well as in heaven. For the invasions and settlement of pagan or Arian Germans within the former Imperial frontiers in the fifth and sixth centuries had led at different times to the creation of a number of separate kingdoms and independent or semi-independent duchies. In the former province of Britain both the native Celtic kingdoms that had been established in the west and the advancing Germanic kingdoms in the centre and east were quite small and warring among themselves for supremacy. On the Continent three major territorial kingdoms had emerged from a prolonged, confused and confusing period of migration and conquest—the Visigothic kingdom in the Iberian peninsula, the Lombard kingdom of north and central Italy and the Frankish kingdom which embraced the former Gaulish and German provinces of the Empire and also extended eastwards beyond the former Rhine frontier.

No single formula will adequately express the relationship of the newcomers with the populations of the territories they conquered or the character of the society that emerged from the clash of two different social systems. Except in Britain, where Romanization had been more superficial than on the Continent, and in a few areas just inside the former frontier, the newcomers did not oust the existing spoken language and replace it by their own: rather, they helped to accelerate certain tendencies already apparent in the Vulgar Latin of the late Empire and enriched the emerging ' Romance ' dialects or languages with elements of their own vocabulary. This implies, of course, that some of the invaders away from the frontier regions continued to speak their original Germanic tongue

2. South-west view of the exterior of the Octagon, formerly Charles' Palace Chapel and now part of Aachen Cathedral (Germany).

23

for many years. In spite of significant local differences, the history of institutions and social organization in these regions is closely parallel to that of language. Hence historians are accustomed to speak of the ' Romano-Germanic synthesis' that was created in the sixth and seventh centuries and provided the framework within which the characteristic features of medieval Europe developed. The German invaders had come as warriors under warrior-leaders, some of whom were accorded the title of king; they recognised social differentiation, certainly between free and unfree, and possibly also between noble and non-noble free, but not a hierarchy of officials acting in the name of the ruler; among them, issues of peace and war were perhaps decided by mass, although hardly universal, deliberation; the suppression and punishment of wrong-doing were primarily a responsibility of neighbourhood and kin, through the workings of vendetta or the agreement to pay compensation which halted it. The written record, coined money and towns were alike unknown to them. By the beginning of the eighth century, kings of Germanic speech were the acknowledged rulers of extensive territories and their various inhabitants; they or the officials who represented them locally punished wrongdoers and acted as arbiters in disputes between individuals or institutions and in the Continental kingdoms the most important officials were usually associated with a town of ancient origin. The transfer of rights over land and men or of other sources of income, not infrequently paid in coin, was regularly the subject of a written document; and the possession of such rights on an extensive scale was the one essential characteristic of men who appear in literary texts of the period as *optimates*, *proceres* and more generally as *nobiles*. The obligation to serve in the royal host was one that in normal circumstances was laid only on magnates and their followers who had been trained to fight and on certain groups of freemen who knew no lord but the king. Finally, both rulers and subjects professed the Catholic Christian faith.

The English kingdoms owed their knowledge of writing, of Latin and of Roman legal concepts to the men who converted them to Christianity and to their successors. The Continental kingdoms had been established in regions in which the late Roman administrative machine still functioned, however ineffectively and uncertainly. But here too the clergy were emerging as essential transmitters of *Romanitas*; and, when responsibility for law and order and carrying out the king's commands was transferred from ' Romans ' to men of Germanic origin and speech, they alone were capable of meeting the continuing need for men capable of writing laws and documents. The Lombard kingdom is often regarded as an exception; but if an educated lay element still existed in the seventh century it was very insignificant and the lay notaries—writers of documents—who are recorded from early eighth century are probably at that date a very recent innovation, perhaps in imitation of current practice in the adjacent Imperial, Byzantine, territories. Yet the church and its ordained servants were not themselves free from the current barbarization of western Romania. In Francia in particular, the Latin they wrote had more in common with current speech than with the Latin of Augustus or even of the Fathers; and at the beginning of the eighth century the texts that were being copied in their cathedral churches and monasteries were mostly, if not exclusively, ones that were of immediate practical use—the Psalter, the Gospels, texts needed for the celebration of the liturgy and a small number of Patristic texts. Even this limited range of books was very rarely available to the ordinary parish priest, working among peasants for whom the adoption of Christianity had generally involved a change of outward and occasional observance rather than a

Fig. 6   Detail from the Altar of Volvinio, S. Ambrogio, Milan.

radical change of belief.

For a less vulgarized Latin, the copying of a wider range of ancient texts—Vergil and Sallust as well as Jerome—and the outstanding achievements of the age in script and the fine arts, it is necessary to turn to Ireland, never part of the Empire but brought within the orbit of the Latin church in the fifth century, and the English kingdoms and in particular to Northumbria. In the space of a few years either side of 700, the monasteries of Wearmouth and Jarrow produced a

Fig. 7   Reconstruction of a seventh/eighth century village near Gladbach, in the middle Rhine area, after excavations in 1937. From a painting in the *Römisch-Germanisches Zentralmuseum, Mainz*.

number of complete Bibles, written in a supremely beautiful version of the 'uncial' script which had been that most widely-favoured in Mediterranean lands from the late fourth to the late sixth century, and also provided Bede with the education of which he made such notable use, while Lindisfarne produced a gospel-book written in a new and distinctive script and decorated in an equally distinctive art-style which skilfully combined features of Mediterranean, Germanic and Celtic origin. From the same area came the first missionaries who attempted to extend the Christian religion to the Germanic peoples who were the eastern neighbours of the Franks, notably Frisians and Saxons, and who, where they succeeded, brought to areas that had never been parts of the Empire the heritage of Rome of which they were now both trustees and principal beneficiaries.

The contrast between the Christian 'Romano-Germanic' kingdoms and pagan Germany beyond the old frontier is very real and it would be foolish to underrate it: but it is equally important not to exaggerate the differences between these two societies. The ' frightful wilderness ' through which the missionary Sturmi travelled in the middle years of the eighth century to bring Christianity to the inhabitants of Hesse and Thuringia, ' seeing nothing but wild beasts, of which there was a great number, birds flying and enormous trees ' and meeting other human beings only where his route took him across well-established but infrequent tracks, had its counterparts in most regions of western Europe: two centuries later a monk of Rheims travelling on a recognised route to Chartres lost his way in the thick woods that at that time lay along the river Marne. Even in areas in which town life had persisted from the Roman period, the majority of inhabitants lived in small villages whose inhabitants had laboriously won their cultivated land from the surrounding forest (fig. 7).

In most of these communities the solidarity of the kin and the possibility of vendetta remained a more powerful check to wrong-doing than the infrequent intervention of agents of the royal authority. Because they were now professed Christians and no longer had their weapons laid in their graves with them, the magnate class had not ceased to regard fighting as their main vocation and physical courage and loyalty to a warrior-leader as the principal virtues: the Old English *Beowulf*-poem, in the form in which it has come down to us, was intended for a Christian audience and the Old High German ' Lay of Hildebrand and Hadubrand ' is most probably of the full eighth century. The standard word for a ruler, and later for a lord of lower rank, in the post-migration Germanic period was adopted partly because it seemed to correspond to Christian Latin terminology; and even Christian kings were still expected to be successful in battle and provide their followers with frequent opportunities for booty. In several kingdoms the lands over which a king ruled, whether acquired by inheritance or by conquest, were regarded as no different from any other patrimony and therefore subject to the rules of succession that were customary in that society.

Among the Franks all sons, whether they were, in terms of Christian or Roman law, legitimate or illegitimate, were entitled to a share in their father's heritage. Hence, when the Merovingian king Clovis died in 511 each of his four sons became ' king of the Franks ' with his own territory. The freedom with which such ' part-kingdoms . could be made and unmade came in the course of the next two and a half centuries to be severely restricted by ' a growing sense of provincial, territorial, divergence of interest ', in the creation of which the personal connections of magnate families combined with geographical factors and elements of historic tradition. This is reflected in the seventh-century use of the terms *Neustria* and *Austr(as)ia*, in addition to the already familiar *Burgundia*, in both a geographical and a political sense. It is still more apparent in the separatist tendencies of some of the regions over which the sixth-century Frankish kings had established their authority by conquest. At the beginning of the eighth century Aquitaine, the land between the Loire and the Garonne, where the barbarian element in society was very small, was effectively as independent as the Germanic duchy of Bavaria, although the dukes of both, as well as of more loyalist Alemannia, were probably of Frankish descent.

The loyalty of the Franks in northern Gaul and Rhineland Germany to kings descended from Clovis long outlasted the ability of its members to restrain dissident subjects or conduct successful military campaigns. The first chapter of Einhard's ' Life of Charles ' has a famous account of the last years of the *gens Meroingorum* when: ' Wealth and power were in the hands of the chief officers of the household, who were called mayors of the palace and who exercised ultimate authority. The king had nothing remaining to him beyond the enjoyment of his title and the satisfaction of sitting on his throne, with his long hair and his trailing beard, there to give the impression of rule and to grant audience to ambassadors from all parts; and he would charge these, at their departure, with answers given in his name but in fact sketched out for him or even prescribed for him.'[1] The mayors of the palace—*maiores domui*, stewards of the (royal) household—referred to by Einhard were Charles, Carloman and Pippin, respectively grandfather, uncle and father of Charles the Great. Their ancestors had first emerged as figures of influence and importance in the early part of the seventh century when Arnulf and an earlier Pippin, whose son and daughter respectively were subsequently joined in marriage, helped to determine the succession to the vacant Austrasian throne. Yet there was nothing inevitable about the rise of their descendants to

[1] transl. J. M. Wallace-Hadrill.

3. Arcade and capitals in the Octagon gallery, Aachen Cathedral.

unique pre-eminence in Francia. They certainly benefited from the extensive internal colonization of the seventh and eighth centuries that established a Germanic-speaking population in what is now eastern Belgium and opened up to cultivation hitherto unsettled territories in the valleys of the middle Rhine and its tributaries: but so did many other magnate families with hereditary lands in the Meuse-Marne-Seine region. And many clergy, bishops, abbots and others, had their own reason for not wishing to see the end of the Merovingians or even their reduction to complete impotence to the benefit of a single family of hereditary courtiers.

The father of the elder Charles was 'duke of the Austrasians' and effective ruler of the kingdom for many years before his death in 714. His son had, none the less, to defeat both external and internal enemies before he was recognised as mayor of the palace to the shadow-king of both Neustria and Austrasia. For more than two decades after this, Charles was engaged almost annually in the campaigns that earned him the nickname, first recorded in the ninth century, of 'the Hammer', *Martellus*—perhaps by analogy with the Jewish leader Judas Maccabeus. His wrath and the savagery of his warriors were vented on the Frisians, who were apparently finding less opportunity for peaceful trading than in the previous century and had inevitably taken to raiding by land and water; on the Saxons, 'detestable pagans who live beyond the Rhine' and who at that time were edging closer to the river; on the Alemannians and Bavarians. They were felt even more severely by the inhabitants of Burgundy, Provence and Aquitaine, all of which offered far greater opportunities for booty than Germanic lands. These opportunities were eagerly seized, and enormously increased Charles' reputation among the Franks.

One military victory brought him fame in a much wider circle. In 711 Moslem armies from Africa defeated and killed the Visigothic king, and in a very few years resistance to the invaders had ceased everywhere in the peninsula except in the far north-west—the nucleus of the later kingdom of Asturias. The Northumbrian Bede noted with concern the successes of the Ishmaelites. In 732 Arab armies crossed the Pyrenees and stormed north to beyond Poitiers, the farthest they were ever to penetrate in western Europe. What happened then may have prompted Bede to insert in the last chapter of his 'Ecclesiastical History of the English People', completed in the previous year, the observation that the unbelievers had earned the punishment due to their wickedness. The invading force was utterly destroyed and a rich booty acquired by the victors when they sacked the tents of the infidel. A Spanish cleric living under Arab rule, to whom we owe the fullest account of the battle, speaks of the victors as *Europenses*, which may be taken as the equivalent of 'Latin Christians'. The decisive defeat of the Moslems, only the second that they had suffered since their advance began a century earlier, was none the less Charles' and the Franks'—and God's.

Shortly after his victory over his internal enemies in 717, Charles had made a gift of land to the monastery of Echternach: its founder and abbot was the Englishman Willibrord who, with duke Pippin's backing, had worked among both the semi-pagan inhabitants of north-eastern Francia and the still predominantly pagan Frisians. Shortly after 732, the mayor of the palace made gifts to several of the old-established churches in the Frankish kingdom, including probably St. Martin's at Tours, and later to the Merovingian foundation of St. Denis. Between these two dates, the English missionary-bishop Boniface had been commissioned by the Pope to tackle the arduous task of preaching the faith to the peoples east of the Rhine and had been taken under the protection of the mayor of the palace. In the

4. Bronze statuette of either Charles the Great or Charles the Bald; ninth century (horse fifteenth century): *Paris, Louvre.*

twenties and thirties Charles' less resounding, and indeed less enduring, military successes against German peoples were followed sooner or later by the establishment of monasteries and bishoprics in regions in which they had hitherto been unknown,[1] and, in the very last years of his life, by the beginnings of missionary activity among the still stoutly pagan Saxons.

When Charles died in 741, his two sons divided Francia and its dependent territories between them and Boniface entered on a new phase of his career, in which he was both irritant and guide in the restoration and improvement of church order and church life within the Frankish kingdom. ' How the law of God and the religion of the church, fallen into decay in the days of former princes, might be re-established and how the Christian people might gain salvation of their souls and not perish through the deceit of false priests' was the declared purpose of the first of several synods that met in Austrasia in the next six years: and since between 737 and 743 there was not even a king of the Franks in name, its decrees were promulgated in the name of Carloman, ' duke and prince of the Franks '. When Carloman abdicated in 747 to become a monk in Italy, his brother Pippin, who had followed his lead, if less enthusiastically, became ruler in all but name of the entire *regnum Francorum*.

Not surprisingly, Boniface's activities provoked antagonism and opposition among the native bishops and abbots, and among the magnate families from which the clerics who ruled over dioceses or monasteries in the north and east of Francia mostly came: there are even hints that some of the measures planned by Boniface and his disciples in conjunction with the Pope were equally unwelcome to the mayors of the palace. Nevertheless, support of the missionaries and reformers was evidently felt to be as politically valuable to the Carolingian dynasty as it was indispensable to the reformers. Even so, it may at first have seemed less important to Pippin than his military campaigns south and east, particularly (after the final reduction of Alemannia (Swabia)) those against the Bavarians. In 749, however, the latter ' submitted to his overlordship and undertook by oath and with hostages not to rebel again '. The promise was soon to be broken, like so many others of the same kind: but ' for two years the land was free of battles '. The next year, 750, the Anglo-Saxon Burchard, disciple of Boniface and bishop of his foundation of Würzburg, and Fulrad, a Frank from the Meuse-Moselle region who had recently added the abbacy of St. Denis to his position as head of the clergy in Pippin's household, set out for Rome. They were to ask the Pope a question that was entirely without precedent, namely, ' whether it was good or not that those called kings in Francia should not have the power of ruling '.

Papal support of the English missionaries in the preceding half-century and their reference to Rome of problems of doctrine and discipline had succeeded in establishing closer links than ever before between Rome and the church in Francia and its lay protectors. Rome and the rest of non-Lombard Italy were still part of the Empire but the Emperor seemed to many a remote and alien figure; and the exercise of temporal authority in the city of Rome and the country districts round about, not yet as desolate and impoverished as they were to be in later centuries, was increasingly in the hands of men who looked to the papal court rather than to the imperial representative at Ravenna. Worse still, the Emperors were also, in the eyes of the bishop of Rome and those associated with him, heretics by reason of their shameful attacks on the pictorial portrayal of Christ, the Virgin Mary and the Saints. And when the deposers, destroyers, insulters or profaners of sacred images were declared excommunicate in 731, the Emperor's counter-moves included transferring the churches in the western Balkans and southern Italy from the 'patriarchal' authority of Rome to that of Constantinople. A Frankish chronicle written under the supervision of Charles Martel's half-brother even claims that in 739 the Pope 'proposed a bargain whereby he should desert the imperial cause and, with the approval of the Roman people, join that of the said prince Charles'. The need of a political ally was the more urgent because the hated Lombards were successfully taking advantage of the discontent in imperial territories; and although king Liutprand's personal respect for St. Peter was such that he was usually ready to reach a compromise with the Pope when the latter felt that his rights and independence were threatened, his successor felt no such restraints.

The Pope's answer to the Frankish request was that the title of king ought to belong to him who had the power and that Pippin was therefore raised to the royal dignity and his family with him. One of the two early sources for these revolutionary happenings says that the Pope gave his decision 'so that order should not be upset'; the other, the writer of which evidently wished to give a greater part in this 'king-making' to the Franks themselves, states that Pippin was chosen by them 'as old-established order demands'. The writers, or the Pope, have clearly in mind the definition of 'order' given by Augustine in his 'City of God': 'the arrangement of equal and unequal creatures, according to each one the place that is appropriate to him'. The leaders of the Franks, having asserted the established Germanic right of naming a king who had the qualities that entitled him to be considered for the position, an additional—and among the Franks a novel—ceremony, sanctioned the replacement of the Merovingians by the Carolingians. In November 751 Pippin was consecrated king, when certain bishops, probably but not certainly including Boniface, anointed him with holy oil: and although there were recent precedents for this procedure in both Visigothic Spain and the Celtic kingdoms, it was surely the Old Testament anointings of Saul, David and Solomon that inspired the ceremony of 751 and gave it an evocative power.

Phrases like 'revolutionary happenings', 'a decisive moment in European history' are easy to write, less easy to justify. Yet the direct involvement of the bishop of Imperial Rome in a change of royal dynasty among a Germanic people, the association of a religious ceremony with the making of a king, and the unavoidable political consequences of a closer link between the Papacy and the largest of the Romano-Germanic kingdoms, surely warrant such language even if the son and successor of Pippin had not turned out to be the man he was.

Some of the implications of the alliance between the Papacy and the Frankish king were soon made clear. The Lombard king Aistulf, having captured Ravenna and all the Imperial territories north of the Apennines except the Venetian littoral and Istria, openly proclaimed his intention of subjecting Rome and its 'duchy'. When Pope Stephen failed to secure a change of heart by penitential processions in which the painting of the Virgin 'made without hands' was displayed (a striking reminder of the Roman rejection of imperial decrees against images), he prepared to set out for the Frankish court. It is by no means excluded that he did so with Imperial approval. On 6th January 754, the Pope, 'worn out', as he later declared, 'by the frost and the snow, by the heat and the swelling of waters, by mighty rivers and most atrocious mountains and various kinds of danger', met Pippin at Ponthion—a royal estate south-east of Chalons-sur-Marne. According to the Papal account, the king dismounted from his horse, prostrated himself and then acted as groom to the still mounted Pope. Next day in the palace

Fig. 8   Detail from the Altar of Volvinio, S. Ambrogio, Milan.

Fig. 9   Detail from the Altar of Volvinio, S. Ambrogio, Milan.

oratory, according to a Frankish source, the Pope, girded with sackcloth and with ashes on his head, prostrated himself and begged the king to ' order the cause of St. Peter and of the commonwealth of the Romans '.

Precisely what the Pope had in mind in this request, what Pippin undertook to do and by what authority the two parties believed themselves to be acting are matters that can never be finally settled: the available sources are too scanty, ambiguously phrased and at least in part deliberately tendentious. These problems are inseparable from that of the date and purpose of the famous, indeed notorious, ' Donation of Constantine ', in which the first Christian emperor is made to resign his crown and empire into the hands of Pope Sylvester I as compensation for being cured of leprosy by the Pope. The authenticity of this remarkable document was already denied at the end of the tenth century, although not finally proved until the fifteenth century, and it even had a new lease of life in sixteenth and seventeenth century Russia. Its partial dependence on the legend of Constantine's miraculous healing put together in the later fifth century is beyond doubt but it included much that was new. Most attention has been paid to the chapters in which the Pope was given the emperor's own diadem, which he then declined to wear, and, in addition to the Lateran palace and the city of Rome, ' all the provinces, districts and cities of Italy and all the western regions '. Hardly less interesting, however, is the chapter in which the various orders of 'Roman' clergy are equated with and given the same privileges as the senate and the different grades of imperial court official. This throws light on the direction in which ideas were moving at the Papal court—from which it certainly originates—at the time it was being prepared. Most scholars now seem inclined to the view that Stephen took the ' Donation ' with him when he crossed the Alps in 753, although it certainly cannot be excluded that it was compiled three or four years later. In either case we must recognise that the writer probably genuinely believed that the papal assertion of the rights ' conveyed ' in the document was just and lawful.

What is certain is that the Pope bestowed on the king and on his two sons the additional title of *patricius*, an imperial dignity borne by the former exarch and the duke of Rome among others, that he re-anointed Pippin and anointed his sons in a ceremony at St. Denis; and that the king of the Franks led expeditions into Italy—the first for over a century—in 755 (less probably in 754) and again in 756. What took place on the second occasion when the Lombard king Aistulf was trapped within the walls of his capital, Pavia, is described in a semi-official Frankish account in these words: ' Observing what was happening and appreciating that no hope of escape now remained, Aistulf again implored the king's pardon and peace through the Frankish bishops and nobles . . . By their judgement he had to yield to king Pippin one-third of his treasure in Pavia and, in addition, give him many more gifts than on the previous occasion. Aistulf further bound himself by oath and by surrender of hostages never again to rebel against Pippin and the Frankish nobility.' Finally, the Lombard king surrendered to the Pope twenty-two cities and castles north and east of the Appennines and one on their west side which, with the duchy of Rome, formed the nucleus of the later Papal States, the medieval ' Patrimony of St. Peter '. But perhaps significantly it was the Frank Fulrad who took formal delivery of the cities from Lombard officials and their own leading inhabitants, and laid the keys that he received as a symbol of their surrender on the tomb of St. Peter at Rome.

The ' heap of treasures and gifts ' with which the Franks returned home in 756 may have reconciled them to a military adventure which many of them had

Fig. 10 Ivory and silver chalice, reputedly of St. Lebuin, a missionary in Saxony who died in 773. Rectangular decoration perhaps copied from the bronze railings in the Octagon, Aachen Cathedral (see pl. 15); eighth/ninth century. *Utrecht, Aartsbisschoppelijk Museum.* (*Height* 11.8 cm. *Diameter* 18 cm.)

5. Molsheim Brooch: seventh/eighth century, Frankish: *Darmstadt, Hessischen Landesmuseum. Width* 8.5 cm.

5

undertaken without enthusiasm. The loyalty of a warrior to his chosen leader, whether captain of a war-band or anointed king, was not a light matter in the earlier Middle Ages: but it was never a one-sided relationship and it could not be automatically assumed in all circumstances. It was least powerful a sentiment when the warrior was also a substantial landowner and had authority over others away from a royal court: hence the successive attempts in all early medieval kingdoms to create a circle of men in immediate dependence on the monarch and to use them to give effect to the royal will. Pippin's immediate ancestors, as ' rulers without the name of king ', and Pippin himself, as the founder of a new royal dynasty, were more than normally in need of loyal companions in war and peace. The steps they took to secure such support were to have unexpectedly long-lasting consequences.

Although the mayors were not responsible for a significant change of meaning of the word *vassus*, hitherto predominantly used of a dependent of a humble kind, it seems to have been in their circle that it first came to be used consistently of a man of free birth who put himself under a superior who in turn assumed reciprocal obligations towards him. The bond created between the two was symbolized by the inferior's placing his hand between those of his superior, a characteristically Germanic ceremony, so far as we can see, for which the Latin term was *se commendare* or *se tradere*. Since, however, such a ' surrender ' could, and in other contexts did, involve a loss of personal freedom, at an early date it was usual for the inferior subsequently to swear an oath of fidelity. And because this oath was linked with the act of commendation, it was different in function if not in form from, say, the submission offered and promises made by the Frankish magnates in 751 or by king Aistulf in 755. This is emphasized by an annalist's account, admittedly written forty years later, of what happened to the boy-duke Tassilo III of Bavaria, at that time under the tutelage of his Frankish royal uncle, when he reached his majority in 757: ' Tassilo came [to court] and commended himself into vassalage by his hands; he swore many and innumerable oaths . . . and he promised fidelity to king Pippin and to his sons . . . as a vassal lawfully must do, with uprightness and firm devotion, acting as a vassal ought to towards his lords '.

Tassilo had fought by his uncle's side in the previous year and it was as a potential warrior that a *vassus* was, originally, taken into his superior's service and became part of his household. The point was soon reached, however, at which *vassi* wished to set up their own households. One solution was for a lord to grant to his vassal a benefice (*beneficium*), land held not in complete proprietorship nor for a rent but in return for the continued service of its holder. For some years, possibly for some decades, before 744 the mayors of the palace had been using the lands of cathedral churches and monasteries as an additional, or perhaps indeed the main, means of rewarding followers. The holder of a benefice created in this way, which was usually a substantial estate or group of estates, comprising many score peasant households, normally paid a rent to the church and later in the century a fifth, of the produce but did service, usually military, to the mayor and afterwards to the king. Why the Arnulfing mayors expropriated the church so systematically (the unsystematic seizure of church lands was, of course, in no way unusual in most medieval centuries) is anything but clear. A desire to hold on to their own estates is hardly an adequate reason and in the early part of the century they needed the support of the higher clergy at least as much as of other laymen.

The explanation first put forward more than a century ago, and until recently almost universally accepted, was that Charles Martel and his sons wanted to

6. Detail from the stone altar frontal, Cividale Cathedral (Italy); Christ in Majesty; c. 745.

create a more effective fighting-force of *mounted* warriors and felt obliged to provide their followers with exceptionally large endowments to this end. It may well be that for a man to provide himself with a horse and with suitable weapons was an expensive business: in 761 a landowner near Lake Constance gave what seems to have been a fairly substantial piece of property to the monastery of St. Gall in return for a horse and a sword. But it has recently been argued that the Arabs of Spain did not become a predominantly cavalry army until nearly two decades after the invasion of 732—the supposed stimulus to the change among the Franks— and, less plausibly, that the Franks were accustomed to fighting from horseback long before that date. A recent attempt to make the Frankish ' discovery ' of the stirrup the decisive (or catalytic) factor is still less satisfactory. This would probably be irrelevant even if there was proof that the device had first reached Francia in the early eighth century. There is no proof: there are no early written references and the earliest pictorial representation seems to be on the Sant'Ambrogio gold altar, Milan, of c. 840 (pl. 48). The one stirrup discovered in a pre-ninth-century context in the West is an unpublished example from a Lombard cemetery near Vicenza. The practical advantages it gave to a horseman trying to charge the enemy are not in doubt: but, as we shall see, contemporary accounts of the earlier campaigns of Charles the Great suggest that cavalry played at most a minor part and there is ample evidence that throughout this period horsed warriors won most of their victories with, literally, fire and sword or with lances used as cutting or thrusting weapons and never with lances held rigid.

Two other possible explanations suggest themselves. The first is that the mayors wanted to give *vassi* lands that were distributed over a much greater area of Francia than their own estates, which were concentrated in the north-east. The second, which gets some support from the precise wording of the key texts, is that as the obligation of military service was beginning to be regarded as dependent on lands rather than on every legally free man, the growing wealth of the Frankish church was seriously depleting the royal host, because its lands were, or ought to be, exempt from *expeditio*, and the mayors were therefore simply using the lands of the church to provide much-needed extra troops.

However Pippin's army was levied and whatever its techniques of fighting there is no doubt as to how it was used. In the late 750s, Frankish armies finally ousted the Saracens from Septimania, the coastal territory and its hinterland from the eastern Pyrenees to Nimes, with Narbonne as its most important town, and they were probably as much to blame as the infidel invaders for the impoverishment of this once-wealthy region. For the last nine years of his life Pippin was occupied almost annually in trying to put an end for ever to Aquitanian and Gascon separatism. Assembling usually in May, the date first adopted in connection with the invasions of Italy in place of the customary March or early April, the Frankish army spent one to three months south of the Loire before returning home with booty, hostages and prisoners. The account of these campaigns given in the family chronicle of the period leaves no doubt as to the savagery and destructiveness with which they were conducted. City walls were demolished, rural estates burnt, monasteries emptied of their monks; in 763 Pippin ' tore up all the vineyards around Issoudun from which almost all Aquitaine, churches and monasteries, rich and poor, used to obtain wine; in 768 one of the Aquitanian leaders ' laid waste the districts of Berry and Limoges annexed by the king, so effectively that not a peasant dared work in the fields and vineyards '. Recovery from such ravages is far more difficult and protracted in a technologically undeveloped society

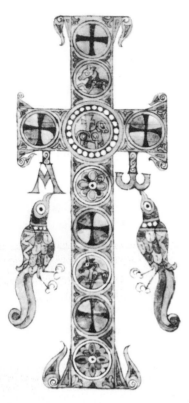

Fig. 11 A motif from an ornamental page of the Gelasian Sacramentary, written in Northern France (?Chelles) in the mid-eighth century. *Biblioteca Apostolica Vaticana, Rome.* Reg. Lat. 316, fol 3v.

7. Interior west wall of S. Maria in Valle (Tempietto), Cividale (Italy); c. 770.

homo

leo

uitulus

aquila

than it is in modern Europe and the effects of these wars were reflected in the economy of the region for generations. Before he died, however, Pippin could claim that he had won control of ' the whole of Aquitaine '.

Pippin was, as his last Merovingian predecessors had not been, a man whose fame was known beyond the boundaries of his own kingdom, whose friendship was sought and who sought the friendship of other rulers. The dissemination of the news of Boniface's martyrdom in Frisia in 754 and of the melancholy journey of his body first down the Rhine to Mainz and then overland to Fulda doubtless played its part in this. The Frankish king exchanged gifts with King Eadbert of Northumbria. His campaigns against the Lombards seem to have persuaded the Imperial court that here was an ally worth having: in 757 a legation from Constantinople reached the Frankish court with gifts that included an organ—which made a great impression on the recipients; and in the same year a Frankish legation was sent to the Imperial capital. Ten years later another legation arrived. It took part in a discussion on the Trinity and on images and it may also have brought a request that the king's daughter Gisla, a future abbess of Chelles, should be given in marriage to the heir to the Imperial throne which, if true, was a startling concession to a ' barbarian ' royal line. At the beginning of 768 legates whom Pippin had sent three years previously to the Muslim Caliph al-Mansur, founder of the city of Baghdad, landed at Marseilles with other legates bearing gifts from the caliph. They had perhaps travelled with some of the ' Jewish merchants called Raadanites ' whose journeys from Frankish Mediterranean ports to Baghdad and beyond are described by a ninth-century Arab writer. Above all, legates passed almost annually after 755, and in some years more than once, between the Papal and Frankish courts. They brought or sought exhortation, advice, instruction or manuscripts that could only be found in Rome or its neighbourhood. Several Franks obtained ecclesiastical office in Italy and two bishops from the sees round Rome, whose incumbents had a special relationship to the Pope and were later known as cardinals, were persuaded to remain in Francia.

The exceptional position now claimed for the Franks and their kings among the kingdoms of the Latin West is evident in alterations made in this period to texts of two very different kinds. In the sacramentary (mass-book) of Roman origin, which Pippin wished to see more widely adopted in his kingdom, intercessions for the emperor, the Romans or the empire were replaced by others for the king or kingdom of the Franks; and a new prologue that was added to the ancient Frankish Lex Salica hails ' The illustrious people of the Franks, established by God the creator, bold in war, loyal to treaties, profound in counsel, noble in body . . . free from heresy . . . eager for justice, the guardian of piety '. The God of the Old Testament and of the New had acquired a new chosen people.

8. Manuscript; Evangelist symbols: *Trier, Cathedral Treasury*, ms. 61 (ex 134), fol iv; third quarter of the eighth century. *Size* 30.5 × 25 cm.

The Apprenticeship of a King

2

On 24th September 768, King Pippin died in his fifty-fourth year and was buried, like Charles Martel and several Merovingian kings, at St. Denis. According to a tradition reported by its twelfth-century abbot Suger, he was placed ' outside [to the west], face downward and not recumbent, because of the sins of his father '. A few days previously, ' with the consent of the Frankish magnates and of the bishops ' and in accordance with an established practice from which he would neither have been able nor have wished to depart, he had divided the kingdom between his two sons. Charles, the elder, was given a great belt of territory that contained the greater part of the old Austrasian kingdom, the whole of Neustria and that part of Aquitaine that lay nearer to the Atlantic coast; the younger, Carloman, received what the chronicler, writing ' by the authority of ' Pippin's half-cousin (whose narrative ends with the events of this year), refers to as ' the kingdom of Burgundy, Provence, Septimania, Alsace and Alamannia ' and the other half of Aquitaine. We are not told what principles, if any, lay behind this division. It is possible that the actual limits of the two territories did not seem very important to contemporaries; but it may be that it was hoped to give both brothers a roughly equal share of the resources of the monarchy. It is perhaps significant that, although Charles acquired most of the Carolingian family-lands, the boundary ran through the Ardennes: and the evidence of ninth-century partitions suggests that it was necessary to take account of the interests of particular magnates.

Both sons became *reges Francorum*: on the same day, October 9th, at their respective ' capitals ' they formally entered into their royal heritage by the acclaim of their great men and through priestly anointing with holy oil. Nineteen-year-old Carloman was to live for only three years. Charles, who was probably then aged twenty-six, was to reign for over forty-five years, a long period at any time and, in the conditions of the early Middle Ages, quite exceptional.

It never seems to have bothered contemporaries and near-contemporaries that at the time of Charles' birth, in 742 or thereabouts, Pippin was not yet married to his mother. She was the daughter of a count of Laon of distinguished ancestry whose cousin married a sister of Pippin. In the early lifetime of Charles churchmen began to make a sharper distinction between concubinage and lawful marriage and to insist on the binding nature of the latter; and it is perhaps significant that Einhard omits from his list of Charles' wives and the mistresses of his later years the name of the mistress who had borne him a son before his first marriage and that this son was never given any position in the kingdom.[1] Einhard, however, saw no incongruity in including this list in a section devoted to the monarch's moral qualities and constancy; and it was only in the third quarter of the ninth century that a Pope insisted that the church's rules about marriage were unequivocal and applied to Emperors as much as to lesser men.

Virtually nothing is known of Charles' boyhood. Einhard observed later that he ' gave himself eagerly to riding and hunting, arts into which he was, as a Frank, born '; and he recorded that he made his sons, when they were of the right age,

[1]But he was a hunchback and this also might have debarred him.

40

' according to the custom of the Franks, ride and be practised in the use of arms and ways of hunting '. From this we may reasonably infer that acquiring these skills formed a major part of his own early education. There is nothing that convincingly suggests this also included a grounding in ' letters '. It was several centuries before kings and great nobles felt that the equation of ' lay ' with ' illiterate ' was shameful. In a famous passage, Einhard tells how Charles tried to learn to write and kept writing-tablets and leaves of parchment on which he could practice under his pillows; but he adds that he had little success because he had taken this up too late in life. It is not improbable that one of the clerics in his father's houschold (men who not only performed the liturgy for its members but also provided the writers of his diplomas: see below, p. 79) had taught him the *Pater noster, Credo* and perhaps even part of the Psalter. These were the standard texts of elementary education during much of the Middle Ages. This at least would provide some basis for the claims made by Einhard that Charles ' practised the Christian religion, in which he had been instructed from infancy, devotedly and most scrupulously ' and that he took a close interest in chant. The monarch's biographer also asserted that he later ' knew Latin so well that he could express himself equally in that language and in his mother-tongue '. By the latter Einhard meant Frankish or more specifically the dialect spoken westwards of Cologne. But Charles must also have been familiar from boyhood with the *rustica romana lingua* into which spoken Latin had evolved and which in his lifetime became sharply distinguished from the written language of the educated. When, later in life, Charles had scholars around him who could satisfy his curiosity, he showed a particular and for once well-authenticated interest in the stars: it is one that follows naturally, as many know from personal experience, from the open-air life that was normal to the well-born young man of the Middle Ages.

Charles' apprenticeship in the public duties and responsibilities to which it was assumed he would succeed began, as with any well-born child of the period, at an carly age. At the end of 753 he was sent by his father to meet the Pope and accompany him on the last stages of his journey to Ponthion and, with his brother was subsequently annointed king by the Pope at St. Denis. When the young duke Tassilo III of Bavaria made his submission in 757 he promised fidelity, according to the later Royal Annals, both to Pippin and to his two sons. In 761, again according to contemporary annals, Charles accompanied his father on a punitive and perhaps more than normally savage expedition into Aquitaine. In 762 he ' consented ' to a grant of land and privileges made by his father and mother to the abbey of Prüm. He may have been present when the already unreliable Tassilo renewed his promises in 763. For the next four years the sources are silent.

The biographer of a modern figure usually has at his disposal material of various kinds that allows him to describe his subject's appearance at different phases of his life. For Charles, to all intents and purposes, this does not exist. A life-size statue of Charles in stucco at Münster in Grisons (Müstair), (jacket front and pl. 59), which has usually been associated with the ' canonization ' of the Emperor in 1165 (below, p. 202), has recently been claimed as a work of the very early ninth century: but even if it is of this date, which is plausible but not proved, it cannot be regarded as a portrait. The last remains of the eighth-century Papal Lateran Palace in Rome include a ruthlessly restored version of a contemporary representation of Charles in mosaic (below, p. 149 and fig. 39) and another one formerly existed at the church of S. Susanna in the same city. A small bronze statuette, formerly at Metz, of a king on horseback (pl. 4) is generally regarded

Fig. 12 Stucco work from Germigny-des-Prés. *Musée de Peinture, Orléans.*

41

as a work of the ninth century although the horse is a Renaissance replacement. It is not established, however, that the figure was intended to represent Charles the Great rather than one of the later Carolingians such as Charles the Bald, in whose time it was almost certainly made.

The common features of these early or probably early representations are the long drooping moustaches, beard and the hair cut all round in a straight fringe. Einhard describes Charles as heavily built and 'seven times the length of his own foot' in height and nineteenth-century examination of his reputed skeletal remains suggests that he was in fact a man of over six feet which, in view of the lower average height of people at this period, means that he would have towered over most of his court and followers. Einhard also speaks of him as having light coloured hair and being bright-eyed and of good bearing. In other respects, however, his description—admittedly based on acquaintance with the king only later in life—does not suggest a particularly impressive-looking person: his neck was short and thick, he had a paunch and his nose was on the long side. His voice was *clara*, by which is probably meant shrill rather than clear, especially as Einhard says that it didn't really match his body. He was, on the other hand, a vigorous and healthy man until the last years of his long life. His normal wear according to his biographer was what he describes as 'the Frankish national costume', that is to say linen undershirt and drawers, over them a tunic and breeches and leggings. In winter a cape of otter or marten skins covered his shoulders and chest and at all times a sword hung from his sword-belt. His usual outer garment was a blue cloak. This is more or less the garb worn by the layman (representing 'Justice'?) in the frontispiece to an early manuscript of the Capitularies (pl. 60) and in the stylistically much superior representation of Charles' son and successor Louis in a manuscript from Fulda (fig. 13). Einhard is almost certainly right in suggesting that similar costume was worn by the Frankish magnates (compare the representation of one of them in the painting at Malles, pl. 71). Only on ceremonial occasions, when he wore a cloak of more magnificent design and material and carried the royal or Imperial insignia would Charles' dress have distinguished him clearly from his greater subjects.

For whatever reason, tension between Charles and his younger brother began within a very few months of their accession. When Aquitaine and Gascony broke into rebellion yet again, Charles was compelled to undertake two expeditions without Carloman's assistance (769). In 770 a temporary reconciliation was achieved through the intervention of their mother Berta, who like many medieval queens emerged only after her husband's death as a woman of strong personality. She went on to secure the re-establishment of friendly relations between the Frankish kings and the duke of Bavaria and to negotiate a marriage between Charles and a daughter of the Lombard king. Such a step seemed calculated to leave the Bishop of Rome isolated in the face of any further Lombard expeditions in central Italy and it provoked him to send a passionately and even violently worded letter. What the Frankish court proposed, he insisted, would not be a marriage but an association of the most evil kind; 'what folly is this that your illustrious Frankish race, which shines supreme above all other nations, and that that most noble royal line of yours should be fouled—perish the thought!—by the treacherous and most foul race of the Lombards, which is not to be numbered among the nations'; for a king of the Franks to enter into any sort of alliance with the enemies of the Papacy would be intolerable and unforgivable; if he does so, by the authority of St. Peter 'on whose tomb we have placed a copy of our

Fig. 13 Representation of Louis the Pious in a manuscript written at Fulda in the second quarter of the ninth century. *Biblioteca Apostolica Vaticana, Rome.* Reg. Lat. 124, fol 4v.

9. The Tassilo Chalice; 781: *Kremsmünster, Stiftsbibliothek.* Height 25 cm.

warning', he will be damned to all eternity. Shortly afterwards the Pope was inextricably involved in a complicated conspiracy and counter-conspiracy of some of the leading Roman laymen associated with his Court, in which the purported aim of one party was to deliver the city to the Lombards. By this time the marriage had taken place, in complete defiance of the Papal threats.

After only a year, however, Charles repudiated his Lombard wife, without incurring any recorded protest from the Frankish clergy and subsequently married Hildegard, 'a Swabian, of the highest nobility'. A number of scholars have supposed that the rise and fall of the Carolingian Empire can be explained almost entirely in terms of marriage alliances and family rivalries—which, in the extreme form in which this view has sometimes been expounded, is certainly not true. There is a particular temptation to look for a political purpose behind Charles' second marriage. Hildegard was, through her mother, a great-great-grand-daughter of the heroic Swabian duke Godfrey, whose sons and grandson had continued to oppose Charles' ancestors as usurpers of the authority of the Mero-vingian kings. Her father, however, was a Frank from the middle Rhine region whose association with the Carolingians brought profit and influence to himself and his descendants—the later untypical emphasis on his daughter's maternal ancestry is good evidence that he himself was a ' new man '—and probably already before 768 a Swabian uncle had succeeded another Rhineland Frank as count in a substantial area of the old duchy. Even the unexpected fact that writers of documents in this part of Swabia were dating them with reference to Charles, and not Carloman while the latter was still alive, is not conclusive proof that Charles' second marriage was one of policy rather than of personal choice.

Carloman died at the end of 771. A number of prominent figures in his kingdom offered their allegiance to King Charles: among them were abbot Fulrad of St. Denis, who had been encouraged to establish close links with western Swabia, and the so-called ' archbishop of the Gauls ' Wilchar, one of the two Papal envoys whom Pippin had persuaded to take office in Francia. Carloman's widow and small children, in company with the once influential Burgundian Autchar and other nobles, judged it wiser to leave Francia and eventually found refuge at the Lombard royal court with king Desiderius. His elder brother ' happily acquired the monarchy of the whole kingdom of the Franks '. In the light of Charles' later career, it is possible to say, as many scholars have done, that Carloman's early death and the re-uniting of the territories over which Pippin had been sole king was fortunate both for Francia and for the future history of Europe. The vast increase of Charles' resources and authority, without a military campaign, unquestionably had momentous results. Had he subsequently achieved less, however, more stress might have been laid on his ruthlessness and apparent disregard of the possible rights of his nephews, even conceding that at this time there was no law to challenge practical convenience when the heir to a kingdom was a minor. The events of these months certainly show the opportunism and ability to take prompt and decisive action that were to characterize Charles' kingship for many years to come.

Indirectly these events helped finally to establish the predominance of northern and Rhineland Austrasia within the ' kingdom of the Franks '. Charles is not known ever to have re-visited Noyon, the city where he was acclaimed king in 768, nor to have visited Paris except briefly in 800, although he stayed several times at St. Denis and also visited his brother's former ' capital ' of Soissons with its tomb of St. Medard (fig. 14). In the first half of his reign, he was frequently on the move for months on end and often over considerable distances. Yet there were few

10. Interior of the west side of the Octagon gallery, showing Charles' throne, Aachen Cathedral.

45

Fig. 14 ' Confessio ' of St. Medard, Soissons, as revealed by recent excavations.

years in which he did not take up residence for several weeks at a time at Herstal, near the Meuse north-east of Liège, or at Worms on the middle Rhine; and these places were particularly favoured for the great feasts of the Christian year and for other occasions when the king required a specially large gathering of his subjects. The first of these was of Frankish origin and possibly an old family estate of Charles' ancestors, like Jupille on the opposite bank of the river. The extent of both can apparently be approximately reconstructed from later parish-boundaries. Worms, by contrast, had been a Roman town of secondary importance which achieved a temporary prominence in the fifth century but after its conquest by the Franks it seems to have played only a minor rôle until Pippin held a ' general assembly ' there in 764. Diplomas of Charles speak of ' the royal city ' and later evidence shows that it was the centre of a complex of royal estates and other sources of revenue. The earlier history of most of these domains is unknown and it is only a guess that many of them were acquired by the Carolingians when they were still Mayors of the Palace.

It was to Worms that Charles summoned his warriors, whom we should probably think of as numbered in hundreds rather than thousands, in the early summer of 772. The leadership of regular military expeditions, of a kind that are perhaps better described as glorified raiding-parties, were still expected of a Germanic king and one at this juncture could help to forestall any latent discontent. The host crossed Hesse, slowly being opened up to settlement with the help of missionaries and monks, and entered the land of the Saxons probably just north of the Frankish fortified settlement of Buraburg, which overlooks what was certainly the principal road through this area a century or two later. The main objective of the expedition was the Saxon fortified settlement or refuge of Eresburg and the heathen sanctuary of the ' Universe tree ' (*Irminsûl*) associated with it, both of which were sacked and looted. Subsequently the army advanced a short distance farther, to the river Weser, where Charles received the submission of some of the inhabitants of the region and twelve hostages. The ' Royal Annalist ' later

noted only that this was the ' first time ' Charles entered Saxony: participants and contemporaries, the former richer for the gold and silver taken from the sanctuary, were probably more interested in its successful conclusion. By October the expedition had dispersed and Charles and his court were at Herstal: the hunting-season had succeeded the fighting-season.

Early in 773 a Papal emissary arrived at the Frankish court, having been forced to travel by ship from Rome to Marseilles because the land-route through north Italy was closed to him. He brought a request for Frankish help, once again to prevent the Lombards from overrunning the former Imperial territories over which the bishops of Rome had an only partially effective territorial authority. Hadrian I, the last Pope to include in the dating-clauses of his official documents the name of the Emperor then ruling in Constantinople, had been elected bishop of the Roman see in February 772. He came from one of the leading families of the city whose members had naturally held high places in both the local Imperial and Papal administration and which had extensive estates in the rural areas to the north of the city. Immediately after his accession he recalled or released those who had suffered at the hands of the ' pro-Lombard ' intriguers and the Pope they had manipulated, thus effectively demonstrating in whose hands temporal authority in the city and duchy of Rome now was. When Desiderius sent an embassy to propose a renewal of friendly relations between the two courts, Hadrian's reply was uncompromising: he declared that his ' predecessor in office told me that Desiderius had lied to him in everything which he had promised with an oath on the body of the blessed Peter, as to restoring the rights of God's holy Church: and further that it was only under the persuasion of the unjust arguments of the same Desiderius that he caused the eyes of Christopher and Sergius to be dug out, and executed the will of the Lombard on those two officers of the Church'. Desiderius' answer was to send troops to occupy some of the cities along the Adriatic coast and in the eastern Apennines that his predecessor had abandoned in 756/7 and to move the frontier on the Via Flaminia nearer to Rome; and to launch the ' general army ' of Lombard Tuscany against the territory of Bieda where it fell upon the city's inhabitants who ' in the expectation of peace had gone out with their wives and children and dependants to gather in the crops ', killing them in large numbers and carrying away what they did not destroy.

According to the Royal Annals, Charles ' took counsel with the Franks as to what he should do ' and the *Liber Pontificalis* has a detailed record of the embassies that travelled between the Frankish, Lombard and Papal courts in the early months of 773. The usual assumption that Charles had been waiting for an opportunity to intervene south of the Alps is almost certainly false. It is not even wise to suppose that when the host was finally ordered to Geneva, all search for a peaceful solution having failed, Charles had a clearly-formed intention of putting himself in the place of the native Lombard king.

The Franks moved south in two separate armies, Charles himself leading one over the Mont Cenis while an uncle brought the other over the Great St. Bernard and down the Val d'Aosta, which was nominally part of the Frankish dominions. Desiderius, we are told, first tried to check the invasion at the necks of the two valleys but was outflanked and beat a retreat to Pavia. A length of wall extending out from precipitous rock on the south side of the Val di Susa at Chiusa is still locally connected with this episode. It would be rash to assume that this belief reflects an unbroken oral tradition and the wall, which is being steadily destroyed, has never been studied by an archaeologist. It does, however, appear to be men-

12. Manuscript; Canon-tables; *London, British Museum* Harley 2788, fol 11v; end of eighth century. *Size* 37 × 25.5 cm.

49

tioned in an eleventh-century chronicle and, in view of the similar earthworks of
seventh or eighth century date in many parts of Europe, it is not unlikely that the
Lombards had in fact built a three-quarter-mile wall and ditch across the valley
at this point. The bulk of the Lombard army was disbanded before Pavia. Desiderius sought security in that city, while his son went with Carloman's widow to
Verona, ' the strongest of all the cities of the Lombards ' because the wall built
round it in the fourth century was still in good repair.

The Lombard capital held out against the Franks for nine months. While the
siege was still in progress, Charles took an expedition to Verona, without apparently
capturing the city or any other of the main towns of north Italy. He subsequently
travelled to Rome, where at Easter-time, 774, he renewed (according to the Papal
biographer) the concession of ' cities and territories ' in central and southern Italy
made to the Pope by his father in 754. At the beginning of June 774 Pavia at last
succumbed, Desiderius and his court and palace officials were captured together
with an immense treasure and ' the whole Lombard kingdom ' accepted Charles'
authority. Henceforward his full royal style was ' King of the Franks and of the
Lombards and patrician of the Romans '.

Even historians convinced of ' the historic destiny of Charlemagne ' have felt
called on to account for the apparently sudden and total collapse of the two-
hundred-year-old Lombard kingdom, which is all the more striking in contrast
with the decades of resistance offered by the Saxons. Stress is commonly laid on
the persistent challenge to the authority of the Lombard kings by the dukes and on
the discontent among lesser magnates in the last decades of the kingdom's history.
There is, however, evidence of similar discontent in the Frankish kingdoms in the
same period. The supposed independence of the dukes, other than those of Spoleto
and Benevento, is by no means an obvious feature of the eighth century; and unless
the evidence from Liutprand's reign (712-44) is wholly deceptive, he had under his

Journeys and campaigns undertaken by Charles.

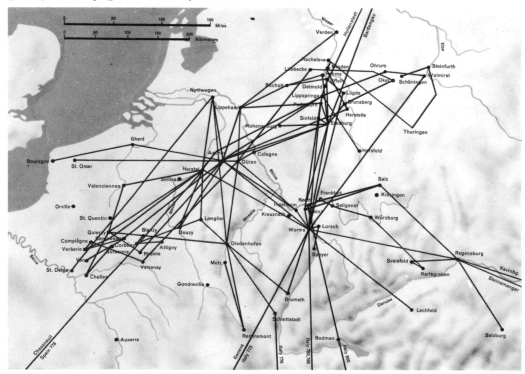

Fig. 15 Figure initial from a
mid-eighth century manuscript.
Paris, Bibliothèque Nationale
Ms. Lat. 4884, fol 1.

control a wider range of resources and exercised a greater authority over his subjects than any of his contemporaries in the West. It is not unlikely, however, that his successors' behaviour towards the bishop of Rome—successor of St. Peter, vicar of Christ—had antagonized many of their leading subjects; and the transfers of allegiance by Lombard magnates many months before Pavia fell to the Franks certainly suggests that Desiderius, and the son who had been designated to follow him, commanded no great respect. Here surely is the crux of the matter. The primary loyalty of magnates at this time was not to a national or patriotic ideal— although regional loyalties there certainly were—but to the person of a king or other acknowledged leader, less commonly to a line of kings. Except when the conflict was sharpened by a major difference of religious belief, the defeat and capture or death of a king were compelling reasons for many magnates—on whom the continuance of the struggle depended—to transfer their allegiance to the victor: only where there was a strong dynastic loyalty had they any serious alternative. The opportunity of gaining control of resources sufficient to provide the basis of a successful counter-attack was very rarely given to a leader who emerged later. It is instructive to compare the overthrow of the Lombard kingdom in 773/4 with that of the Visigothic kingdom in Spain in 711 and of the Anglo-Saxon kingdom in 1066. Perhaps it is relevant to add that when Charles returned north of the Alps he took with him a number of bishops and landowning laymen as hostages—a crude but not ineffective way of guaranteeing the continued good behaviour of others of their class.

One consequence of Charles' prolonged absence from Francia with his warriors is hardly unexpected. The southern Saxons launched a retaliatory raid against the area round Buraburg and were only prevented from burning the monastery of Fritzlar, consecrated by Boniface, by a miracle. Having returned to Ingelheim in the late summer of 774 Charles sent four raiding-parties into Saxony. Three are said to have fought and beaten the Saxons, the fourth to have collected a quantity of booty without a battle. Neither the social structure of the Saxons nor the terrain in which they lived made the task of an invader an easy one or a defeat like that of the Lombards easily envisageable. None the less, a year later Charles assembled his troops for what was obviously intended to be a more effective demonstration of Frankish power. The expedition advanced up the valley of the Ruhr, crossed the watershed to Eresburg and then followed the line of the Weser northwards before turning west near where the modern town of Minden stands. In two places groups of Saxons, under their local leaders, made acts of submission and handed over hostages. One of the leaders was a certain Hessi whose daughter was later to marry a Frankish magnate and who himself died as a monk at Fulda. On three other occasions Charles' armies had to fight and once the Franks clearly were only just saved from destruction. The unknown writer who partially rewrote the Royal Annals for the late eighth century shortly after 814 claimed that already at the beginning of 775 Charles had decided to subject the Saxons and make them Christian. The weight of the evidence is against this view: the only difference between the invasion of 775 and earlier ones by Frankish armies, apart perhaps from its duration, was that the king left behind garrisons in the two Saxon castles nearest the western and southern boundaries, in a situation that evidently had much in common with the frontier-forts of eighteenth-century British North America or of twentieth-century French Sahara.

By 775 letters written by Anglo-Saxon clergy living in Charles' dominions to the king himself or to their fellow-countrymen and others from England show that

Fig. 16 A seal of Charles the Great. *Paris, Archives Nationales.*

51

Charles' successes were bringing both fame and responsibility. A certain Cathwulf congratulated him on his series of triumphs which (he said) were pleasing to God and earning him a high repute among men. About the same time, however, one from Lul, Boniface's successor at Mainz, to the archbishop of York spoke unhappily of the ' modern princes who introduce new ways and new laws according to their desires '. The successes, indeed, were not very securely based. Immediately after Christmas 775 the Frankish king and his warriors were on their way to Italy: rebellion had broken out in the north-east—always a danger-area because it was a frontier region—and in Tuscany. Moreover, famine conditions that had apparently lasted over several years had provoked a more general discontent. When the rebel duke of Friuli, a Lombard who had been confirmed in or given office by Charles, was defeated and killed by the Frankish armies, his followers and allies seem to have given up the struggle very quickly and the king was able to set off homewards again with yet more hostages in his train. By this time he and his warriors had suffered another set-back: the garrison at Eresburg had been overrun by the Saxons and that at Syburg had only been able to beat them off with difficulty. A new assembly of the host had to be summoned for the late summer. But having again entered Saxony from the south, Charles' actions suggest that he had in mind for the future something more than annual punitive expeditions which left the mass of the Saxon warriors free to re-emerge from their hideouts once he had withdrawn.

The Christian Breton inhabitants of the Armorican peninsula had, rather surprisingly, succeeded in maintaining their independence of successive *reges Francorum*, although the frontier was in constant flux—now east, now west of Vannes and Rennes. Probably already before the death of Pippin the insecurely held Frankish frontier regions were made the responsibility of a man who in Charles' time appears with the title of ' prefect of the [Breton] march ' and who presumably had a more independent authority and more soldiers at his disposal than other local representatives of the monarch. Charles now evidently had something similar in mind for southern Saxony. Eresburg was rebuilt and an entirely new castle, Karlsburg, was built on the left bank of the upper Lippe: permanent garrisons were installed in both. The modification of captured Saxon *castra* and the building of new ones that could house a substantial community were to become a common feature of Frankish policy in Saxony over the next quarter of a century; and it is not unlikely that the first of the quite distinct smaller forts, which subsequently proliferated along the southern approaches to Saxony and were later built elsewhere in the territory, belong to this time. By contrast with the Saxons the conquerors made use of mortared stone in their fortifications. The same technique was naturally used for the chapels or small churches which became a normal feature of the larger castles (cf. the plan of Hohensyburg, page 58) and of which the earliest recorded dedication is almost invariably to St. Peter. It is impossible to show that any one of these chapels goes back to 776 but they none the less reflect a change in the Frankish king's attitude to the Saxon problem which is evident in this year. Now for the first time the submission of large groups of Saxons was accompanied not only by the giving of tribute and the surrender of hostages but also by the Christian baptism of the local population of both sexes and all ages by compulsion rather than by their own desire and in the vicinity of Karlsburg, symbol of Frankish military power. The kind of elementary catechism or baptismal vow used on this and similar occasions can be gathered from the one or two examples that scribes of the ninth century and later took the trouble to copy: the

13. Royal (Imperial) throne in west gallery, Aachen Cathedral.

14. Bronze lion's head on the west door of Aachen Cathedral. *Diameter of head* 29 cm.

15. Bronze railings of the Octagon gallery in Aachen Cathedral.

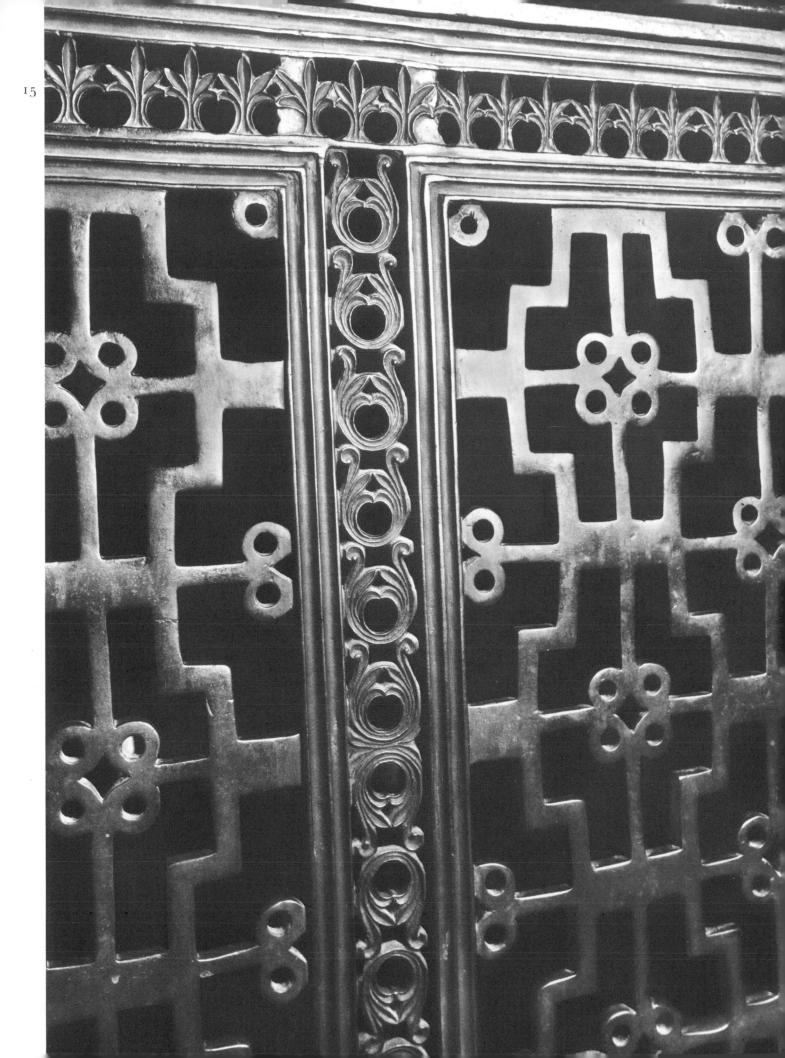

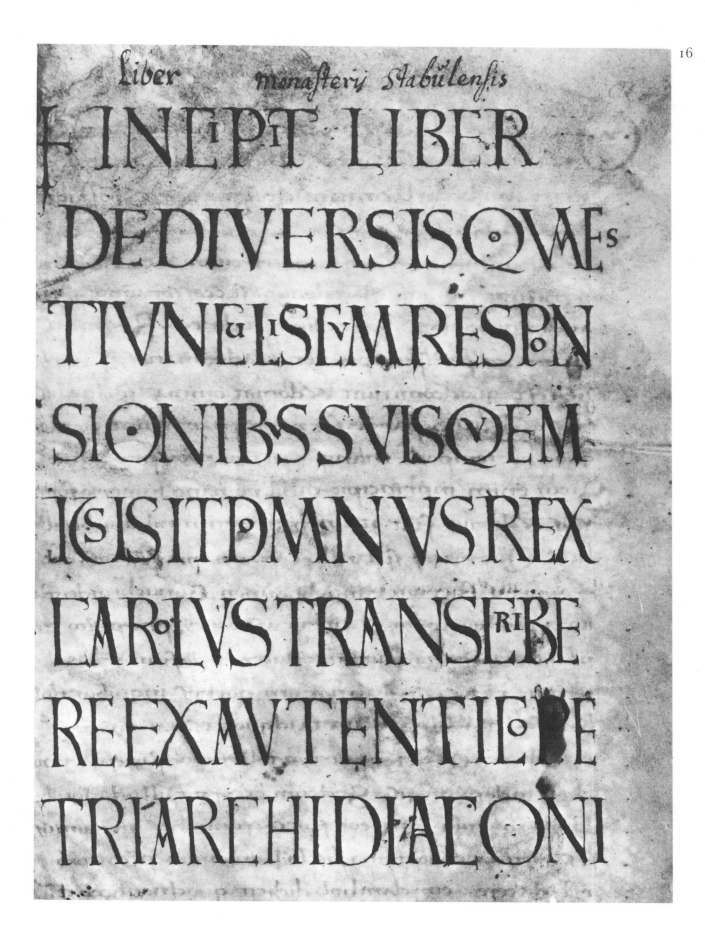

renunciation of Thunaer, Uuoden and Saxnot is at least as prominent as the profession of the new faith.

The monks of Fulda later tried to make out that already at the date of abbot Sturmi's death in 779 he and his monastery had become the main base of an organized missionary activity among the pagan Saxons. Although their community was certainly one of the earliest to benefit from the pious donations of recent converts, there seems little substance in the claim. The process was certainly much slower and success more difficult to achieve than ' Lives ', written in the ninth century, suggest. In the 780s, the most notable contributions to the task of conversion seem to have come from the work of Willehad, a Northumbrian who had been sent by his fellow-countrymen and king to work in the area of Frisia in which Boniface had been martyred but had been persuaded by Charles to work farther east; and by the bishopric of Würzburg, which controlled and staffed early mission-stations at Paderborn and elsewhere in south and central Saxony. The future importance of Paderborn was foreshadowed when Charles ordered a ' general assembly ' to meet there in the summer of 777. The fact that he had for the first time chosen a meeting-place not even in the Frankish march but in Saxony proper suggests a growing and, as it proved, dangerous self-confidence. He could not have foreseen that those Saxons under the leadership of Widukind, whose name appears in Frankish records for the first time, who failed to present themselves at court were to occupy Frankish energies considerably more in the next decade than the others who were prepared to adopt the Christian faith.

It has been boldly argued that the Saxon wars henceforward had some of the elements of a class-struggle, in that the landowning class or aristocracy sold itself to the invaders while the ordinary people sought to free their land of both their existing and their threatened masters. This has been equally vigorously denied, not least on the grounds that the notions of a popular revolt and of independent action by the non-noble free are equally anachronistic. There is no doubt, however, that many prominent Saxons sought to and in some cases did secure their position by coming to terms with the invader: the Annals for 777 refer specifically to the surrender of personal freedom and property to the king, which later evidence suggests was often only a preliminary to receiving them back from the monarch, and some of those involved in these transactions subsequently became men of greater power and influence by being entrusted with an official position at court or in the kingdom.

The 777 assembly brought Charles even more exciting prospects of military success in a region in which the material rewards—treasure of all sorts—were likely to be substantial. For nearly twenty years neither the Spanish Arabs nor the Franks had made any recorded incursion across the Pyrenean frontier. Charles' reputation as a warrior leader had, however, evidently spread across the mountains, for legates arrived at Paderborn with a request from the son of a one-time Amir of Cordoba for help against the man who had ousted him. It may be, although it cannot be proved, that appeals had also come from some of the Christian elements in Spain and it is a fact, although it is not likely that Charles was well-informed on the point, that the representatives of the Amir in some of the most important communities north of the river Ebro were of Visigothic origin. To say that Charles envisaged establishing a protectorate either over this border region or over all the Christians of Spain is to attribute to him more than either the sources or probability permit. What is clear is that Charles, grandson of the man who forty-five years earlier had inflicted a decisive defeat on Moslem armies, was persuaded of the opportunity that lay at hand, regardless of the problems of moving an army over

16. Display page of ' court ' manuscript: *Brussels, Bibliothèque Royale de Belgique* Ms II 2572, fol 1. *Size* 25.5 × 19 cm.

57

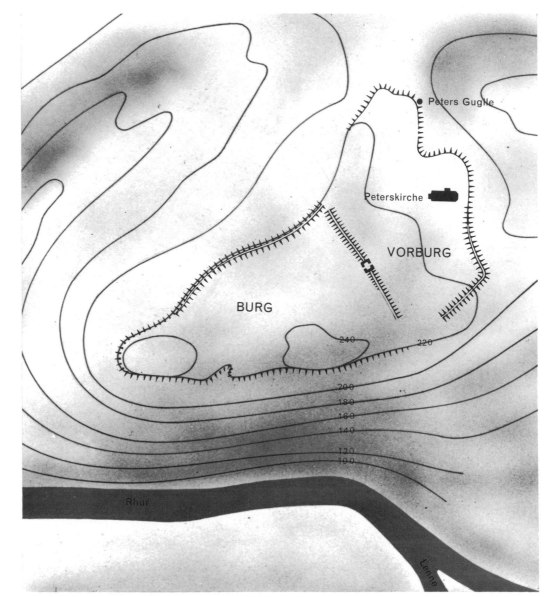

Plan of Hohensyburg (*height* in metres)

longer distances and more difficult country than he had yet attempted.

Charles summoned what the annalists imply was much the largest army that he and probably his predecessors had ever brought together. In the early summer of 778 two columns moved to and crossed the Pyrenees. They joined up at Saragossa on the middle Ebro and Charles received the nominal surrender of the city. Shortly afterwards the expedition began its journey back to Francia, taking with it hostages and doubtless also treasure. In a gesture of defiance and superiority that was not untypical of much of the warfare of the period, the walls of Pampeluna were razed. What happened to the army as it retreated across the Pyrenees in early August provided the stuff of a memorable legend which three centuries later acquired poetic grandeur and imperishability in the first great work of Romance literature, the *Chanson de Roland*. The original version of the Royal Annals are silent. The unknown reviser who was at work shortly after Charles' death knew and recorded the uncomfortable truth; and Einhard subsequently added a few more details. In one of the notoriously difficult high passes of the Pyrenees, which the later poet

' remembered ' as Roncevalles, the mountain Basques fell on the expedition's rearguard. The chronicler's account of what then befell the Franks reflects the perennial resentment of the heavily-armed and encumbered professional soldier towards the lightly-armed irregular who skilfully turns difficult country to his advantage. The Frankish rearguard seems in fact to have been cut to pieces: the dead included Charles' steward or seneschal and his count of the palace and also Roland, ' commander of the Breton march '.

The king is reported to have returned to Francia a much-saddened man. Worse was to follow. At Auxerre news was brought to the king that the Saxons, under Widukind's leadership, had risen against the Franks. By the time the detachment sent to deal with them made contact with the rebels they had penetrated to the Rhine opposite Cologne and had ravaged the country on its right bank—in which many of Charles' leading magnates and the monasteries most closely associated with him had substantial estates—as far south as Coblenz, and then withdrawn up the Lahn, frightening the monks of Fulda into quitting the abbey with the body of its founder. It is possible that the former Lombard kingdom was showing signs of restlessness at the same time: and the Pope sent an appeal for help against a threat from Lombard Benevento whose prince had never submitted to the Frankish king and who was reported to have gained Byzantine backing. Men who were not involved in the king's expeditions and regions far away from the frontiers had misfortunes of their own: in 779 the king sought to put a stop to the raising of private armies, whose purpose was clearly not to reinforce the Frankish host. (At the same time he prohibited the export of metal-reinforced tunics and attempted to prevent the misuse of associations privately organised for mutual help.)

The years 778-9 have been described as ' a crisis in the reign of Charlemagne '. The setbacks suffered by the Frankish king and the consequent loss of prestige at this time, when his fame had been steadily increasing for a decade, were certainly serious: but the judgement quoted seems to exaggerate the contrast between these years and other years of his reign. In the winter of 785/6 Charles had to meet what the well-informed reviser of the Royal Annals regarded as the most dangerous threat in his career: possibly partly as a protest against too-frequent campaigns which brought no obvious reward, a number of magnates east of the Rhine associated themselves with a local count, in whom the king had clearly placed great trust, in planning a rebellion that was, however, forestalled; and when the king was in Italy a year later, he found cause for deporting as hostages a number of Lombard landowners who had unsuspectingly answered a summons to his court. 792 and 793 were apparently abnormally wet years, with serious consequences for the harvest; and in the space of twelve months Charles had to face successively an attempt by discontented magnates, including his eldest, illegitimate, son, to kill him; the failure of an expedition led by his other sons against Benevento—from which, incidentally, at least one substantial Italian landowner is know to have deserted; a widespread famine; the cutting to pieces by Saxon rebels of a body of troops on its way from Frisia to join the main Frankish host which forced Charles to abandon the expedition planned for that year; and a successful Saracen counter-offensive against the region south of the eastern Pyrenees over which Frankish domination had been established in the preceding eight years.

Dangers and disasters such as these, however, provided Charles with exceptional opportunities for displaying those qualities which enabled him to impress contemporaries with his personality and gave his reign a lasting importance in the history of the areas over which he ruled. Even in the midst of apparent disaster, the king seems to have been able to give attention to the wider problems that faced him as a ruler of territories and men and each setback only encouraged him to pursue his ambitions and aims with even more determination. In retrospect the periodic years of crisis seem to be an essential preliminary to further advance and achievement.

The years 778 and 779 were ones in which for the first time, so far as we know, Charles sought to create a more solid basis for the exercise of royal authority and to provide for the greater security of his subjects and of what belonged to them. In 780 he led an expedition which, for the first time in the history of the Franks, advanced right across Saxony to the lower Elbe; at the end of that year he set out with his army for Italy and in 781 he took new steps to solve that country's particular problems; and, again in 781, he compelled the duke of Bavaria to acknowledge once more the superior authority of the king of the Franks by swearing oaths and sending hostages. The attempt to restrain the duke's freedom of action was only a little more lasting than the effect of getting hostages from the Saxons and compelling them to accept Christian baptism. In 782 Charles held his summer assembly inside Saxony. It was attended by emissaries of the king of the Danes and of the kagan of the Avars. He dispatched an army that included Saxons against the Slavs who were settled across the lower Elbe: it came face-to-face with an army of rebel Saxons, among them many whom the king had thought he could trust, roused and led by Widukind. Although a second army was hastily sent from Francia, the leaders of the original expeditionary force committed their troops to battle so that the commander of the reinforcements, Charles' relative Thierry, should not earn the credit of the expected victory—and they were decisively and disastrously beaten. The account of the battle given in the revised Royal Annals and clearly obtained from a participant suggests that on this occasion the Frankish armies may have intended, if not actually attempted, to launch a cavalry charge.

Once again, an expedition led by Charles in person was necessary to save the situation: on the Weser not far from Verden the main Saxon army was compelled to surrender. Charles' patience, however, had been tried once too often: according to the royal annalist 4,500 prisoners were then put to death. A succession of scholars has suggested that the number of Saxons massacred at the royal command must in fact have been very much smaller or even that the annalist made a mistake of another kind and that the 4,500 were deported, not killed. To suppose that Charles was incapable of such an act is to attribute to him a moral virtue above almost all Christian kings of the Middle Ages: the slaughter of a defeated enemy on the battle-field was common practice, except where enslavement or ransomming seemed likely to prove profitable; and it is commonly forgotten that most of the hostages taken year by year by the Frankish king would have been put to death when those who had handed them over as a pledge of their good behaviour once again challenged royal authority. Only the magnitude of Charles' revenge distinguished it from other acts of the same kind.

Widukind had evaded capture and death, taking refuge among the Danes. Opposition to Frankish domination and the Christian religion by the inhabitants of east Saxony was weakening: in 783, immediately after what the annalists imply was a mass revolt involving all those who had previously acknowledged Charles' overlordship and doubtless causing the death of priests and the destruction of churches, and again in 784 the Frankish king was able to lead his armies through that region as far as the Elbe with relatively little trouble. The hard core of resistance was to be found among the Westphalians. There are, however, hints in the

Frankish annals for these years that they had none the less been compelled to make a change in their tactics which, on the usual assumption that horsed warriors already formed an important part of the Frankish armies, must ultimately have been to their disadvantage. They were apparently committing themselves to battle in open country presumably because they recognized that they were engaged in a war of survival and perhaps also because their main fortified refuges were in Frankish hands. Charles and his armies were in the field for almost the whole of 784 and it is probably not merely due to chance that there is no extant diploma of that year or of the next. At the beginning of 785 the king moved his family to the Eresburg. He was clearly determined that this would be the last year of Saxon resistance and by now he had grasped that without a broad strategic plan he was unlikely to succeed. Accordingly, several months were spent in skirmishes, the demolition of fortresses and the opening-up of lines of advance. In June the host left Paderborn on a destructive advance through central and northern Saxony to the lower Elbe. The Saxons settled to the north of the Elbe, in Nordalbingia, were still beyond his reach and the marshy territory between the Weser and Elbe estuaries remained safe from invasion. But the spirit of Saxon resistance was broken and even Widukind was prepared to come to terms with the conqueror. In the autumn of 785 the Saxon leader and those who had stood by him to the end accepted Christian baptism. When news reached the Pope that ' the savage and inimical Saxons ' were at last subjected to Frankish authority and that through the submission of their chiefs ' the whole Saxon people ' had become Christian, he ordered three days of litanies of thanksgiving, not only in the Frankish dominions but in the whole Christian west.

In 785 Saxony, which had been for many generations the one serious external threat to the Frankish ' heart-land ', became a part of the ' kingdom of the Franks ' and the territorial organization of the Latin church was extended gradually,

Fig. 17 A portable reliquary from the monastery of Enger (Saxony) reputedly given by its founder, Widukind, who in turn had received it on the occasion of his baptism from the Frankish king. *Berlin, Staatliche Museen.* See pl. 78. (*Size at base* 16 × 14.5 cm.)

beginning with the see of Bremen, to which Willehad was consecrated in 787, over the whole area between the Rhine, the foot of the Danish peninsula and the lower Elbe. Between 793 and 797 Charles was forced to lead or send several expeditions to Saxony: in 795 a strictly contemporary source reports that he levied more hostages than he or anyone else was ever known to have done before. However, except in the coastal district between the Weser and the Elbe which only became Frankish in this period, the purpose of these expeditions was the suppression of rebellions, not the conquest of independent peoples, and however unwelcome these may have been as a challenge to royal authority they were not peculiar to this region. After 785 Charles was free to direct the main military strength of his kingdom and to use the annual or near-annual assembly of the host, which now usually included a substantial element from the conquered territories, to other ends.

Only in one region along his frontiers was Charles' sovereignty spontaneously sought. In 785, according to the annals of a south French monastery, the inhabitants of Gerona, just across the Pyrenees, rejected the authority of the Amir and ' delivered their town [and, of course, its territory] to Charles '. About the same time something similar must have happened in the Pyrenean territories of Urgel, Cerdagne and Besalù. Even so, for some years the Frankish hold on this predominantly wild and difficult region was anything but secure. Immediately to the west was the country of the Basques (Gascons) who once again created a dangerous situation in 790; and in 793 the Spanish Arabs delivered a counter-attack along the coast. The successful penetration of this host into Septimania is reported with gloomy relish by the anonymous reviser of the Royal Annals. There was more than one good reason, therefore, for giving special treatment to Frankish Spain. Later evidence shows, in fact, that Charles formally recognized the different legal and judicial traditions of the Gothic territories incorporated in his kingdom and granted exceptional privileges to the magnates and others who had offered him their allegiance—privileges that were extended to the inhabitants of Barcelona after its capture from the Saracens in 801. *Gothia* was none the less several times the scene of rebellion in the next three-quarters of a century but the explanation is usually to be sought in local magnate rivalries rather than in nationalist or even anti-alien feelings.

To the *Hispani* of this limited area in or near the Pyrenees the Frankish king Charles may have come as a liberator from the infidel yoke. To the other peoples who bordered his dominions, Christian and non-Christian alike, he was an oppressive enemy, like so many others before and after him. In 786 an army was sent into Brittany, on the grounds that its inhabitants were not keeping up payment of the tribute offered to his predecessors. Towards the end of that same year, at a time when normally only the Montgenèvre crossing is open in the western Alps, Charles and the Frankish host left Worms for Italy. By the time he reached Rome the prince of Benevento had concluded, rightly or wrongly, that his territory—which the later reviser of the Royal Annals not unreasonably described as the last part of the former Lombard kingdom to remain outside his control—was the object of the Frankish expedition. He hastily sought a peaceful settlement of a long-standing border dispute with the nominally Imperial, but effectively independent, duchy of Naples; and sent his younger son to persuade the king to accept his submission but to stay away from the principality. Somewhat surprisingly Charles seems to have been inclined to agree: and on this occasion it was his magnates backed up by the Pope, who hoped to recover papal estates that had been previously seized, who insisted on continuing the expedition. Advancing down the ancient Via Latina past Monte

17. Detail from ivory diptych in the Cathedral Treasury, Aachen. *Width of panel* 10 cm.

18. Manuscript: *Fons Vitae;* opening words of the Gospel for Vigil of Christmas from the Godescalc Evangelistary: *Paris, Bibliothèque Nationale* Lat. 1203, fol 3v and fol 4; 781-783. *Size* 30.5 × 21 cm.

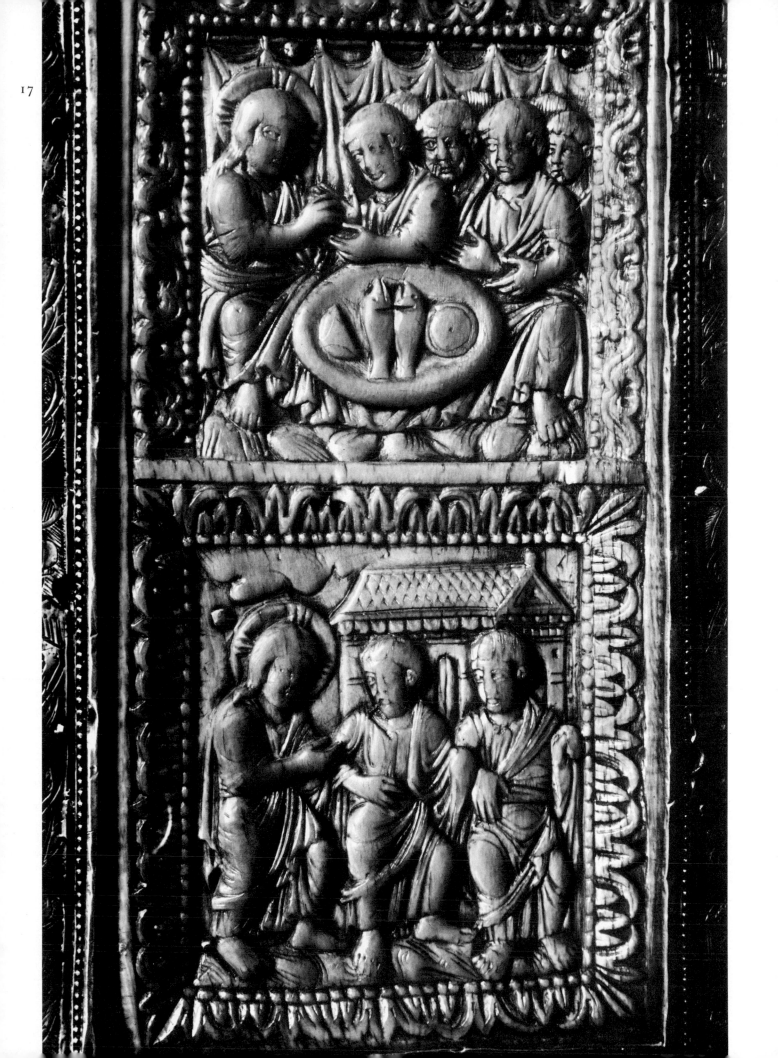

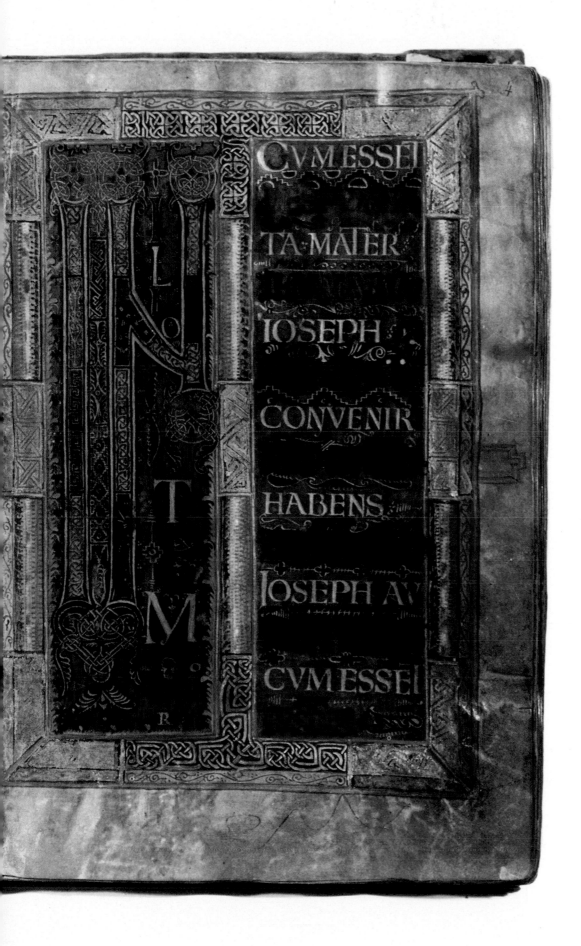

CVM ESSE[T]

TA·MATER

IOSEPH

CONVENIR

HABENS

IOSEPH AV[T]

CVM ESSE[T]

Cassino, now once again a flourishing centre of monastic life, the Frankish army occupied Capua which at this date was still on its ancient site (the modern S. Maria Capua Vetere). Prince Arichis had taken refuge in his second capital, Salerno, and a negotiated settlement was soon agreed: the prince acknowledged Charles' sovereignty, promised not to dispossess bishoprics and monasteries and handed over his elder son Grimoald and the customary twelve others as hostages. When Arichis died next year the Frankish king let his son return to the principality only on condition that he recognized his superior authority by including Charles' name also in the dating-clauses of documents and on coins. The avoidance of an expedition was probably well-judged: in later campaigns, which had been forced on the Franks by Grimoald's repudiation of Frankish sovereignty only three years later, southern fevers were an ever-present and very real threat—as Alcuin had occasion to remind one of the counts taking part in that of 801; and in another letter the same writer warned one of his disciples who was travelling to Italy of the dangers of its food and wine.

Charles' growing power and his greater freedom of action after the successful conclusion of the Saxon wars was a matter of increasing concern to duke Tassilo of Bavaria. In the 760s he had emancipated himself from Frankish tutelage and did not appear at the Frankish court until 781 when he renewed his earlier promises and gave hostages. Between those dates he had confirmed the Bavarian hold on the transalpine valleys of the Isarco, Rienza and upper Adige to beyond Bolzano; he had inflicted a notable defeat on the Slavs of Carantania and he favoured the church and senior clergy with gifts of land and sought their support in his administration of the duchy. In 769 the duke founded the monastery that subsequently gave the present town of S. Candido its name so that its community 'might lead the unbelieving race of the Slovenes to the path of truth' and nine years later he established a monastery at Kremsmünster, nearly on the north-east frontier of his duchy. In 772 an Irish cleric acclaimed Tassilo's successes against the pagans and invoked God to treat him as another Abraham, another David, even as another 'Constantine son of Helen'.

The fall of Pavia in 774, however, effectively put a stop to the duke's ambitions southwards and pro-Frankish sympathies were already apparent in one group of clergy, centring on bishop Arbeo of Freising, and apparently among nobles in the same region. When Arbeo resigned in 782/3, he was succeeded by the abbot of S. Candido; but when the independent-minded bishop Virgil of Salzburg died in 784, the former Freising deacon Arno returned from Francia to become his successor. In the early spring of 787 Arno and an abbot were sent by Tassilo to Rome to seek a settlement with the Frankish king. The Pope insisted that the duke's earlier promises were still binding on him and he sent the legates back with the warning that if Charles and his army were forced to invade Bavaria to secure his obedience they would have the church's absolution and would not be to blame for any misfortunes that befell the duchy and its inhabitants. But when on his return to Francia Charles called on Tassilo to fulfil his obligations, he declined to do so, only to change his mind when Charles dispatched armies from the north-west, west and south and his own 'faithful men' showed no desire to fight for him against the king of the Franks. The duke once again 'commended himself' as a vassal, swore oaths and handed over the customary twelve hostages and his son. A year later, on what can properly be described as trumped-up charges, the duke was deprived of his duchy and condemned to death: only because of Charles' 'Christian clemency' was the sentence commuted to one of confinement to a monastery, while his supporters were sent into exile.

19. Sepulchral Inscription of Hadrian I, St. Peter's, Rome.

The final incorporation of Bavaria in the Frankish kingdom after so many abortive attempts made the leaders of the Franks decidedly more aware of the pagan Slavs who faced them along eight hundred miles of frontier. And through the tribes in the Danube valley and eastern Alps the Franks were brought into contact with a new and potentially more fearsome enemy—the still partly nomadic Avars who for a century and a half had exercised a rough authority over their Slav neighbours. The campaigns against the Slavs before Charles' death in 814 belong perhaps to the pre-history of the German ' Drang nach Osten '. Only in the Julian Alps, in Carantania, and along the middle reaches of the river Drau did they have enduring consequences. The Avars, on the other hand, were decisively defeated and their leaders converted to Christianity within two decades in campaigns that were described by Einhard as ' the greatest of all Charles' wars except the Saxon '. This was the prelude to their complete disappearance in only a few years more as a distinct ethnic group.

Any complete assessment of Charles must recognize that he had learnt many valuable lessons from the bitter experiences of the Saxon wars. Immediately after the deposition of Tassilo he extended the ' march ' organization to the Bavarian-Avar frontier region, entrusting it to a man who was apparently a brother of his first wife. From early 791 to late 793 he and his court remained uninterruptedly in the south-east, making use for much of this period of estates that had passed into direct royal control as a result of Tassilo's fall. The Royal Annalist's account of the campaign of 791 shows clearly that Charles was now capable of devising an overall strategic plan and that he commanded the resources necessary to put it into effect: the king himself led one of three armies that advanced simultaneously into the lands of the Avars between Alps and Danube; and for the first time, so far as we know, a flotilla of Danube river-boats was used in conjunction with the land forces. As a result the Avars were forced to abandon their advance defences just beyond Krems and the Frankish expedition penetrated as far as the Raab before turning back. Charles had even bolder ideas to ensure the success of future campaigns. In 792 he had a movable bridge of boats built (the first since Antiquity?) so that his troops could more easily cross the Danube and its main tributaries. His ambitious plans for 793 were, however, abruptly checked by a revolt in Saxony that compelled him to send troops there. In the late summer of that year he moved his court to east Franconia and assembled a vast labour-force to begin work on an immense canal that would have linked navigable tributaries of the Danube and the Main and simplified the movements of his soldiers. The project had to be abandoned when less than a thousand metres had been dug, because of the constant collapse of the banks. But the completed fragment, which incredibly is still to be seen north-east of the river Altmühl above Eichstätt, shows the grandeur of the plan; and it was actually revived in 1800 by one of Napoleon's generals and two of his technical staff, only to be given up when it was recognized that the geology of the area created almost insuperable difficulties. By 793, however, Charles was in his fiftieth year or more: his fighting-days were virtually over, and when Frankish attacks on the Slavs and Avars were resumed he was content to leave the actual conduct of the campaigns to his sons and others. From 794 he usually spent a substantial part of the year on an estate near the Ardennes hunting-country, *Aquae, Aquisgrana*, Aachen, close by some of the roads along which his earlier journeys had often taken him and where he could enjoy the warm springs that gave the place its name. Here he began to build himself an unusually grand residence. A new phase of his reign was beginning.

Fig. 18 ' Karlsgrab ', the fragment of the canal planned by Charles:

(*a*) eastern portion looking from the west

(*b*) south-west portion.

Ordo et Justitia

3

The enormous extension of the territories that recognized Charles as a king, the constant campaigning that did not always produce immediate results inevitably created new problems for the monarch and those who advised him. Every Germanic king was at least vaguely conscious that, in addition to leading his followers to victory in war, he was responsible for ' guaranteeing to each man his particular law ', as Charles and others put it, and neglect of this principle was a legitimate ground for rebellion and even deposition. The ancient concept of public order had not been entirely destroyed by the establishment of barbarians within the Empire: and as it became weaker its place was partly taken by churchmen's notions of ' peace ' and ' right order '. It required no profound speculation on the notion of kingship, therefore, no close acquaintance with Old Testament or Augustinian concepts, for a king of the Franks, whose father had been raised to that dignity with the co-operation of the church, to feel that his commands should be obeyed and disorder eliminated throughout his kingdom. If he were ever tempted to forget, there were soon those ready to remind him. Cathwulf, in the letter previously quoted, after congratulating the king on having won success and eminence, goes on to say what is expected of him hereafter: he must uphold the law and protect and regulate the church and its servants; he must be scrupulous in his own behaviour and see that unbiased justice is done to all; and he must accept all the help he can from the spiritual armoury of the church. But how, in the circumstances of the time, was the king to carry out this programme?

The way in which his problems were seen by a well-informed writer of the next generation and the manner in which they were tackled in one part of the Frankish dominions are illustrated by a striking passage in the anonymous biography of Louis the Pious. When Charles returned north from the disastrous expedition of 778 (above, p. 59) he resolved to create a kingdom of Aquitaine for his new-born son. ' Since, however, the most wise and percipient king Charles knew that a kingdom is like a body and is agitated now by this and now by that trouble if it is not cared for by good advice and strength as doctors keep a body in health, he bound the bishops to himself [by an oath?] so far as was necessary. He then established throughout Aquitaine counts, abbots and many men who are popularly called *vassi*, drawn from the Frankish people, from whose foresight and courage no one would be protected either by cunning or strength; to them he gave the care of the kingdom, so far as he judged it of benefit, the guarding of the frontiers and the management of the royal estates '. And the biographer concludes this section by naming the nine men who were established as counts in the main towns and territories between Loire, Rhone and Garonne. Three years later (781) Louis and his brother Pippin, who had just been baptized by the Pope in his Lateran baptistery, were annointed by Hadrian as kings respectively ' in Aquitaine ' and ' in Italy ' (or ' of the Lombards '). Courts were created for each of the boy-kings and shortly after Charles' death a writer claimed that Francia had been denuded of royal servants to provide for the subordinate kingdoms.

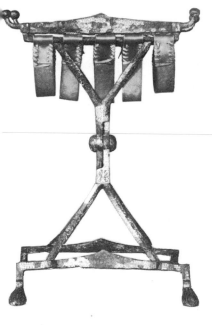

Fig. 19   A folding stool (*sella plicalis*), presumably made for a monarch or other high dignitary and found at Pavia; early ninth century (?). *Civici Istituti di Arte e Storia, Pavia.*

69

As these texts imply, the two pivots on which the government of Charles' dominions turned were the royal court or courts and the territorial counts. The Frankish court was very different from the Imperial court at Constantinople with its luxurious palace, complex ceremonial, strict protocol (shown for example in a list drawn up at the end of the ninth century to decide precedence at an Imperial banquet) and stipended bureaucracy. In the later seventh and eighth centuries the Lombard kings normally resided at Pavia, where they had a substantial palace built in the standard late-Antique manner by the Ostrogothic king Theodoric: at the time of the Frankish conquest it was already the permanent base of a tiny professional class, the ' notaries of the king ' or ' of the royal power ', and housed both the royal treasure and an archive of important documents. King Pippin and his advisers took over and made good use of these unique resources and the palace organization was greatly developed by his successors as rulers of the Italian kingdom. Nothing similar, however, existed north of the Alps at the beginning of Charles' reign, although his Merovingian predecessors had naturally had their favourite residences and their itinerant writing-offices. When they were not actually campaigning the Frankish kings, with their entire court, moved at intervals of a few days, a few weeks or, exceptionally, a few months from one rural estate or town residence (cf. above, p. 46) to another.

Such places made up the royal domain or fisc (*fiscus*, the Latin word originally for a large basket and then for the Imperial privy purse); and the individual properties were usually known, north of the Alps, as *fisci* or *villae* (*v. regales, v. publicae*: the use of the two terms interchangeably is revealing) and in German as *fronehof*, south of the Alps, as *curtes regis* or *villae*. Their origins were various—estates that had previously belonged to the Merovingian kings, especially around Compiègne and Paris, estates that were family lands of Charles' ancestors, estates that had been acquired by conquest or confiscation. As a result they were widely scattered, although with a marked concentration in the regions between the Seine and the lower Rhine and along the middle Rhine and, south of the Alps, in or near the valley of the Po. Where the itinerant court was an infrequent visitor but where none the less there was a reason for maintaining the character of a property as a royal estate—to provide hospitality, for example, for royal servants journeying to distant parts of the kingdom—it might be entrusted to some local figure of prominence who was required to pay a rent in cash. This is perhaps reflected in the previously-quoted remark of the biographer of Louis the Pious about the situation in Aquitaine after 778 and it explains the apparent paradox that royal estates in areas that are usually regarded as economically backward, such as the central Alps, were prominent among those that made money payments to the court. It was particularly because the interests of the fisc were directly involved, but also perhaps because he wished to encourage the payment of compensation instead of vendetta, that Charles actively concerned himself with the character and quality of the coinage in use in his dominions and the circumstances of its production. In the early years of his reign he completed or confirmed the change from private to royal minting which had been attempted by his father—a change reflected in the substitution of the king's for the moneyer's name on the Frankish silver coins of the period. In 781 the gold tremisses hitherto circulating in the Lombard kingdom ceased to be lawful currency and Italian mints, all of course working by the king's authority, began to strike silver coins similar to those in use north of the Alps, characterized by 'rude workmanship and light weight'. In 793 or early 794 he introduced *novi denarii*, which were both of a more regular pattern and heavier,

20. Manuscript; Evangelist portrait (Saint Mark): *Abbeville, Bibliothèque Municipale* No. 4, fol 66v. *Size* 35.5 × 25 cm.

21 and 22. Ivory diptych (from book-cover of Lorsch Gospels): *Biblioteca Apostolica Vaticana, Rome* and the *Victoria and Albert Museum, London. Size* 37 × 25.5 cm.

20

INITIVM SCRIPTV
EVANGELII EST IN
IHV XPI ESAIA
FILII DI PROPHE
SICVT ELEGI EX

being struck on the standard of 240 to the pound. Profits of minting presumably went partly to the moneyer, although this is less certain than is sometimes assumed, and partly to join the other ' treasure ' at the royal court.

The use of coin was however much more restricted than it is today. In the comparatively small area in which most of the royal travels took place, royal servants of modest status had the task of seeing that the produce of a particular estate or group of estates was available for consumption by the court, either on the spot or at some not-too-distant place. If the royal itinerary were to be planned with any care, and except in emergencies it could never have been left entirely to chance, knowledge of what resources were available at particular places and steps to keep the management of royal estates up to scratch were essential. One of the most interesting illustrations of the new vigour injected into Frankish royal administration in Charles' time and a significant by-product of his encouragement of the written word is the preparation of estate inventories. Indeed, shortly before 800 someone at court prepared an elaborate set of instructions for the guidance of the administrators of royal estates, the so-called *Capitulare de villis*, which incidentally gives us much evidence about early medieval agricultural practice not to be found elsewhere, even if its list of plants is the product of the study rather than the field (it is based on glossaries and late-Antique herbals). Although it now exists in a unique copy, there is evidence that it was widely-known and used in the earlier ninth century.

Several of the places regularly visited by the court are sometimes, although by no means consistently, dignified with the title of *palatium*. From time to time in the early part of this century substantial stone-built and stone- or mosaic-floored domestic buildings, with which other smaller buildings are commonly associated, were excavated in the vicinity of several of the places in question and identified as eighth or ninth century *palatia*: with the exception of Ingelheim, most if not all have been supposed by other scholars to be Gallo-Roman villas. Since the Second World War, however, excavations at Frankfort-am-Main, Forscheim, Bâle and at a number of other places have produced remains that are unquestionably those of Carolingian royal *villae* or *palatia*. A precise dating is, of course, rarely possible and it is unlikely that the elaborate complex of stone buildings, including a substantial church, uncovered at Frankfort had already been built when the royal court resided there in the 790s. It is none the less clear that the early ninth-century description of the buildings on a group of estates around Lille—a stone ' royal hall ' or ' royal house ' of two or three rooms plus attics and perhaps attached ' lean-to ' sheds in the more important places, a more modest similar building on the less important ones with a miscellany of one- or two-roomed wooden huts for dependants and storage, the whole being surrounded by a precinct wall or stout fence— would be broadly accurate of many more. The more modest *villae* were probably no different from the residences of most of the Frankish magnates of the period. Not until the building of his residence at Aachen, and perhaps not even then, did Charles have a palace that would have been recognized as such by a visitor from Imperial Constantinople.

When eighth-century writers use the word *palatium*, they are referring more often than not, except in Italy, to the itinerant court—the king and his family, his advisers, followers and servants—whatever it might be: the only fixed element in this ' palace ' was the person of the king. When, however, they wished to refer collectively to the men around the king they commonly used another word that in an almost equally long history had undergone less change of meaning, *comitatus*.

23. Manuscript: *Incipit* of St. Luke's Gospel: *London, British Museum* Harley 2788, fol 109. *Size* 37 × 25.5 cm.

75

The Frankish court, in fact, was still very much a ' companionable ' one. Einhard leaves us in no doubt, in spite of the literary derivation of some of his remarks, that Charles was a hearty eater (a pleasure that he was reluctant to abandon for Lent), particularly of roast meats—the product usually of hunting—and that he hated to be alone. And Alcuin was clearly not the only cleric who was worried by excessive drinking at court, his own and other peoples'. Close association with the king meant for most men that one hunted with him in peace and fought with him in war, ate and drank at the same table, or at any rate in his presence, and gave him advice. Court protocol was extremely simple and no more than is to be expected in any group around a person in authority, although in the latter part of the reign, when the court was an Imperial one, it may have become a little more formal and elaborate. Nithard, an illegitimate son of one of Charles' daughters, declares that when Louis succeeded his father in 814 he made three of the latter's illegitimate sons his *participes mensae*. The looseness of court morals in his father's time was something against which Louis was to react very strongly.

Distinctions of rank or office among the royal courtiers, of course, there always had been. Most important in terms of function, although never allowed to attain the unique influence that Charles' ancestors had attained as mayors, was the Count of the Palace: he exercised a general power of supervision and discipline, and later had a special part to play in legal proceedings that came before the king himself, either because of the eminence of the parties, such as duke Tassilo, or because the decisions of a local court had been ignored. The supervision of particular aspects of domestic court life was the responsibility of men who are referred to in literary sources as *dapifer*, *comes stabuli* and so on, but who were clearly known to most of their associates by the Germanic titles that are the origin of our words ' seneschal ', ' marshal '. Their court offices were no honorific ones, but as courtiers they were all likely to be given other and greater responsibilities also: the seneschal Eggihard fell with Roland at Roncevalles; one of the legates sent to Tassilo in 781 was the master-butler; the marshal, chamberlain and count of the palace were the commanders of the armies in Saxony in 782 who behaved so imprudently. Apart from the well-born youths who had been sent or invited to court at the age of twelve or thereabouts to serve a rough knockabout apprenticeship, most of the other laymen at court who did not form part of the anonymous mass of menial servants are probably to be numbered among the royal vassals, *vassi dominici*. Their primary task was doubtless to form an élite fighting-troop around the king in battle but in times of peace they, or some of them, undertook a wide variety of missions, from being a royal legate to the papal court to investing the recipient of a royal grant with the property in question; and at least one vassal, a certain Leo who was probably not even a Frank but of north Italian origin, became a key figure in the administration of the subordinate ' kingdom of the Lombards '. In the last analysis it was personal acceptability and proving worthy of the royal trust that gave a man high standing with the king and influence in the kingdom.

These qualities can, of course, only be assumed from the recorded activities of the men in question: for to us they inevitably remain mere names or at most puppets jerked by some chronicler's strings. Only two laymen at Charles' court emerge momentarily as persons of flesh and blood. The first is the large limbed and paunchy warrior Wibodus, lumbering awkwardly and menacingly as he hears himself described by a sharp-eyed poet. The second is the dwarfish but talented and well-liked Einhard—one of the early products of a new era in which even a select

24. Fresco fragment from S. Sofia, Benevento (S. Italy); late eighth century.

25. Fresco fragment from S. Sofia, Benevento.

26. Manuscript; Evangelist symbol and portrait from *Codex Millenarius*: Kremsmünster, *Stiftsbibliothek* 1, fol 174v and fol 175. *Size* 30 × 20 cm.

few laymen may acquire book-learning and write good Latin—described by the same poet as ' little Nard, who runs back and forth with ceaseless pace like some tiny ant; laden like the ant with his burden, books or heavy packages '.

At the time of Charles' accession, those in the royal *comitatus* who could write and were familiar with books, were entirely clergy. The clerics who were permanently attached to the court were known as *cappellani*, from the *cappa* or cloak of St. Martin which had been acquired by one of the Arnulfing mayors. In addition to guarding the relics which helped to protect the mayoral and later royal dynasty, they celebrated mass and performed the other ceremonies of the church's liturgical year for the household. It was also from the ranks of the chaplains that the writers of royal diplomas were now drawn—a change from Merovingian practice that had been an immediate consequence of Pippin's elevation to the royal dignity and one that seems to have involved incidentally a marked ' Germanization ' of the writing-office. Since we cannot even hazard a guess at the number of Charles' diplomas that have disappeared without trace—almost none survive, for example, of those given to laymen—there is no means of telling how much work was involved. We know only that at any one time the writing-office included men of several different grades from the lowly ' fair copyist ' of the main part of the diploma to the man who authorized its preparation and ensured that it had all the characteristics that gave it legal force. In the latter part of the reign the cleric in charge may already have been called *cancellarius*, a title that was to have a long and momentous career at the courts of the monarchs of Europe. Rather surprisingly, the preparation of the draft texts of capitularies that were considered by the Frankish magnates when they came to court in great numbers in the spring or autumn and of the copies that these same men took away or had sent to them, was normally the work of other court clergy—at any rate north of the Alps, for in the Italian kingdom these tasks seem to have been performed by the (lay) notaries of the palace. The composition and copying of the king's letters to the Pope and others, which at some points in the reign was evidently a burdensome responsibility, and the copying of manuscripts of many other kinds (see below, ch. 4) were tasks that were evidently widely shared. At the head of the entire complex was the arch-chaplain. Such a man was exceptionally well-placed to influence royal policy towards the church and its ordained members: we know that Charles' first arch-chaplain, Fulrad who died in 784, was a prominent figure in several key episodes in the early history of the dynasty and was high in the royal favour without our being able to say what use he made of his position. His successors, bishop Angilram of Metz, who died during the great Avar expedition of 791, and bishop Hildebold of Cologne played a less conspicuous part in the history of the next fifteen years; and it is likely that at the court they were overshadowed by a cleric who never had any official position and who never rose above deacon's orders, the Northumbrian-born Alcuin.

The interesting fact that Charles sought permission from Pope Hadrian to keep Angilram at court and from an assembly of the leaders of the Frankish clergy to keep his successor Hildebold there ' for ecclesiastical services ' should not mislead us into talking of a Carolingian ' central administration '. This was as foreign to the personal system of government of the period as the notion of a strict hierarchy of officials with neatly-defined functions. It was not, in fact, assumed that an abbot or a bishop who became arch-chaplain, or indeed acquired any other dignity at the royal court, would sever his connection with his previous charge, like an outsider seconded to a government post today: and the evidence for Fulrad and Hildebold shows them taking an active and constructive interest in their churches,

27. Fresco from south wall of S. Procolo, Naturno (Italian Tyrol): St. Paul escaping from Damascus; ?eighth century.

even if the pastoral side of their duties can hardly have had much attention. In any case this particular kind of pluralism, which benefited many other court clergy also, was the natural, if not quite the inevitable corollary of a social and economic structure in which coined money was not universally used and in some regions, such as east of the Rhine, did not circulate at all. The major churches and monasteries of the kingdom were drawing a substantial revenue from the land at the beginning of Charles' reign and in most cases an even more substantial one by the end of it: the royal abbey of Lorsch for instance, of which the court cleric Ricbod became abbot in 784, benefited from over three thousand separate gifts of land between the arrival of the bones of St. Nazarius from Italy in 764 and the death of Charles. Grants of land from the fisc, whether outright ' in proprietorship ' or conditionally, usually ' as a benefice '—in Charles' lifetime almost invariably the latter—were the obvious ways of rewarding a king's lay followers. They were also the expected ones for without land men could make no provision for the next generation and their standing in the kingdom at large would always be weak, however highly they were regarded by the ruler they served; and although the transporting of the produce of an estate over considerable distances was not entirely unknown—letters of Einhard show it happening and reveal some of the snags— it was obviously exceptional. The married and ' landed ' layman was unlikely to remain a courtier—Charles' court was in fact, his own family apart, largely a bachelor establishment. But the process could be turned to the advantage of the monarch for the royal vassals who were established with families and land in annexed territories—Aquitaine, Italy, where exceptionally vassals are even found *buying* land, and so on—or even in Francia proper were, like their counterparts the thegns in the English kingdoms, ' a prop to royal power ' in these regions.

The mainstay and principal channel of royal authority in the different parts of the kingdom was, however, the local count: for Charles went far beyond his father in establishing or re-establishing the doctrine that the title, and the power that went with it, came only from the king, that it was a royal or public office and from 778/9 the burdens and responsibilities laid on the individual count increased steadily for many years. No comprehensive account of the early Carolingian count has ever been attempted, and if it were, the result would probably not prove very satisfying: there are no personal documents and there are too many other gaps in our knowledge. The most certain facts about them are that their job was no sinecure and that they were comparatively few in number. In a territory that eventually extended over six hundred miles from north to south and from east to west, there were, in Professor Ganshof's view, between two hundred and fifty and three hundred counts at any one time. I would myself put the figure at the end of the eighth century even lower—in the entire *regnum Langobardorum*, for example, there were perhaps less than thirty—but it is impossible to be precise: the total number named in the sources for Charles' lifetime is under one hundred and twenty. From texts that rarely record failure and the fates of individuals, ten counts are *known* to have been killed in battle in the first thirty-one years of the reign; and an unspecified number were executed or mutilated when they took part in the rebellion of 786, or in that of 792, because they could no longer tolerate the behaviour of Charles' queen.

In addition to taking part in military expeditions, they were expected to come to court at intervals to hear the royal commands. The capitularies that embodied these commands laid on them the responsibility of suppressing wanton disorder and encouraging the peaceful termination of lawful feud, of ensuring that criminals

28. Ivory book-cover from the Dagulf Psalter; *Louvre, Paris.* *Size* 17 × 8 cm.

29. Stucco from S. Salvatore, Brescia.

30. Facade of the cathedral, Torcello (Italy), after ?early ninth century reconstruction.

did not escape justice by taking refuge in some place from which the count's jurisdiction was excluded (an 'immunity') of seeing that justice was done to all free disputants in the public courts, of protecting those who were least able to protect themselves—widows and orphans (of freeborn landowners, naturally), monasteries and churches; and of ensuring that those freemen who were called to serve in the host set out with proper equipment and provisions. In addition, where counts were not directly responsible for the lands of the fisc, they might have to keep a watchful eye on those who were and in some areas, as we have seen, they were responsible for the permanent defence of some portion of the frontier, a select few of them getting extra powers to enable them to do so more effectively.

A casual reading of the sources might suggest that the territorial units in which the counts exercised their day-to-day responsibilities, their counties, were everywhere more or less the same: but the opposite is true. In Francia east of the Rhine, both in those areas that were Frankish in 768 and those which Charles annexed and divided between counts for the first time, their authority seems generally to have been based on a group of royal estates which in some cases mingled with those entrusted to other counts and could easily be increased or reduced. West of the Rhine the territorial county was, with rare exceptions, an area with definite boundaries, corresponding to the territory long associated with a city of Roman origin—from which the count usually took his title—or to a part of such a territory —in which case it was often known as a *pagus*—or very occasionally to a group of city-territories. In Italy, too, where Frankish counts replaced the native Lombard dukes—gradually over two decades rather than suddenly in 774 or 776, as some sources misleadingly suggest—counties had settled territorial boundaries, sometimes even marked with stones or wooden posts, that were, except in old frontier-regions, largely of Roman origin. Even so, there were wide differences of size, character and strategic importance between one county and another—from the

Fig. 20 'Baptism by immersion', from a theological miscellany with texts in old High German as well as Latin; early ninth century, Bavaria. *Munich, Bayerische Staatsbibliothek* Clm. 22053, fol 16.

31. **Exterior of Germigny-des-Prés (France) from the east.**

counties of Toulouse, nearly eighty kilometres from north to south and reaching almost to the one-time Pyrenean frontier, and of Parma, which controlled forty-five kilometres of the Via Emilia and a similar stretch of the River Po to the tiny Pyrenean county of Conflent or the almost equally small and poor *pagus* of Flanders.

There were obviously correspondingly wide differences of responsibility and power among the men whose areas of territorial authority these were but other factors, too, helped to determine the prestige and influence with the king or his counsellors of individual counts. Who were they? Where did they come from? At the end of the reign quite a number were certainly or probably sons of counts, or their nephews or other close relatives. At this period it is still very exceptional to find a son following his father in a particular county: quite often he was given office elsewhere in his father's lifetime and, if he did succeed to his father's county on the latter's death, we may be sure that it was by specific royal or Imperial concession. Nevertheless being born into certain families offered a reasonable certainty of future comital office. From one of these came William, count of Toulouse from 790 until his retirement in 804 to a monastery he had founded; from another came the descendants of the men who had patronised the writers of the chronicle recording the rise of the Carolingians; a third was that from which Charles' second wife had come. Significantly, the first two were not only of Austrasian origin but shared an ancestor with Charles. It has already been suggested that the third family came of a marriage between a well-born Swabian and a man from Austrasia of undistinguished background. By giving comital office to men who were in a very special sense Franks and either closely associated with the royal family or ' new men ' whose fortunes were intimately bound up with his, Charles presumably expected that he would retain both the loyalty of the individual and of the conquered region over which he had been placed. In the early part of the reign, most of the free-born laymen who agreed to become the king's *vassi* could reasonably hope that one day they would be rewarded with a county somewhere in his dominions. It is likely, although not certain, that the relationship between some of the Frankish magnate families who had been among the ' aristocracy ' of the kingdom in Merovingian times and the Carolingian king changed significantly as the reign proceeded. As their members saw office and the advantages that went with it going to other men and, since the king had a growing need of men of substance in his service, they sought access and were admitted to the privileged group around him. And it is possible that in the process a sharper distinction began to be drawn within the circle of *commendati* between the ordinary vassal and the ' faithful men ', *fideles*, of higher standing.

Commendation and comital office were, however, at no time a monopoly of the Franks, still less of a restricted group among their magnate families: at the time of Charles' death the counts in the ' kingdom of Italy ' included Swabians, Bavarians and the occasional ' Lombard '; and north of the Alps Saxons and Goths, as well as the first two, are found side by side with Neustrian and Austrasian Franks. This mingling of men drawn from various parts of Charles' dominions was not part of a conscious ' policy of unification ' in the sense in which that expression may legitimately be used of some later medieval kings. The unity of the Carolingian kingdom, such as it was, rested on the personal bond between separate individuals and the king and their coming together at intervals at his court or at the courts of his sons. But even if the subordinate kingdoms in Aquitaine and Italy were created in 781, so that there would be resident royal courts in regions which Charles visited only in emergencies, and not merely as a concession to their particularist

32. Interior of Germigny-des-Prés.

traditions, they certainly strengthened them in the long run. Whatever the practice, the principle that a man was to be judged according to the law of his ' tribe ' remained in vigour: partially-revised texts of the old written codes of law were put into circulation in this period and new codes compiled by royal authority for the Saxons and other peoples who had hitherto lacked them. And in spite of the impression given by the capitularies that the forms and procedure of local courts of justice were everywhere the same, marked regional differences persisted.

Throughout the whole kingdom there was an insistence that law and order should prevail and that the courts should enforce them in the name of the king. This is one of the two main themes in the capitulary ' agreed ' between the king and his magnates at Herstal in March 779—the first text of its kind from Charles' reign—with its condemnation of murder, robbery, perjury and the various ways in which criminals evade due punishment of their crimes. The fact that these crimes and abuses figure again and again in the capitularies of the next thirty-four years, together with new ones ranging from desertion from the royal host to counts' exacting servile labours from free men, should rightly arouse scepticism about the effectiveness of Charles' measures. But violence was endemic in the Middle Ages and the pursuit and punishment of offenders by official agents of the monarch could never be more than a qualified success.

Not surprisingly, therefore, Charles recognised that private vendetta still had a part to play in the maintenance of order and justice, although we find him insisting, as did the English king Alfred in the later ninth century, that where monetary compensation was offered it was not to be refused. The regular local courts, *malli* (germ. *mahal*, etc) and *placita generalia*, were royal in the sense that they were presided over and their decisions executed by a *iudex*—whether the count or someone who took his place—who acted in the name of the king. They were popular in the sense that ordinary law-worthy men supported the parties to a dispute, saw that the established procedure was observed and declared the law. Even this arrangement was not safe from abuse or indifference. It seems that until c. 780 in most parts of the pre-768 *regnum Francorum* judgment-finders were nominated from those present when a court assembled but the position elsewhere is far from clear. In 780 Charles apparently ordered that henceforth each county or each court should have a regular panel of judgement-finders, known as *scabini*. They may theoretically, although rarely in practice, have been seven in number and were later nominated by the count with the approval of a visiting royal representative. North of the Alps they were invariably drawn from the ranks of the substantial landowners of the county, south of the Alps the *scabinus* in the ninth century was commonly a professional notary. Probably at the same time that *scabini* were instituted, it was laid down that the presence of all free men at a court should be limited to three occasions in the year. It is not clear, because the texts are ambiguous and indeed contradictory, whether these three occasions were henceforth the only ones when the count was expected to attend in person and whether they were assemblies of the whole or of a part of a territorial county. It is clear only that in those areas in which the *scabini* were effectively established, which was by no means everywhere, they later often acted collectively as *iudices* in place of the absent count. In the light of resources available and the contemporary view of who was and was not law-worthy, there can be no quarrel with the traditional laudatory judgements on the steps taken by Charles to check violence and make justice readily available to ' all ': as Alcuin was to put it, ' I am quite certain of the good will ' of the king, although he has ' fewer abettors than subverters of justice '.

33. Manuscript; St. Augustine:
Berlin, Deutsche Staatsbibliothek
Phill. 1676, fol 18v. *Size* 39 × 31 cm.

The greater authority entrusted to the counts and the more urgent insistence on their duty of pursuing and punishing crime created ample opportunities for corruption and what in other reigns might be acceptable or at any rate pass uncondemned was regarded at this time as an abuse of true justice. The improper levying of services, the demand for free hospitality when travelling, the misappropriation of fiscal or church property—these examples are one aspect of this abuse. The taking of bribes by those who were supposed to dispense justice—a recurrent theme in the writings of clerics associated with the court—is another. How established a practice this was is shown by the admission of one critic, the court cleric and poet Theodulf, in the preliminary section of his versified advice to judges, that he had judged it less upsetting to accept than to refuse small gifts— eggs, fowls, wine, bread and fodder—while remaining uninfluenced by them. (Those acquainted with the practice of *racommandazioni* in present-day Italy will find the situation a familiar one.) The poem was based on the author's experiences when, with another court cleric, the Bavarian Leidrad, and future archbishop of Lyons, he toured the south-west as royal *missus* in 797. The word *missus* means simply ' messenger ' or legate; but it was already used in the Merovingian period particularly of a man who had been sent from the court with special powers. Pippin may already have used itinerant *missi* as an occasional check on the activities of counts and administrators of royal domains. From the late 780s if not earlier Charles followed the same practice much more freely and perhaps widened the scope of his legates' activities, particularly in areas like Aquitaine and Italy where his own itinerary did not normally take him. The main problem—apart from discovering the misdemeanours and injustices that were to be dealt with—which was never satisfactorily solved by Charles or by his successors, was who to use for this purpose. If *vassi* or lesser men in the royal service were used, as was usually the case in the early part of the reign, they might lack the prestige necessary to be effective instruments of the royal displeasure; if a count were used he would either be judge in his own cause or be taken away from his already considerable regular responsibilities; and the use of clerics of high standing, whether jointly with a layman or, as in the example already quoted, by themselves, was not a solution that could be used in all circumstances.

The employment of clergy connected with the court as royal *missi* checking the behaviour of counts and other laymen was a logical extension of the duties they performed at the court itself. The association of bishops and other clerics with the day-to-day tasks of secular administration was no novelty in the Romano-Germanic kingdoms but in Charles' reign it took new forms and was extended far beyond anything previously known. It is entirely characteristic that where a bishop had taken over the functions of a count in his diocese or a substantial part of it, as in the case of Trier, these were now taken away from him and the territorial countship re-established: but at the same time bishops were commanded, at any rate in some parts of the Frankish dominions, to sit in the regular local courts side by side with the counts. Many episcopal churches and abbeys received a royal grant of *emunitas*, which in its developed form meant both exemption from the payment of levies in kind and in cash (the latter ultimately of Roman origin and much less important now than in the seventh century), and the exclusion of royal officials in normal circumstances from the lands of the church. Immune churches had, however, to have their own advocate (*advocatus*) to act for them in the public courts and to deal with breaches of the law by those on the church's lands; and since these advocates had to be men of substance, some of them may already have been, as they certainly

34. Manuscript; Evangelist portrait: *Brussels, Bibliothèque Royale* Ms 18 1723, fol 17v. *Size* 26 × 19 cm.

were later, the local count in another guise.

The organisation of the church and the obligations of the king's lay subjects to it provide the second major theme of the capitulary of 779 and of many subsequent ones. The task of reforming the Frankish church had begun, as we have seen, nearly thirty years before Charles' accession: and although the success of the measures taken by Charles' uncle and father was often only local or temporary they provided the guide-lines and foundations on which Charles built so energetically and with lasting consequence. The enormous enlargement of the scope of such reforms in the second decade of Charles' reign and the new awareness of the rules (canons) laid down by and for the church in the past, as well as the king's assumption that he is responsible for seeing that they are enforced, are strikingly illustrated by the extant capitularies. At Herstal in 779 the first six chapters deal briefly but categorically with bishops and their authority over the clergy in their dioceses and with monasteries, without reference to specific earlier laws. Ten years later Charles issued a 'General Admonition' to his clergy, comprising more than eighty separate chapters, some of them of considerable length—the entire text fills nine pages in the modern printed edition—and drawing heavily on the decrees of councils and bishops of Rome of the fourth and fifth centuries. In between he had established at least one new bishopric without reference to the Pope. The regulation of monastic life and the maintenance and endowment of local churches are a prominent feature of the earliest written instructions to *missi*. In later 'general assemblies' at the royal court, bishops and abbots often met separately to propose new measures to the monarch or to consider others that he laid before them for the elimination of abuses within the church. By the mid-790s metropolitan (arch-) bishops, whose authority the king had helped to re-establish and whose number was steadily being increased, were holding synods of their suffragan bishops and other clergy to reinforce the royal decrees and subsequently the more energetic of the bishops took similar steps in their own dioceses.

There can be no doubt that in the short term the effects of Charles' reforming endeavours were far more apparent at the higher, 'aristocratic', levels of the church than at the level of the humble clerics who served the parish churches—in many areas still comparatively few in number—their dependent oratories (later also known as chapels) and the churches on private estates. In the early ninth century it was necessary to prohibit priests from using churches for the storage of hay and from forcing others to get intoxicated—a reference apparently to the ritual drinkings that had survived from pre-Christian time and which in their dubiously Christianized form had at least the tacit approval of many of the most cultivated churchmen of the age. Sharing the superstitions of those among whom they lived, often barely literate in spite of the notable educational advances of the period, materially ill-provided for, 'the life of the lower clergy', it has been justly said, 'was not only parallel to but actually was a part of the life lived by the lay poor'.[1] The capitulary of Herstal in 779 contained one major novelty: the seventh chapter, which marks the transition from the clauses concerned with the church to those concerned with secular matters, lays the obligation of paying tithe—the one-tenth of the products of a man's labours due to the church—on each of the king's subjects; what has hitherto been a voluntary payment, or at any rate only a moral obligation, is now one that the king requires and that his agents will enforce. The voluntary payment was traditionally made to be dispensed to those in need; later Carolingian evidence shows that the compulsory payment was supposed to be paid to the clergy of the church where a man received the sacraments or more

[1] H. Fichtenau *The Carolingian Empire*

35. Ivory book-cover from the *Bodleian Library, Oxford:* Ms Douce 176. *Size* 21 × 12.5 cm.

specifically, notably in Italy, to the baptismal or parish as distinct from the private church. But if Charles' decree originally had in mind the needs of the suffering, the poor and the parochial clergy, the many derogations from these principles that rapidly appeared in practice, from payment to the private chapels on royal estates by their tenants to alienation to monasteries, force us to conclude that it soon failed in its purpose.

Historians who have sought a simple and comprehensive definition of Charles' 'policy towards the church' have rarely succeeded in their self-appointed task or, if they have found one, it has usually failed to win the approval of others. This is partly because Charles' ideas undoubtedly altered and evolved as his reign proceeded, partly because the church was not a monolithic structure, distinct and set apart from the fabric of secular society. But how does one judge a ruler who, on the one hand, endowed monasteries and protected and increased the lands and incomes of churches and, on the other, exploited them to provide rewards for followers; or who commanded in 779 that where there were vacancies in episcopal sees they were to be filled, and that monks were to live according to their Rule and abbots were not to abandon their monasteries; yet who in the mid-780s put forward an abbot for the see of Pavia so that he could help administer the 'kingdom of the Lombards' and kept him there for many years although the Pope, whose right it was to consecrate him, declined to do so; and who, when Angilram of Metz died in 791, left the see vacant for the rest of the reign?

These evident contradictions, which show in another field something of the opportunism that Charles displayed on his brother's death or in his treatment of duke Tassilo, perhaps help to provide us with the answer we are seeking. Charles was king of all who lived within the area of his territorial authority, whether laymen or ordained clergy, called by God to rule, guide, reward and punish them. A deep personal religion, the compelling inner force of the Christian imperative, the striving for spiritual unity with God Himself—familiar to St. Paul and the great Saints and recognized by the ordinary Christians who at various times have sought to be like them—were alien to Charles as they were to everyone else in the first Carolingian generation. But the king had no doubt that the Saints gave help in this world to the generous giver and that he would answer for the way he had used his authority at the Day of Judgement. There was nothing false or cynical in the claim that in putting forward abbot Waldo for the bishopric of Pavia he was fulfilling the will of God, nor in his holding out against the Pope, who on other occasions was eventually persuaded of the rightness of his actions; nor even in his using the material resources of the church if that were a means of securing peace, justice and the triumph of the Christian faith. As it was put in a letter written by Alcuin in Charles' name to Pope Leo III shortly after the latter's accession in 795, 'It is my duty by Divine aid to defend everywhere the holy church of Christ externally with arms against inroads by pagans and ravaging by unbelievers . . .; it is your task, holy father, to support our fighting by hands raised to God as those of Moses'.

The inseparability, in Charles' mind, of his duties and rights as a ruler and the worldly and other-worldly functions of the church and its servants is very apparent at three critical moments in the middle years of his reign. Shortly after the surrender of the leaders of Saxon resistance in 785, Charles promulgated a capitulary specifically for the conquered territory. The implication of most of the first fourteen chapters, the *capitula maiora*, is that the policy of 'conversion by the sword' is extended to times of peace: whoever enters a church by force will be executed;

Fig. 21 Carolingian footsoldiers; an illustration from the St. Gall 'Golden Psalter'; end ninth century. *St. Gallen, Stiftsbibliothek* Cod 22, p. 141.

whoever kills a bishop, priest or deacon will be executed; whoever cremates the body of a dead man (pagan fashion) will be executed, and this at a time when under other laws even homicide made the offender liable only to the payment of compensation to a man's relatives or his lord and possibly a fine to the fisc and the death penalty was normally restricted to offences against the king personally. The *capitula minora* lay down, among other things, that the inhabitants of each parish—forcibly created—will provide its church with a minimum endowment of land and dependent cultivators, that tithes will be paid by all and children shall everywhere be baptised within the year. Finally, there is to be no public assembly except on the instructions of a royal *missus*. The likelihood that these draconian laws reflect Charles' own ideas rather than those of his favourite advisers or else that the Saxon rebellion that broke out in 793 threw doubt on their wisdom, is suggested by a group of letters written by Alcuin in 796. In one to bishop Arno of Salzburg, who was then in Avar country evidently initiating the mission activity in that region for which later sources show his church to have been responsible, he tells him to be ' a preacher of piety, not an exactor of tithes ', which were turning the Saxons away from the faith. And in a letter to the king he develops the same point at greater length: ' even we, who have been born, raised and trained in the catholic faith, are barely willing to tithe our property fully; how much more unwilling are those of tender faith and childish spirit and grasping dispositions? ' Although there is no evidence of a relaxation of the rules on this point, it is very striking that after the rebellion had been finally suppressed in the summer of 797, a capitulary was promulgated in an assembly that included Saxons as well as Franks by which the penalties henceforth imposed on Saxon offenders were brought more or less into line with those due from the king's other subjects.

To those mature in the faith and not yet made cynical by the changes of allegiance and the making and unmaking of promises that marked the thirty years after Charles' death, the belief in Divine punishment for the breaking of an oath—particularly one made on the relics of the saints—was still the most powerful of sanctions. But even this could be exploited by a king who felt compelled to inflict abnormally severe earthly punishments. When a potentially serious rebellion planned for 786 was forestalled by the arrest of the conspirators (above, p. 59), Charles forced them to visit sanctuaries in Italy, Neustria or Aquitaine and swear fidelity to him and his sons; then, on their return, he had them blinded, exiled or executed, and their property confiscated on the grounds of their infidelity. An oath of this kind, however, could also, it was realised, be used in more normal circumstances as a means of guaranteeing for the future the loyalty of the king's subjects who were not his *commendati*. *Missi* sent from court in 789 were ordered to take an oath from all free men that: ' I promise to my lord king Charles and his sons that I am faithful and will be so all the days of my life without fraud of evil design '. Less than three years later Charles was faced with another rebellion coinciding with other misfortunes in his kingdom (above, p. 59). Some of those involved, when taken prisoner, declared that they had never sworn an oath of fidelity and we can well believe that the instructions given to the *missi* in 789 had been carried out very haphazardly. Early in 793 from his court at Ratisbon, therefore, the king sent out *missi* once again with the responsibility of ensuring that every man over the age of twelve took the oath of loyalty to the king: they were to explain why this was necessary and that it was an old custom; they were to take it personally from counts, royal vassals, bishops, abbots and other men of substance; ordinary men were to take the oath in the presence of the count of their area, whose responsibility it was

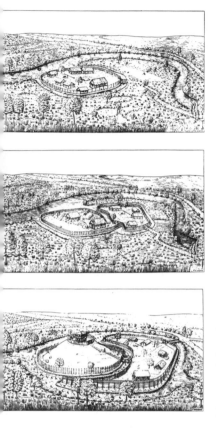

Fig. 22 The development of a ninth century *villa* (upper and middle illustrations) and the castle which later evolved from it (after Dr. A. Herrnbrodt).

95

to produce written lists of those who had sworn—a noteworthy illustration of the increasing use and importance of the written record. The fact that counts and royal vassals are included shows that this oath was felt to have a different purpose from that which they had sworn to the king in person. Whatever a combination of administrative technique and religious belief could do to remind men of their unequivocal duty of obedience to their royal master had been done.

Yet no king was entirely master of his own destiny. God, who was a jealous god, the Righteous Avenger as well as the Lord of Hosts, had many ways of punishing and of helping his sinful people and their leaders. Charles had come to Ratisbon at a time when his kingdom was suffering from a disastrous famine, to make preparations for an expedition against the pagan Avars. God must be appeased and invoked. In the same months in which he sent his legates to receive oaths of loyalty he ordered the celebration of masses and the reciting of penitential psalms by bishops, priests and monks throughout his dominions first for the king, secondly for the army, thirdly for the present affliction; clergy and laity alike were to fast for two days whenever possible, although by a characteristic gesture of privilege counts could redeem this obligation by money; and all were to give alms according to their means. *Sacrificium* and *officium*, it had been said, had at least as important a place in Charles' plans as military preparations. Was it then the work of God or the work of the Devil that the Avar expedition never took place because of the ' great damage ' brought about by the Saxon uprising, news of which was brought to the king in the early summer of 793?

It would certainly have seemed to many a Divine judgement when the young queen Fastrada died in August 794. And when, two months previously, an unusually large ' general assembly ', perhaps indeed the largest of the reign, gathered at Frankfort, it was clearly still under the shadow of the disasters of the previous two years. After due deliberation by lay magnates and by bishops and abbots meeting separately, Charles promulgated a capitulary that affected both orders of his subjects. The church and its organisation got most attention. Current heresies having been condemned (below, p. 112), the powers of the metropolitans were confirmed and clarified; clerics were not to move from one church to another without special permission; bishops were to avoid involvement in worldly affairs; the monastic character of religious communities was to be safeguarded and monks were to live in full accordance with the Rule of St. Benedict; and a novelty—clergy were to be tried for secular offences committed by them in a court presided over by the bishop, although the count would attend to keep an eye on proceedings and take the action necessary after the court had delivered judgement, while immediate penal action was no longer permitted against a cleric caught *in flagrante*. On the secular side, Tassilo was brought out of his cloister—Jumièges, according to the later traditions of that monastery—and submitted a written renunciation of his ducal rights, of which a copy was to be kept in the royal chapel. The practice of exploiting famine conditions by selling grain at high prices was condemned and maximum prices fixed; standard measures or weights that had recently been introduced were alone to be used and the acceptance of the new standard pennies was enjoined on all. There were, the Frankfort decrees implied, to be no limits on the king's responsibility for peace, order and justice in his realms.

36. The Pleiades in a Rheims Aratus manuscript, c. 840: *Bibliotheek der Rijksuniversiteit te Leiden* Ms Voss. Lat. Qu 79, fol 42v. *Size* 22 × 20 cm.

36

A Court of Scholars
and the Revival of Learning

4

In the later months of 781 or shortly afterwards a certain Godescalc, who had accompanied Charles to Rome earlier that year and was presumably one of the clerics in his chapel, wrote at the royal command a Gospel lectionary (i.e. passages from the Gospels appointed to be read at mass on Sundays and feast-days), calendar and Easter tables. The manuscript was a luxury one—silver and gold writing on fine purple parchment (or vellum). The way of preparing the parchment to receive the text links it with earlier manuscripts written in the British Isles. The script of most of the manuscript is a stylish but un-fluent ' uncial ', revived for almost the last time. A few pages, however, are in a different script, a round ' minuscule ', close in form to modern lower-case type, clear and orderly but more compact than uncial. The arrangement of the lectionary and the choice of Gospel passages followed the usage of the Roman churches most closely connected with the Pope. The dedicatory verses composed by Godescalc make clear the connection between the commissioning of the manuscript and the baptism of Pippin, ' born again in the font ' at Rome at Easter-time 781. They refer to Charles as *consul* and speak of his fourteenth *fasces* (the ancient Roman word for ' a year of office ') and they commemorate Pope Hadrian, now Pippin's *compater* or godfather, in words that are partly derived from the funerary inscriptions of an early sixth-century and an early seventh-century Pope. (Appropriately, the manuscript entered the French public collections in the early nineteenth century because it was given to Napoleon by the citizens of Toulouse in 1811 on the occasion of *his* son's baptism.)

In the later 780s or early 790s Dagulf and a second anonymous writer, both presumably belonging to the royal chapel, produced a Psalter of equally luxurious appearance for presentation to Pope Hadrian. The manuscript was made up in a similar way to the Godescalc Evangelistiary and the scribes write in a minuscule hand not very different from his. Probably in the 790s ' by order of the king ' several writers using a similar script copied a number of grammatical and other works entirely or in large part from the ' original ' of a recently-deceased arch-deacon Peter, and prefaced it with a handsome title-page written in almost epigraphic capitals (pl. 16). In the same decade an unknown writer of Italian origin, who seems to have been resident at the royal court, added to another manuscript of grammatical texts a collection of verse of recent composition and a list of manuscripts, many of Classical texts—including several unusual ones—that evidently records the contents of the library to which this volume then belonged.

These four manuscripts, the first two of which also share a distinctive style of decoration (see below, ch. 5)—the chance survivors of centuries of dispersion and destruction—provide a revealing if obviously incomplete picture of the activities of the literate, clerical element at Charles' court in the last two decades of the eighth century. The earlier manuscripts link the glorification of the Frankish monarch and his court with the practical needs of a worshipping church. The first of them already shows the importance of *imitatio*, the search for parallels and

99

sources of inspiration in the past—occasionally in the world of pagan Rome but more commonly in the Rome of the first Christian Emperors and of the successors of St. Peter. But the script of the final pages, very different from the minuscule scripts then in use in most parts of Europe yet less formidable to the average scribe than the calligraphic scripts favoured for luxury products in earlier centuries, is a witness to something different: here, older models have not merely been drawn on but freely adapted to create something substantially new. The later manuscripts emphasize the international connections of the court and the enlargement of the interests of some of those who belonged to it beyond the immediately practical; and they hint at the important contribution this tiny group was to make to the future development of European literary culture.

Although the ' Godescalc Evangelistiary ' has every claim to be considered the oldest surviving manuscript from Charles' court and has many features that set it apart from other books of the same period, it was not, of course, produced in a void or completely without precursors. For several decades Anglo-Saxon and Irish missionaries had been collecting, copying and disseminating manuscripts in widely-separated parts of Francia and more than one pilgrim had made copies of the epitaphs of popes and others in the churches of Rome. King Pippin's respect for the church of St. Peter was such that he had wished its forms of worship to be adopted throughout his kingdom and he had asked for and been sent Roman sacramentaries and other liturgical texts. By the 770s a scribe, or scribes, of the north French abbey of Corbie, where the angular minuscule writing of the Anglo-Saxons was evidently well-known, had evolved a rather stiff but round minuscule closely modelled on the ' half-uncial ' writing of earlier centuries and not long afterwards a more elegant and refined minuscule script was also being written at not-far-distant St. Amand. A meeting and mingling of the insular and Italian literary traditions had already taken place before 781, if not in Francia proper certainly in Bavaria—as may be seen in the writings of or those associated with bishop Arbeo of Freising or in the ingenious *Cosmographia* that circulated under the name of Aethicus Ister but was actually the work of the Irish bishop Vergil of Salzburg.

The knowledge of Latin displayed even in learned circles such as these is, however, often anything but impressive: the man who added supposed German equivalents to a Latin glossary, perhaps at Freising, failed to see that the words in each entry were merely interpretations or synonyms of the initial one. At the beginning of Charles' reign the texts of royal diplomas, written by clerics who were presumably among the best-educated men in the Francia of the day, were still full of vulgarisms of spelling and grammar, although they were more ' correct ' than their Merovingian predecessors. There was as yet no real parallel to the cultivation of Latin letters at the Lombard royal court. Even in monasteries like Corbie or cathedral churches like Salzburg there was no one of the stature of the Friulian Paul the Deacon, who had already compiled his *Historia Romana*—a revision of the *Breviary* of Eutropius, brought down to the sixth century—and written his first polished if stilted verses before the fall of the Lombard kingdom. It is tempting, therefore, to regard the striking developments that took place at the Frankish court within little more than a decade after Charles' accession as a direct consequence of the annexation of north Italy in 774, and many scholars have not hesitated to do so. It is certainly striking that some of the property confiscated as a result of the rebellion of 776 was given to Paulinus *artis grammaticae magister* who subsequently spent some years at the Frankish court and remained in touch with the king and his circle by correspondence for many years more; and that the deacon Peter ' of

Fig. 23 Carolingian cavalry. Note the stirrups and the manner in which the lance is held. From the St. Gall ' Golden Psalter '. *St. Gallen, Stiftsbibliothek* Cod. 22, p. 141.

Pisa ' (presumably the later arch-deacon) who had been a figure of note at the royal palace at Pavia in the 760s, seems to have joined Charles' court about this time. He was to be remembered by Einhard as the person from whom, ' as an old man ', the king learnt ' letters ' (*grammatica*). There is, however, no justification for claiming Godescalc as a Lombard: and the Italian elements in his manuscript are not their most outstanding feature. It seems better to regard the emergence of the court as a place of creative activity shortly after 780 as a reflection of the wider horizons that a decade of military endeavour and the flattery of educated clergy, from Pope Hadrian to Cathwulf, had opened up for the king of the Franks. The royal court was already a training-ground in practical and manly pursuits for well-born youths. Charles was now persuaded that to have at his court men who could produce fine manuscripts or pass on their knowledge and skills to others would bring him greater prestige and authority; and—as is not uncommon among men of action, particularly when their first youth is past—Charles developed a personal respect for letters and the learned: in the words of Notker a century later, he became an admirer of—an amateur in the older sense of the word—and most greedy for knowledge. Notker begins his account of the ' Doings ' of Charles with the often-quoted story, in which this description of the king occurs, about how learning was saved from oblivion when two wise Irishmen arrived in Francia and offered their wares for sale. This is obviously not authentic history, even if the Irishmen are historical figures: Notker tells it because he thinks it has a moral for his contemporaries. But consciously or unconsciously it also points a rather different moral about the way in which learning was able to flourish under Charles. Already before 780 the future archbishop of Salzburg, Arno, left his native Bavaria for Francia and by 782 was abbot of St. Amand; in 780 a certain Adam, abbot of a monastery in Alsace, dedicated his copy of one of the late Antique grammatical manuals that reappears in the previously mentioned court manuscripts of the 790s to the king to whom he owed his abbacy. In 781 (or 787) Paulinus became Patriarch (bishop) of Aquileia in north-east Italy. In Notker's tale the price of the wisdom the two Irishmen had to sell was low, unlike in his own time, or so he implies, but it was, in fact, the provision of regular sustenance and the fellowship of other gifted men.

Even in the largest and most prosperous religious community books were still few and contact with other scholars was at best intermittent: hence the unique attraction of a court where both these needs were generously met. In the 780s a combination of this natural magnetic pull and the initiative of the king in summoning educated men to his court brought together scholars from many parts of Europe. Incomparably the most important among them was the Northumbrian Alcuin. When Charles met him for the second time—we do not know when or where the first occasion was—at Pàrma on the return journey from Rome in 781, this master of the cathedral school at York was nearly 50, a decade older than the Frankish king. He had been away from his native country only for brief periods. He may have known his Vergil well—his early enthusiasm for profane Latin literature later worried him—but he knew hardly any other Classical writer, and at this date he had almost no literary or scholarly achievement to his credit: only a few of his poems were certainly written at York. Moreover he was and remained always only in deacon's orders. It argues a remarkable percipience on Charles' part that he saw in Alcuin a man who could serve his needs. Alcuin's biography does not say specifically that the king chose him to be the teacher and mentor of his entourage, but this is certainly what he became; and later, in 800, he recorded

Fig. 24 Hercules in a computistic and astronomical collection from Cologne; early ninth century. *Cologne, Dombibliothek* Cod. 83[11].

his conviction that the summons to the Frankish court was his destined vocation, which had been prophesied by a holy man in his youth. Evidence of originality in his writings is hard to find and he cannot be numbered among the more creative of the scholars who gathered round Charles, except perhaps in the field of liturgy. He had instead a rare gift for friendship, which was not broken when personal contact stopped but was maintained and even strengthened—like all true Christian relationships—by prayer as much as by correspondence; and he never forgot what he had learned from his teacher at York, that ' one learns in order to teach '. Hence he was a transmitter of the learning of greater minds than his own, skilled in bringing out the best in his contemporaries and in inspiring the younger generation to rise to greater heights than their masters. He took up residence at the itinerant royal court in 782 and, apart from two visits to England in 786 and 790-3, only left it to live the last years of his life (796-804) as abbot of St. Martin's at Tours. Such was his impact on those he helped to educate in those years that for three-quarters of a century men were proud to remember that they were the pupils or pupils of pupils of Alcuin.

At the very end of 782—the year incidentally of the massacre of Verden—the still small circle of educated men at the Frankish court was enlarged by the arrival of the Italian Paul, an even older man than Alcuin. He had attracted Charles' attention by his petition in verse, begging for the release of his brother who had been in captivity since the rebellion of 776: ' It is now seven years since conflict brought forth many sorrows and shook my heart; for that time my brother has been a captive in your lands, heart-broken, naked, in need; in her homeland his wife begs for food with trembling mouth; she supports four children by this shameful art, by which she scarcely manages to cover them with tatters '. For Paul the call of the cloister was stronger than the call to royal service and he returned to Monte Cassino after less than seven years; but his literary skills left their mark on others of the court circle.

By the time of his departure from Charles' court, it included several younger men. The ablest scholar among them was probably the Spanish Goth Theodulf, one of the Christian inhabitants of northern Spain who had judged it wiser to take refuge north of the Pyrenees in the aftermath of Charles' abortive expedition of 778. His familiarity with the literary traditions of late Antiquity and Biblical knowledge are a reminder that Christian Latin learning still flourished in Arab Spain. Among the others, mostly of less distinction, were several English pupils of Alcuin who followed him to the Frankish court and more than one Irishman, including a certain Cadac, whose methods of Biblical interpretation aroused the wrath of Theodulf, and possibly also Dungal. But the court also contained the first of the native Franks who were to carry on the tradition of learning that stemmed from the court, notably Angilbert, noble-born and no longer young, who became Homer to Alcuin's Flaccus, lover of Charles' daughter Berta and, in 789, abbot of wealthy St. Riquier, although probably never an ordained cleric.

How the younger generation was led on from its ABC to *grammatica*—defined by Alcuin as ' the science of letters and the guardian of right speech and writing: it depends on nature, reason, authority and custom ' and in our terminology embracing literature as well as grammar—can only dimly be discerned from the material at our disposal. All medieval text-books, including both those inherited from Antiquity and those written by Alcuin and his pupils, now seem both repulsive and barely intelligible. If his writings are to be trusted, however, Alcuin encouraged a dialogue between master and pupil. His ' elementary ' treatise on the parts of speech and their use, which Notker later commended to a future bishop of Constance as a work in comparison with which ' Donatus, Nocomachus, Domistheus and our Priscian seem as nothing ', involves both himself, fifteen-year-old ' Saxon ' and fourteen-year-old ' Frank '. The later is made to seem duller than his fellow-pupil. A more elaborate and advanced work takes the form of a dialogue between king Pippin of Italy and Alcuin. It begins with the illuminating questions and answers: ' What is writing? The guardian of history. What is speech? The revealer of the spirit. What gives birth to speech? The tongue ' and then goes on to riddles. (A fuller collection of riddles and arithmetical puzzles which some manuscripts connect with Alcuin includes several which in slightly variant form are to be found in present-day children's annuals and weeklies!) Finally, not long before 800 Alcuin put into writing a dialogue in which the other participant is the king himself. The more advanced nature of the notions that were examined here may be gathered from these two extracts: ' C. Expound the nature of justice. A. Justice is a state of mind which assigns to each thing its proper worth. In it the cult of the divine, the rights of mankind, and the equitable state of the whole of life are preserved '; ' C. How is justice that proceeds from customary use maintained? A. By contract, by equity, by judgement and by law. C. I would like to hear more about these also. A. Contract is an agreement between persons. Equity is that which is fair to all. Judgement is what is established by the opinions of a prominent man or of several. Law is right written down for all the people to know what it is their duty to avoid and what to maintain.'[1]

[1] transl. M. L. W. Laistner

Fig. 25   Portion of a library catalogue from Würzburg in Anglo-Saxon minuscule; c. 800.
Oxford, Bodleian Library Ms. Laud Misc. 126, fol 260. (*Actual size.*)

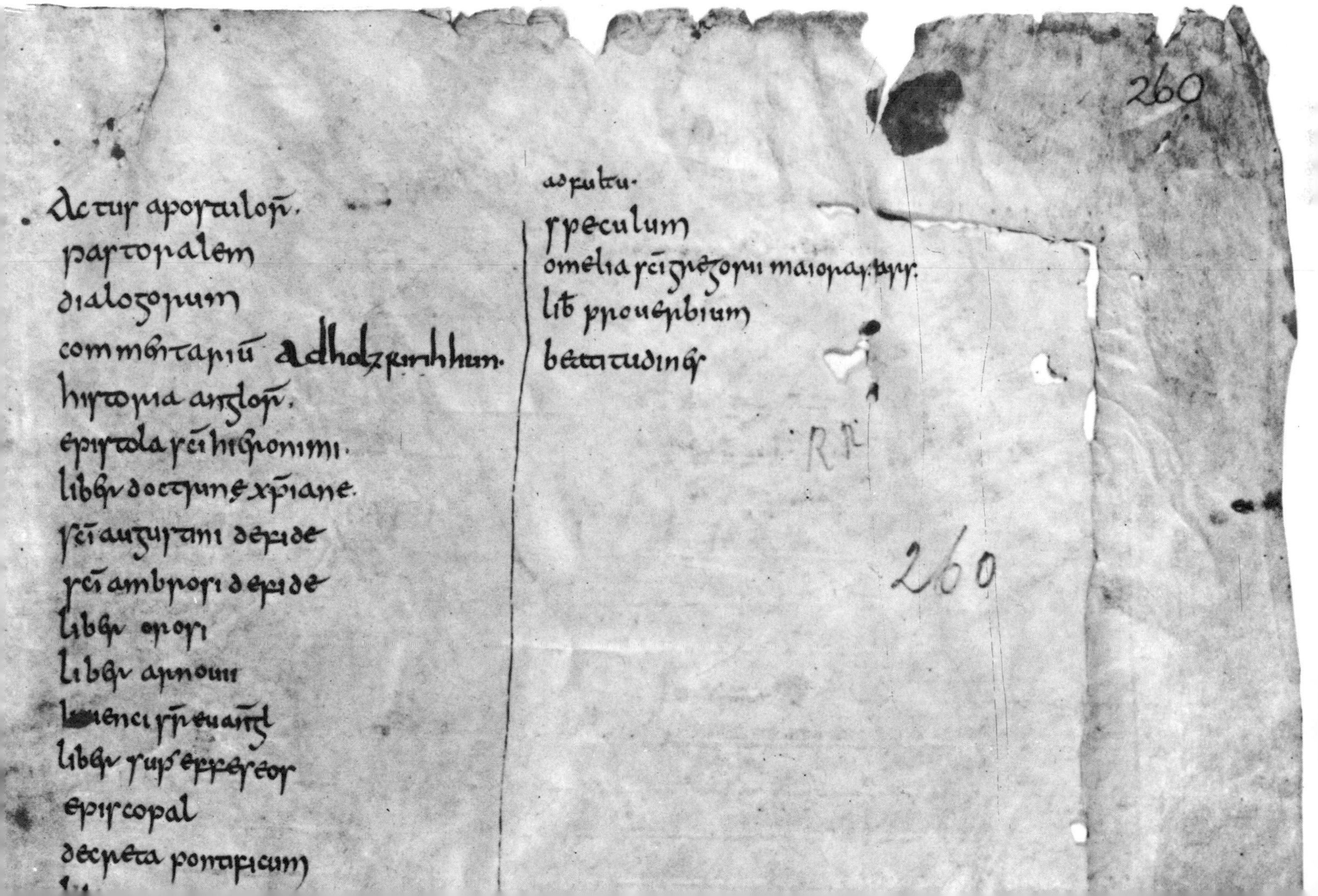

We do not have to suppose that Alcuin was recording a dialogue that had
actually taken place, any more than that the verses standing in Charles' name in
the court collection are his own unaided composition. The previously quoted lively
description by Theodulf of the court circle in 796—with Alcuin enjoying his drink
and the tiny Einhard running about like an ant—is, however, better evidence than
either Alcuin's writings or Einhard's ponderous phrases that the king was treated
as an apt pupil by the scholars he had gathered around him and played an active
part in their intellectual exercises. There is nothing incredible in the picture that
emerges from these and other texts of a middle-aged but energetic king possessed
of a lively intellectual curiosity, a growing awareness of the literary heritage of the
past and an ability to take pleasure in the word-play of others. Scholars in recent
decades have reacted against an older picture of a Carolingian Court Academy
similar to its counterparts in the Italian Renaissance, in which an élite group
indulged in humanistic delight; and more than one has stressed the ' modest and
practical' intentions of Alcuin and his fellows, even defining the scope of their
'intellectual reform and textual criticism ' as the ' indispensable preliminary to
the reform of the clergy and the performance of the *Opus Dei* '. The reaction has
gone too far. Although the judgement quoted is not wrong, it singles out what is
only one aspect of the revival of learning in the early Carolingian period: and it is
truer of the period in which this revival was spreading outwards from the court to
other places where men read and copied than when the ' Court scholars ' of the
first generation were displaying their qualities as *viri ingeniosi*.

It is too easily overlooked that the majority of Alcuin's text-books—the *De
Orthographia* with its frequent Vergil quotations *may* be an exception—the bulk of
his extant letters, his and Theodulf's work on the text of the Vulgate Bible, his
most important and lasting liturgical innovations, the attempt to produce a
' standard ' homiliary and a standard text of the Benedictine Rule all belong to the
period after 787/8. Unless the surviving evidence is wholly deceptive, the educated
men at Charles' court in the previous decade were engaged in very different
activities. Probably not long after his arrival Paul was commissioned by Angilram,
bishop of Metz (and from ?784 simultaneously Charles' arch-chaplain), to write
an account of his predecessors, beginning with Clement who had traditionally been
sent there by the apostle Peter. Paul unfortunately made no use of documents or
other local material, an omission which is also noticeable in his later and much more
widely-read ' History of the Lombards ' and a sharp contrast with Bede earlier in
the same century or with Flodoard of Rheims at the beginning of the tenth century.
The interest of his *Libellus* was twofold: it was the first attempt to do for another see
what ' the Popes' Book ' did for Rome; its account of the incumbency of the saint-
bishop Arnulf, ancestor of the Carolingians, provides an opportunity for stressing
the qualities inherent in the royal line that had stemmed from him and whose
destinies, by implication, were linked with the see of St. Peter. In the same period
someone was beginning to assemble the manuscripts of Classical authors, including
Lucan, Terence, Juvenal and Tibullus, listed in the court library catalogue, although
few of them are known to have been read or copied until the collection had been
dispersed among the major monastic libraries of north-east Francia.

Alcuin and other non-Italians at the royal court showed greater enthusiasm for
literature of a more esoteric and ' learned ' kind, such as the artificial and tedious
' figure poems ' of the fourth-century writer Porfyrius. Their own verse composi-
tions, although not entirely negligible, are the work of writers fascinated by
language and technique (newly discovered and barely mastered) much as a small

38. Manuscript; Christ in Majesty
from the Godescalc Evangelistary:
Paris, Bibliothèque Nationale Lat.
1203, fol 3. *Size* 30.5 × 21 cm.

39. Detail of the ' tower-gateway ',
S. Nazarus, Lorsch (Germany).

40. Detail of Einhard's Church,
Steinbach (Germany).

38

child is fascinated by a new toy, and confident that the fellow-members of their tiny circle will share their delight. The most interesting to the historian are those that directly reflect contemporary events, like the poem of an anonymous Irishman (?Dungal) commemorating the overthrow of duke Tassilo by a bold and heroic Charles. Among the ' court poetry ' of this period only Paul the Deacon's shows any true poetic quality. Because the Frankish court of the 780s and early 790s was an agreeable meeting-place of scholars and poetasters and a major source of stimulus to others, we must beware of rating too highly the literature it produced. The outstanding poetic achievements of the first phase of what is, rightly or wrongly, commonly known as the ' Carolingian Renaissance ', are to be found in the supple and sensitive rhythmic verses of Paulinus after he had returned to north-east Italy; and Paul's polished ' History of the Lombards ' was written at Monte Cassino, although it is probably true that both the form and some of the content of this work were influenced by Paul's sojourn at Charles' court.

No single factor, no one person can be held responsible for the change in emphasis or broadening of activity which is evident at the Frankish court from the late 780s. Respect for Rome, a realization of the implications of the establishment of new churches in Saxony and of the annexation of territories that had their own ecclesiastical traditions, Charles' own grander ideas about the function of a king and his growing respect for the written word stimulated and encouraged by the scholars with whom he had personal contact—all doubtless played their part. Through Paul a royal request went to the Pope in c. 786 for a copy of the sacramentary ' put in order by Pope Gregory '. Extraordinary though this now seems, and an illustration of the striking changes that took place during Charles' reign, Hadrian was unable to meet this request immediately because of a lack of spare copies and of qualified copyists. What he eventually sent may have been a *de luxe* manuscript, but it was hardly suitable for the purposes Charles, or his advisers, had in mind, for it contained only the masses at which the Pope was himself normally the celebrant in the Roman churches and it was not even up-to-date. In spite of this, it was still being copied in 811/12, the date of the one surviving direct copy, made for the bishop of Cambrai (fig. 26).

The book's very real defects if it were taken as the basis of the liturgy to be adopted by all the churches in the Frankish kingdom could not, however, be ignored. Acting perhaps on his own initiative rather than at the king's command, Alcuin accordingly prepared a supplement containing masses for the Sundays lacking in the *Hadrianum*, based on material in other ' Roman ' sacramentaries that had reached Francia earlier, and additional services and prayers—notably, a lengthy series of benedictions, which were a distinctive and well-established feature of the liturgy of Frankish Gaul. It has recently been suggested that a famous notice in many later copies of Alcuin's edition of the Gregorian Sacramentary to the effect that it was written *ex authentico libro bibliothecae cubiculi* is not, as has long been supposed, a reference to the private library of the Pope: it refers instead to the library at the royal court and, after c. 794, presumably at Aachen where the ' authentic ' manuscript of the sacramentary prepared by Alcuin was made available for copying. As an attempt to get the whole Frankish church to celebrate mass in the same way, it was a failure. Sacramentaries of other types continued to be used and copied: a list of the liturgical books available in the monastery of St. Riquier in 831 shows that it had fourteen ' Gelasian missals ', three ' Gregorian missals ' but only one ' Gregorian and Gelasian missal arranged in modern times by Albinus '. But Alcuin had done his work supremely well and although further additions were

41. Manuscript; Canon-tables from the Book of Kells, *Dublin, Trinity College* fol 2. *Size* 33 × 25 cm.

unavoidable and many changes were made at various times in the next seven centuries, his version of the sacramentary was the basis of the missal in universal use in the Roman church from the late sixteenth century.

The church, like any other earthly institution, had to lay down rules or laws for its members. There were probably few decades in the early Middle Ages when a copy of one of the more or less arbitrary collections of conciliar decrees was not being made somewhere in the Christian west and copies were made in even greater numbers during the Carolingian period. Already in 774 Charles obtained from the Pope a text of the most comprehensive collection of canon law then available, that compiled by Dionysius Exiguus in the sixth century, with some later additions—the so-called 'Dionysio-Hadriana'. There are reasons for thinking that this book was not properly utilised for some years to come, but before the end of the century copies had been made for churches in many parts of Francia: at least three manuscripts of later date have a colophon declaring that 'This codex was written from the original (*authenticum*) which Hadrian gave to the Frankish king'. In 787 or not long afterwards Charles asked the abbot of Monte Cassino for a text of the monastic rule of St. Benedict-and was duly sent a copy of what the community believed was the Saint's autograph (probably wrongly, although it may well have been a manuscript of the sixth century). An early ninth-century manuscript from the monastic *scriptorium* (writing-workshop) and library of St. Gall is generally regarded as a very accurate copy of this 'official' text. Perhaps already in the 780s Alcuin had been called on to produce an epistle-lectionary, a list of the portions of the New Testament Epistles or of the Prophetic books of the Old Testament read at the mass, based on Roman practice; and Paul the Deacon, who is described as *familiaris clientulus noster* in the letter by which the king subsequently commended his work to all the *religiosi lectores* of the kingdom, had been commanded to prepare a homiliary, based on the works of the great Fathers of the Church, for use at the night office.

Most early medieval popes had favoured a policy of 'diversity within unity'. It is ironical, in view of the later history of the church, that the first attempt to enforce the use of standard texts came from the secular arm. But to Charles the uniformity of the church's worship and of the rules by which its members were governed was not an end in itself: it was the only way of ensuring that Christian society should be rightly ordered and at the same time of showing respect for the see of St. Peter. It was equally important in the eyes of Charles' advisers that 'right belief' should always prevail throughout the church. Wrong belief at this time, and indeed at all periods of the Middle Ages, was of two basically different kinds. On the one hand there were the notions and practices that were pagan survivals or superstitious perversions of the church's requirements. These were, for example, the pagan Lombard practice of placing an eggshell between the legs of the dead against which St. Carlo Borromeo was still inveighing in the sixteenth century; the ritual drinkings in churches; or the circulation of a supposed letter that had fallen from Heaven, which is attacked in more than one Carolingian capitulary. Raising the standards of the ordinary clergy might save the faithful from these and similar errors but it could never entirely eliminate them. On the other hand, there were the doctrines developed by men of learning and understanding which were judged by others to be heretical and incompatible with eternal salvation. In the last decade of the eighth century the leading scholars of Charles' court and kingdoms were compelled to find counter-arguments to two such doctrines.

The first of them, which usually seems the more important to modern scholars although contemporaries probably thought the opposite, was the newly-defined attitude of the Greek church to images, as it was understood (or, better, misunderstood) in the west. A council summoned to Nicaea in 787 had cancelled earlier decisions ordering the destruction of sacred images as conducive to idolatry and had then attempted a new doctrinal definition, to be binding on the church for the future, which distinguished between the different degrees of veneration to be accorded to icons and divine worship which is proper to God alone. As was so often the case, the Latin translation of the acts of the council was full of errors and, partly for this reason, partly because the theological subtleties of the Greeks and of the undoubtedly orthodox Fathers they had followed were beyond the western theologians of the period, perhaps partly even because they *wished* to misunderstand the theologians of Nicaea, those who formed opinion at the Frankish court rejected their decisions and definitions. They condemned both those who worshipped and those who destroyed images: the adoration of images was heathen; it had been

Fig. 27 Latin version of acts of the Council of Ephesus with marginal indications made by Alcuin. *Paris, Bibliothèque Nationale* Lat. 1572, fol 79. (*Actual size.*)

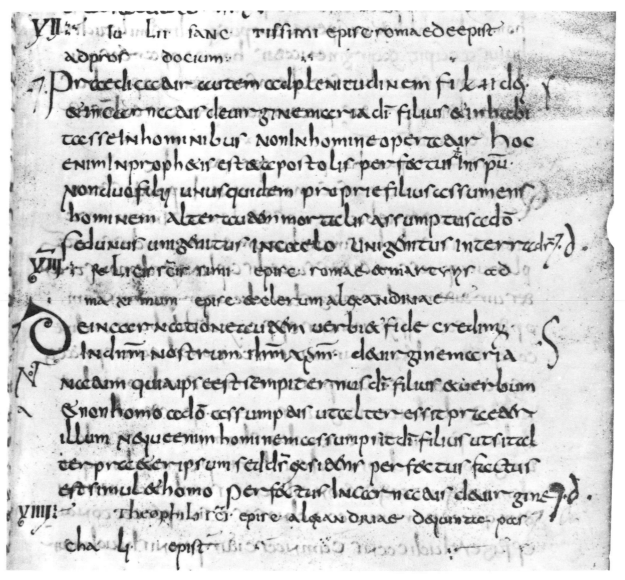

allowed neither by patriarchs nor prophets nor Apostles nor Fathers; but, with Pope Gregory I, they maintained that pictures in church were justified both as decoration and because they instructed the illiterate. The fullest statement of this position is to be found in the so-called ' Caroline Books ', which for all their faults constitute the most considerable and most original piece of theological writing in the west in this period. It is almost certainly substantially the work of Theodulf, reflecting his personal outlook and learning. His draft text was, however, evidently discussed and amended at the Court; and the marginal notes to the manuscript that provide evidence of this editorial activity (now unfortunately incomplete) may preserve some amateurish comments from the king himself. There is no evidence that copies were made for wider circulation and most of those who, at the Council of Frankfort in 794, joined in the public, formal, condemnation of the adoration of the images of the saints and of the Divine Trinity ' as ordered by the recent Greek synod ' must have done so in complete ignorance of both the facts and the arguments.

The same Council re-affirmed an earlier condemnation of the two Spanish bishops and their followers who maintained that ' Jesus Christ Incarnate is, in His manhood, the Son of God only by adoption '. This terrible departure from the established doctrine of the church, first propounded by archbishop Elipand of Toledo (in Arab Spain), had eight years previously brought a stern warning from the Pope to other bishops in Spain ' not to be poisoned by this serpent's venom '. Its acceptance by bishop Felix of Urgel, a Pyrenean diocese in the Spanish March, c. 790, brought the heresy to the active notice of the Frankish court. In 792 a council at Regensburg, attended by bishops from both sides of the Alps, found Felix guilty of grievous error. Such was Alcuin's standing among Frankish clerics in higher orders than himself that, when he returned from England a year later, he was immediately accepted as the authoritative defender of the orthodox doctrine, against a man whom he had hitherto thought of as a friend: he was largely if not wholly responsible for the resolution against adoptionism drawn up at the Council of Frankfort in the name of the Frankish bishops (Paulinus of Aquileia was responsible for another in the name of the Italian bishops); and he was responsible too for the letter in the name of king Charles that was sent with these and other documents to archbishop Elipand. It was apparently as a direct consequence of these dramatic events that the royal chapel—for the first time in the history of the liturgy—included a singing of the Creed in the introductory section of the mass, originally in a version provided by Alcuin, who seems to have used a text of Irish origin, and then from 798 in the version put forward by Paulinus. When, two or three years after Frankfort, Felix re-asserted his views at greater length, Alcuin, now abbot of St. Martin's at Tours, addressed a number of letters both to him (fig. 54) and to the most effective opponent of adoptionism in Spain itself, abbot Beatus of Liébana (Asturias) and wrote two full-length treatises on the subject: a manuscript of the Latin Acts of the council of Ephesus, written at Tours earlier in the century, has indications in the margin where Alcuin found texts that were to provide him with ammunition for the first of these (fig. 27). In spite of such weighty counter-blasts, traces of the heresy lingered on in the south into the next century, but it had lost its force. When Alcuin wrote the last of his works on the doctrine of the Trinity two years before his death it was only incidentally polemical and it confirms that, in spite of his great age, its author had continued to extend both his knowledge of the writings of the Fathers and his understanding of the deeper mysteries of the Christian faith.

42. Brooch reliquary: ' Talisman of Charlemagne '; *Rheims, Cathedral Treasury. Size* 6.5 × 7 cm.

43. The Hon gold plaque; ninth century: *Oslo, Universitetets Oldsaksamling.*

42

43

To defend the fundamentals of Christian belief in learned debate was the privilege of a select few. To maintain and advance the Christian religion was—or ought to be—the obligation of many. But the obligation would be largely meaningless so long as many of the ordinary clergy were as illiterate as the people among whom they worked. Often even those who had received some education had no access to the basic texts of the church's worship and belief. In such circumstances superstition would always win. The task of raising the standards of the entire Frankish church was boldly faced in Charles' ' General Admonition ' of 789, which survives in enough manuscript copies for us to be sure that it was widely disseminated on both sides of the Alps. The first fifty-nine chapters are mostly taken from decrees of early church councils as transmitted by the collection recently brought from Rome. The remainder combine practical exhortation based directly on passages in the Bible with novel regulations directed at clergy of all ranks. ' Let bishops diligently examine their priests throughout their dioceses ', says one chapter ' . . . so that they may hold the right faith, observe catholic baptism and understand well the prayers of the mass; and so that the psalms may be sung worthily according to the divisions of the verses and so that they understand the Lord's Prayer and pass on its meaning to all . . . ' Another commands that all clergy and monks shall live good and worthy lives which will attract to their company ' not only children of servile condition but also the sons of free men. And let there be schools in which the boys read. Correct well the psalms, musical notation, [office- and mass-] chants, chronological works (*compotus*), works on grammar in each monastery and cathedral church and the Catholic books, because often men wish to address God but do so badly because the works are incorrect. And do not allow your boys to corrupt them through reading or copying: if a Gospel-book, psalter or missal has to be copied, let men of mature age do so with every care.'

Some years later Alcuin, as it seems, drafted for the king some new injunctions on the same theme. ' We, together with our faithful ', the king is made to declare in the royal mandate that embodied them, ' have deemed it expedient that the bishoprics and monasteries entrusted by Christ's favour to our government, in addition to the observance of monastic discipline and the practice of the religious life, should vouchsafe instruction also in the exercise of letters to those who, with God's help, are able to learn '; and again, ' in letters sent to us from various monasteries . . . we have observed right sentiments and uncouth language . . .; whence it came that we began to fear lest, as skill in writing was less, wisdom to understand the Sacred Scriptures might be far less than it ought rightly to be '. The only surviving copy of the mandate is addressed to Sturmi's successor as abbot of Fulda, Baugulf; and a slightly different version which may represent the form in which the circular was passed on to other clergy, as the king had ordered, comes from the same place: but there is little doubt that it was originally sent to many other churches.

On the basis of these and other texts, some scholars have attributed to Charles the intention of introducing universal elementary education. This is hardly credible. What they do envisage is, first, that proper arrangements shall be made to teach future generations of clergy all that they need to know to perform their duties properly and for the copying of manuscripts, without which this will be so much wasted effort; secondly, perhaps, that the royal court will not be the only place where laymen can acquire a grounding in ' letters '; and thirdly, that the language used will be clearly distinguished from the *lingua romana* of everyday speech. Even if there were precedents for the first two in, for example, some north

44. The Lorsch ' tower-gateway '.

115

Italian episcopal and parish churches and in the monastery of Fulda (where Einhard had been taught before he came to court), these plans are remarkable enough. How far schools were created as a result of them is not easy to say. Theodulf, as bishop of Orleans (?798-818), tried to do so in his own diocese. A decade or two later, we hear of monastic schools that provided an education for boys who were to return to the world as well as for those who were future monks—at St. Gall and perhaps elsewhere—in a separate establishment outside the precincts of the

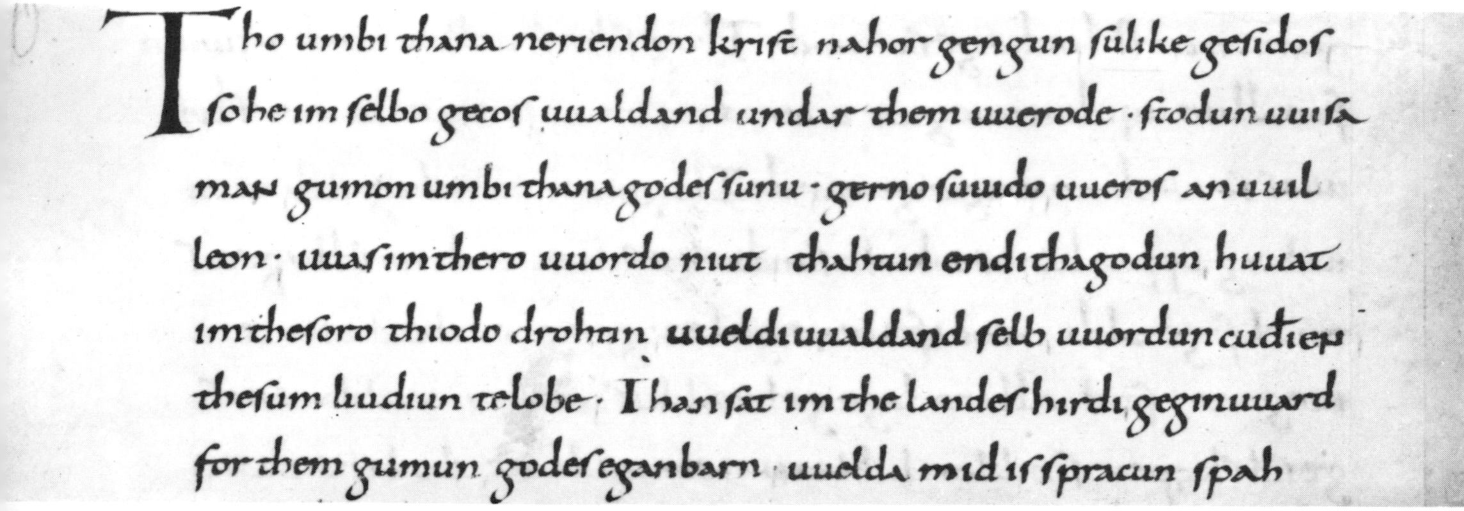

Tho umbi thana neriendon krift nahor gengun fulike gefidos
fohe im felbo gecof uualdand undar them uuerode. ftodun uuifa
man gumon umbi thana godef funu. gerno fuuido uuerof anuuil
leon. uuafim thero uuordo niut thahtun endi thagodun huuat
im thefero thiodo drohan. uueldi uualdand felb uuordun cudiep
thefum liudiun telobe. I han fat im the lander hirdi geginuuard
for them gumun godef eganbarn. uueldi mid if fpracun fpah

Fig. 28   Part of a page from the 'Heliand'. *Munich, Bayerische Staatsbibliothek* Cod. Germ. 25, fol 19v. (*Actual size.*)

monastery; and right at the end of the ninth century at least one cathedral church in Francia, Rheims, made formal provision for teaching the parish clergy of the diocese as well as the cathedral clergy themselves. But these stand almost alone. If the success of Charles' educational endeavours were judged by the number of references to schools, it would be necessary to admit almost complete failure. There is, however, other and better evidence that they had a remarkable degree of success and there are good reasons for accepting the familiar doctrine that 'the Carolingian Renaissance' largely determined the intellectual and literary development of medieval Europe.

When the Council of Frankfort of 794 insisted that it was false to believe that God can be prayed to only in the three sacred languages (Hebrew, Greek and Latin) and, more significantly, when a regional church council held at Tours in 813 laid down that homilies are to be translated into *rustica romana lingua aut thiotisca* so that they could be understood by all, the evident implication was that the reforms were succeeding to the extent that the language normally used by the clergy was again a Latin purged of its vernacular features. It is evident none the less that the prescription that congregations were to know the central documents of the Christian faith, the Lord's Prayer and the Creed—laid down already in 789—posed new problems that had to be solved in a similar way: translations of both into the dialect of Alemannia are found in a pre-800 manuscript now at St. Gall (although 'some unintelligent mistranslations show that the full benefit of the reforms had not yet manifested itself'), as is a translation of the Lord's Prayer into Bavarian in early ninth-century manuscripts from Freising and Regensburg: and two creeds, the *Gloria* and the *Laudamus*, as well as the Lord's Prayer, were available in the Rhine-Frankish dialect by the end of the eighth century. Other vernacular texts for use by the laity, such as baptismal vows (cf. fig. 20), in one or other of the Germanic dialects spoken in Charles' dominions are found scattered through ninth-century manuscripts.

More extensive texts were used in religious communities for the instruction of novices or perhaps to help clergy working among a people whose language was not their own: such are the interlinear translation of the Rule of St. Benedict, now at St. Gall but apparently written at Reichenau, and the similar translation of twenty-six hymns of St. Ambrose. A more remarkable achievement is the translation of the first part of one of Isidore's theological treatises which, alone among surviving vernacular texts, has been connected—on not very adequate grounds—with Charles' court.

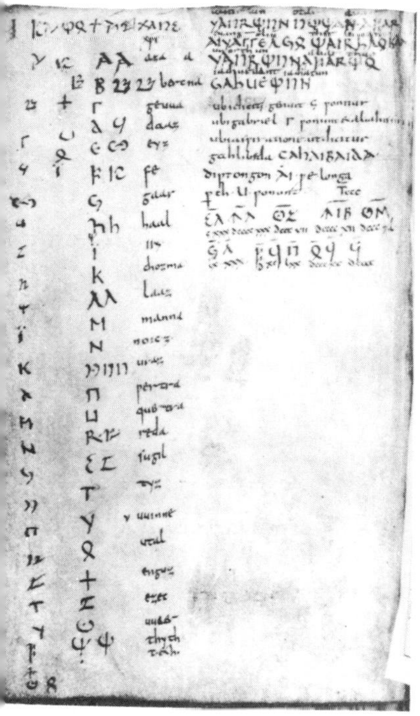

The most outstanding piece of Carolingian religious literature in the vernacular is, however, undoubtedly the Old Saxon *Heliand* (fig. 28) composed (perhaps at Fulda, perhaps at Werden) a few years after Charles' death. Its well-read author casts the Gospel story in the form of a secular epic, with Christ as war-leader and the disciples as his warrior-followers. The latter are appropriately noble-born, the marriage at Cana reads like a court feast and the account of the Sermon on the Mount is one of the most graphic descriptions extant of a barbarian king addressing his faithful followers and subjects. A succession of scholars has commented that these early religious texts come predominantly from monasteries which had been founded by or were otherwise connected with Anglo-Saxon missionaries and has concluded that it was they who first used the Continental Germanic vernaculars for the propagation of the Christian faith. This may well be true, but it is clear that Charles' own endeavours gave considerable encouragement to the practice, since they made it more necessary than ever and provided new facilities for the transmission of the texts. The most inappropriate of the many criticisms that have been directed against Charles' encouragement of learning and literacy is that it was only concerned with the creation of a Christian Latin culture for an élite class.

The Frankish king did not forget and could not have forgotten that he and many of those among whom he moved were of Germanic origin and speech. In a famous section of his biography, Einhard tells us that Charles devised (Rhine-) Frankish names for all twelve months of the year and for the twelve winds listed by Isidore and earlier Latin encyclopaedists—and not merely for the winds from the four cardinal points which were all the language had hitherto known. An even more famous passage immediately before this claims that, in addition to having the tribal laws recorded in writing (which in broad terms is true), the king was responsible for the copying of ' very ancient barbarian poems in which were sung the deeds and wars of kings of old ' and that he planned a grammar of his native language. In reaction against those who have even been prepared to describe the lost poems which went into these lost manuscripts, some scholars have suggested that Einhard simply invented the whole thing. This seems unnecessarily sceptical. The existence of bilingual glosses, the known interest of the period in languages and language—which took many forms, including even the collection of runic and other alphabets (fig. 29) and their use for short transliterations—and the court's familiarity with Latin grammatical treatises makes the *idea* of a German grammar by no means incredible, even if it were many centuries before one was produced. The existence of an oral Germanic literature is not in doubt and it is clear that an important part of it preserved a tradition—distorted with the passage of time

Fig. 29   A collection of alphabets added in the mid-ninth century to a Salzburg manuscript of the works of Alcuin.
Vienna, Österreichische Nationalbibliothek Cod. 795, fol 20v.

but none the less containing a core of historical reminiscence—of the wars and invasions of the fourth and fifth centuries, particularly those involving the Ostrogothic king Theodoric. Alcuin's exclamation—admittedly in a letter addressed to the bishop of Lindisfarne—' What has Hinield [a legendary Germanic king] to do with Christ? ' and his criticism of the reciting of pagan songs at table; the inclusion in Paul the Deacon's ' History of the Lombards ' of versions of several of the familiar stories from the common stock of Germanic folk-tale and his attempt to produce an acceptable Latin version of the early saga-history of people (which makes his ' History ' in some respects more valuable as a source for early Germanic history than for seventh-century Italy); evidence elsewhere of Charles' interest in Theodoric and his recognition of him as a great precursor of his own strivings and achievements; Louis' repudiation of the ' pagan songs ' of his youth: taken together facts such as these suggest that the collecting of texts of ' ancient barbarian poems ' at Charles' court is more than possible. It is useless to speculate on what relations they had to later German epic poetry or to what extent they had hitherto been transmitted by the Lombards rather than by the Franks: the only extant text that gives an idea of what they may have been like is the fragmentary ' Lay of Hildebrand and Hadubrand ', the tale of a father compelled to fight his son which, to those capable of mastering the linguistic complexities of a text that is an Old Saxon rendering of a version in Old High German (Bavarian) or even in translation, is still deeply moving.

Directly or indirectly as a result of Charles' measures, his reign constitutes a definite if ill-defined phase in the development of Germanic literature. With the degree of standardization imposed by the writing down in religious communities of texts hitherto transmitted orally and because of the need to create an enlarged vocabulary to express new concepts, it was also an important period in the history of the Germanic languages. It is none the less true that the European literary and intellectual tradition, of which Charles' work was and was to be for centuries part, even into the period in which (as the title and content of Ernst Robert Curtius' great book reminds us)[1] the greatest creative writers had already adopted the vernacular as their medium, was primarily a Latin one. And the true measure and enduring significance of the Frankish king's ' reforms ' lie in the greatly improved standards of Latinity, the wider range of words available to the literature, the considerable enlargement of the number of those who could read and write and the considerable improvement in the appearance and practicality of scripts and manuscript books.

The consequences are apparent, in the first place, in the more regular and less ' vulgar ' Latinity of the diplomas prepared in the royal writing-office in the second half of the reign; and in the similar change—which has never been studied in detail—evident in the charters written by local clerics, and in Italy by laymen, in different parts of the kingdom. They are apparent, secondly, in the language of the Royal Annals, put together by someone closely connected with the court shortly after 790 and continued thereafter year by year (above, p. 13); in the production of a version with greater literary pretensions not long after Charles' death; and in the widespread dissemination, copying and continuation of these annals in the ninth century. They are apparent above all in the number, appearance and content of the manuscripts written in all parts of the kingdom and empire in Charles' later years.

This evidence is not always easy to use or to interpret convincingly. At the present time our knowledge of manuscripts certainly or probably written before

[1]*Europäische Literatur und Lateinisches Mittelalter*, Bern, 1948

45. Einhard's Church, Steinbach.

the year 800 is much more complete than that of manuscripts written in the next
two decades; even where a particular manuscript is unquestionably the product of
a particular *scriptorium*, a precise dating is rarely possible; and chance survival
falsifies the overall picture. A selective account of what happened in a few specific
places none the less provides the best approach to an understanding of ' the
Carolingian Renaissance ', of how the initiative of Charles and his court eventually
affected all parts of his dominions.

At the time of the surrender of Pavia to the Frankish king, Verona had a well-
established tradition of copying and annotating manuscripts and the cathedral
church already had a substantial library. (The additions made to an *orationale*
brought from Spain, via Cagliari and Pisa, include what is usually regarded as the
earliest example of an Italian literary vernacular—a riddle about the ox pulling
the plough across the field, which is apparently a reference to the act of moving
the pen across the page.) The manuscripts produced there or acquired for the
library in the decades either side of the year 800 constitute a relatively numerous
group. They include canon-law collections, works of the Fathers, *compoti* and school-
books. When, however, a particularly splendid homiliary was written at the command of bishop Egino (?796-99), it was not in the version prepared by Paul but
an older one. And similarly the text of the ' Rule of St. Benedict ' written there in
the same period and subsequently taken to Swabia to become the source of a copy
that not long afterwards entered the library of Freising (and probably also of the
Reichenau copy with interlinear translation) was not in accordance with the
royally authorized version; and an unrevised text is also found in a manuscript that
entered the Verona library from elsewhere. Yet new texts could and did circulate
surprisingly rapidly. Round about the turn of the century a copy was made at
Verona of a manuscript, presumably from St. Martin's at Tours, containing works
by Alcuin and others and apparently put together as an educational and theological
manual (fig. 31): very shortly afterwards it was taken to Freising and the first part
copied. Verona scribes had made several attempts to produce an acceptable
minuscule from semi-uncial and cursive elements. Egino brought with him or
rapidly trained a small group of scribes who wrote a much superior minuscule,
comparable with but quite distinct from that used by Godescalc and his successors
at the court, and a script of real beauty when penned by an accomplished scribe.
Other Verona clergy continued to write in the way to which they were accustomed.
When Egino retired to the island of Reichenau (Lake Constance), taking with him
a number of the manuscripts written on his initiative, his best scribes seem to have
departed also. The seven scribes who made the copy of the Alcuin manuscript a
year or two later displayed hands of very different kinds, from ones similar to the
Egino script to others which show a marked influence of the older scripts. Among
the latter, however, was the cleric Pacificus (fig. 31, left) who, as arch-deacon of the
cathedral church, subsequently encouraged the adoption of the type of minuscule
which was becoming the standard one in the Carolingian Empire and had manuscripts on a wide variety of topics, including several original works of his own,
copied and added to the Verona library.

At Salzburg the tradition of writing was only a few decades old when Arno
arrived in 785. The forty or so manuscripts written there in the next fifteen or
twenty years probably give us a good picture of the kind of library that was being
built up in many other centres in the same period. They include, of course, texts
of the Scriptures, texts for use in worship, Saints' lives, canons of councils, peniten-
tials, together with works by Jerome, Ambrose, Isidore and other Fathers: the fact

46. Manuscript; Perseus:
*Bibliotheek der Rijksuniversiteit te
Leiden* Ms. Voss. Lat. Qu 79,
fol 40v. *Size* 22 × 20 cm.

that the works of Cyprian exist in two bulky manuscripts identical in text, size and script suggests ' a flourishing scriptorium which produced books for other houses ' (E. A. Lowe). Other works include a text of the *Liber Pontificalis* and the earliest manuscript of a selection of Alcuin's letters (fig. 54). Apart from a certain Cuthbert, whose name as well as his writing proclaim him to be an Englishman, the Salzburg scribes wrote either in a round minuscule with letters of rather broad proportions or in a much more delicate and refined script—one of the most advanced minu-

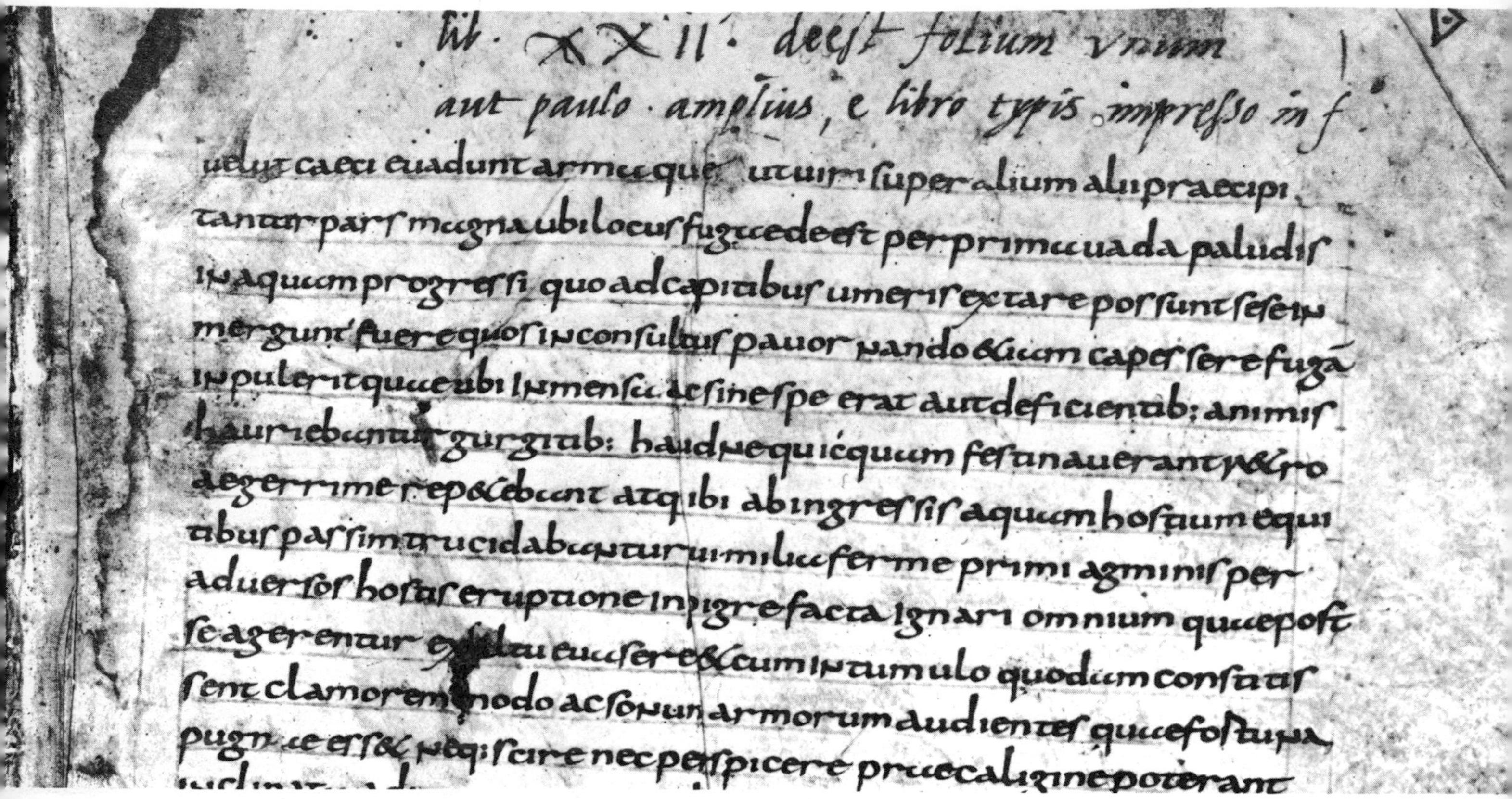
lib. XXII. deest folium unum
aut paulo amplius, e libro typis impresso in f.
uelutcaeci euaduntarmaque etuiri superalium aliipraecipi
tantur pars magna ubilocus fugaedeest perprimauada paludis
inaquam progressi quoadcapitibus umeris extare possunt sesein
mergunt fuere quos inconsultus pauor nando &cum capessere fugã
inpuleritquaeubi inmensa acsinespe erat autdeficientib; animis
hauriebantur gurgitib; haudnequicquam festinauerant retro
aegerrime repetebant atqibi abingressis aquam hostium equi
tibus passim trucidabantur sexmilia ferme primi agminis per
aduersos hostes eruptione inpigre facta ignari omnium quaepost
seagerentur exsaltu euasere &cum intumulo quodam constitis
sent clamorem modo acsonum armorum audientes quaefortuna
pugnae esset nequi scire necperspicere praecaligine poterant

Fig. 30 Extract from the ' Third Decade ' of Livy, written at Tours during Alcuin's abbacy. *Rome, Biblioteca Apostolica Vaticana* Vat. Reg. Lat. 762, fol 1. (*Actual size.*)

scules in use in the period—the origin of which seems to be the north French abbey of St. Amand. Arno seems to have shared to the full the interest in the Heavens that is recorded of both Charles and his daughters and is evident in Annals and other writings of the period: the early manuscripts include Gregory of Tours' *De cursu stellarum*, an excessively rare text; and in the last years of Arno's pontificate (he died in 821) the Salzburg *scriptorium* produced at least two volumes of computistic and astronomical texts with illustrations of—in part—exceptional quality (pl. 46 cf. fig.).

The immediate source of most of the contents of these two manuscripts may have come from St. Amand but the place of origin of the astronomical sections was very probably Italy. Alcuin's letters show that Tours was another source of texts copied at Salzburg. The little we know of the St. Martin's library in the eighth century suggests that it was a rather miscellaneous collection and not particularly impressive. In 799 Alcuin complained about his daily battle with ' Turonic rusticity ' and this gets some confirmation from the manuscripts themselves. Before his

47. Detail of a fragment of an altar frontal in silver-gilt from Conques (France); eighth or tenth century.

48. The Altar of Volvinio. S. Ambrogio, Milan, mid-ninth century.

48

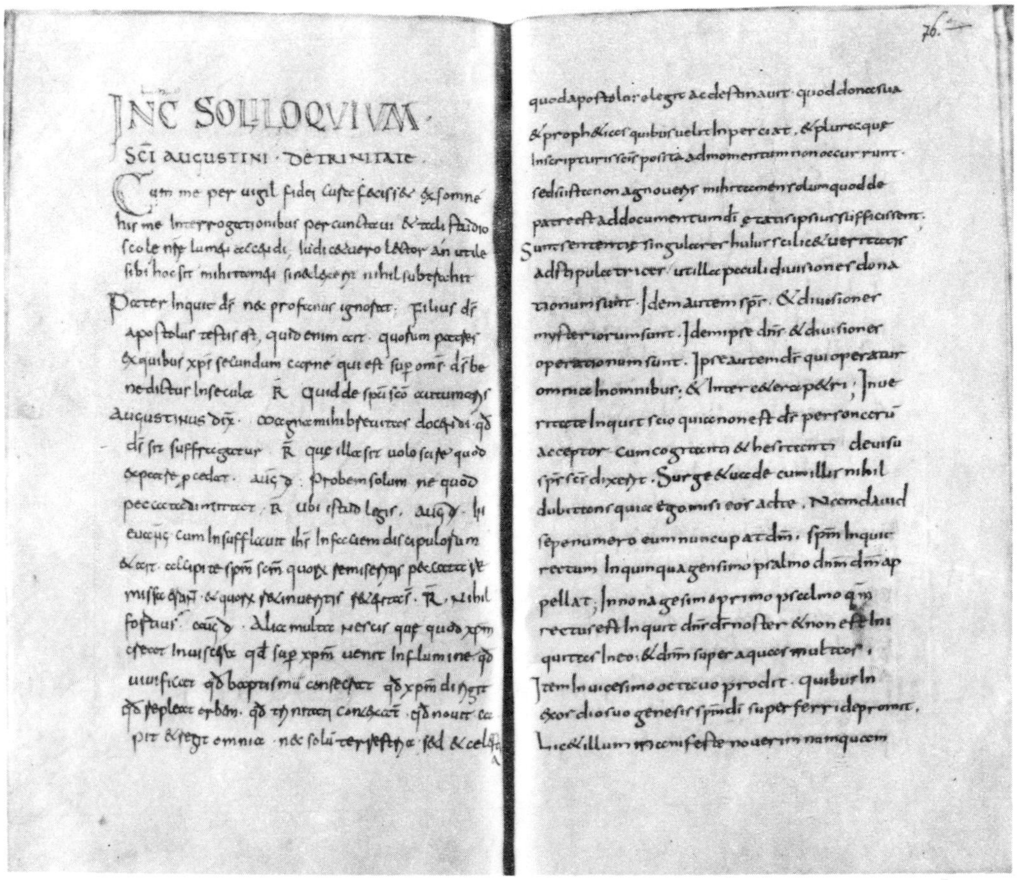

Fig. 31 Part of a theological miscellany written at Verona c. 800; left hand autograph of Pacificus (776-844/6). *Munich, Bayerische Staatsbibliothek* Lat. 6407, fol 75v and 76.

49. Detail of the Altar of
Volvinio.

death however, eight St. Martin's scribes, writing a round minuscule of varying degrees of competence, had made a copy of Livy's ' Third Decade ' (fig. 30) from a fifth-century Italian manuscript (at this time probably at the palace and only later in the library of Corbie)—the earliest, or almost the earliest evidence of an interest in the major Classical prose writers away from the court. And someone at Tours was sufficiently accomplished to design and cut on local marble the remarkably classical lettering of the verse epitaph of Pope Hadrian I (pl. 19), composed by Alcuin with the help of earlier papal and other funerary inscriptions and the standard commonplaces of Classical and post-Classical panegyric. The use of written capitals for main headings and uncial for subsidiary headings, in conjunction with an unusually consistent and comely round minuscule for the text (what is often called ' the hierarchy of scripts '), and the particular care shown in the preparation of the writing-material and the layout of the page, become distinctive features of the St. Martin's *scriptorium* in the time of Alcuin's successor as abbot, his former pupil Fridugis: and they give the Tours manuscripts a special place in the history of the medieval book.

The spread of this particular variety of round minuscule to most other centres within the Carolingian dominions and its subsequent adoption in countries that had never been subject to Charles' authority—to be consciously imitated by Florentine humanists in the fifteenth century and thence to become the model for the first Italian and most subsequent European printing-types—was, however, closely linked with the dissemination of a text for which Alcuin was himself responsible. Somewhat unexpectedly, Charles seems never to have commissioned a standard edition of the Bible or of any part of it although, as was the case with other texts in regular use at the beginning of Charles' reign, the more recent manuscripts were usually 'corrupt' one way or another. The wide differences between copies contemporaneously in use in different parts of the Frankish kingdom can be seen by comparing the Gospel-texts in, for example, the Trier Gospels (preserved

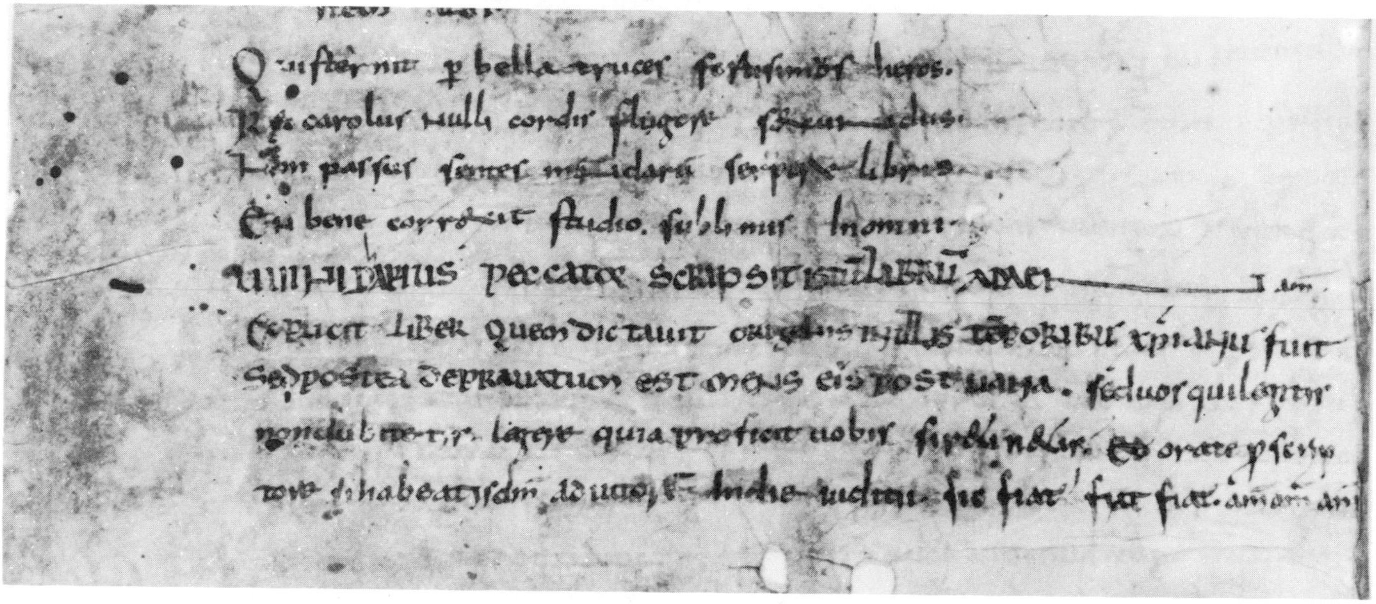

Fig. 32 Winidarius' verses dedicating his work to king Charles. *Vienna, Österreichische Nationalbibliothek* Cod. 743, fol 78v. (*Actual size.*)

in the area in which they were written) with an Insular background and in the so-called *Codex Millenarius* from Kremsmünster with predominantly Italian connections (cf. pl. 26). The need for an improved version had already been recognized at the abbey of Corbie in the early years of the reign. The most interesting attempt to produce a critical edition from the texts currently available was Theodulf's: to him we owe one in which the main variant readings found in his sources were included in his exemplar (cf. fig. 33). Alcuin, with his usual modest good sense, set himself a less ambitious task when, in the last years of the eighth century, he began—doubtless as he claimed, at the king's command—to establish a text from which the worst imperfections had been eliminated. That he was still working on it at Easter 800 is apparent from a letter written to Charles' sister Gisla, abbess of Chelles which was one of the few nunneries known to have produced manuscripts. The completed version was presented to Charles either on the very day on which he was crowned Emperor at Rome, 25th December 800, or on the first anniversary of that occasion. In the ensuing decades the scribes of St. Martin's at Tours made innumerable copies available to other monasteries and cathedral churches within the Frankish Empire.

The scribe from south-west Germany who wrote, in his copy of a commentary on Paul's Epistle to the Romans, verses which acclaimed the king as one who not only engaged in ruthless wars but applied his zeal to the correction of books (fig. 32) was not entirely indulging in a flight of fancy.

50. Manuscript; celestial map: *Munich, Staatsbibliothek* Clm 210, fol 113v; 818. *Size* 32 × 25 cm.

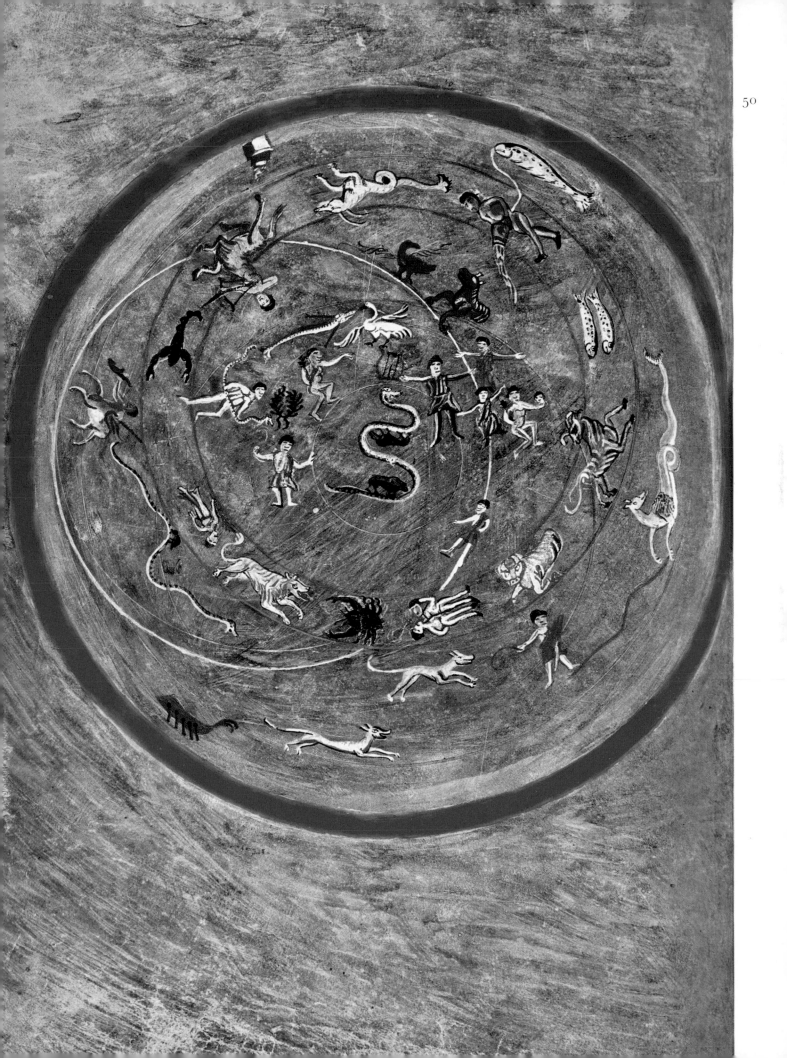

The Beginnings of Carolingian Art and Architecture

5

The electicism of early Carolingian scholarship, the assembling of knowledgeable men from all parts of Latin Europe, the attempt to provide standard texts, the key part played in this process by the royal court: all these had their counterpart in the history of art and architecture in the same period. But in these fields creative originality is already a conspicuous feature of the first two-thirds of Charles' reign, a period in which the king often seemed to be struggling for the very survival of his kingdom. Here the idea of *renovatio* possessed the same force and meaning that it had had for the early preachers and expounders of the Gospel—men who had sought to express in a single work the implications of Christ's message: from the motifs, styles and techniques inherited from the past, artists and builders evolved something entirely new and in a startlingly short space of time.

To say, as does a recent admirable history of Carolingian art, that ' in a sense, it grew out of nothing ' is perhaps no more than a dramatic way of drawing attention to this achievement and stressing its novel contribution to the European experience. It may, however, be easily misunderstood. The pictorial representation of Christian themes, and the association of figural narrative representation with decorative schemes that had no other purpose than to appeal to the senses, were both well-established by the sixth century. In a famous letter that was quoted with approval in the ' Caroline Books ', Pope Gregory I praised the bishop of Marseilles of the time for having put a stop to the cult of images in his diocese but criticized him for obliterating the actual picture: ' painting ', he declared, ' is admissable in churches in order that those who are unlettered may yet read by gazing at the walls what they cannot read in books '. And on the reasonable assumption that clergy were assumed to be capable of distinguishing between the material image and the objects that it represented, and therefore would not accord the former a superstitious reverence, he did not think it necessary to justify the decoration commonly found on the vessels and other objects used in the celebration of the liturgy in most major churches. When some thirty years after the Frankish condemnation of iconoclasm the Spanish-born bishop Claudius of Turin, who was never loath to take up an unorthodox position against his contemporaries, renewed the attack on images of saints, he provoked a well-documented if furious reply from the Irishman Dungal: citing St. Augustine and other Fathers he had no difficulty in establishing —as the Greek council of 787 had maintained—that there were many degrees of veneration besides the worship that is proper to God and that there can be no objection to images as such.

In the late Roman period, a wide variety of books on non-Christian subjects was provided with illustrations, although manuscripts of this kind were probably never numerous and—except for some tiny fragments—they are known only from copies made in the Middle Ages: some early ninth-century astronomical manuscripts probably give a very accurate impression of fifth/sixth century bookpainting (see pls. 46, 54, 55). At this time the illustration of Biblical and other Christian texts was even less common, at least among *Latin* Christians. The church

51. East end of S. Benedetto, Malles (Italian Tyrol).

131

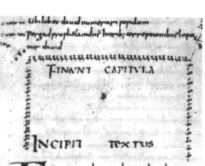

did, however, take over from the Ancient World the idea of the ' author-portrait ' as a frontispiece and at an early date, although we do not know when and where, some or all of the authors of the four Gospels were represented in the act of writing —unlike their pagan predecessors who were gentlemen and therefore not their own scribes. In addition, the existence of at least one fifth-century Latin Bible with a few pages of narrative scenes and other illustrations has been inferred from manuscripts produced at Tours c. 840 (cf. pl. 63). At an early date simple decoration was applied to the ' Eusebian canon-tables ', that is to say, the standard lists of parallel and unique chapters in the Gospels. Pages of pure decoration, combining ornamental motifs derived from different sources, are found for the first time in the luxury products of seventh and eighth century Irish and northern English monasteries, whose achievements in this field have never been surpassed. The same centres also introduced the use of the four Evangelist symbols as full-page or quarter-page decoration (pl. 8) and created and developed the elaborately decorated initial; an English monastery in the eighth century was responsible for the first known instance of the representation of a human figure within an initial letter.

Some of the monasteries founded on the Continent by missionaries from the British Isles remained for decades to all intents and purposes colonies in a foreign land, in which the script and decoration of their manuscripts continued the traditions of their homeland without noticeable change (pl. 8 and fig. 25). Other examples of their book-art were widely distributed throughout Europe and some of the motifs that they used were soon being taken up in other centres (cf. fig. 15). A manuscript of the Gospels precisely dated to 754, now at Autun and probably originating in that region, has both symbols and ornament of an insular type. But it combines the former with a representation of the Christ in Majesty which was evidently based on a similar illustration in an Italian manuscript that, like the crudely but vigorously carved mid-eighth century altar at Cividale del Friuli (pl. 6), had taken over and adapted an originally east Mediterranean theme. It is unfortunately only through copies, which may often in fact depart considerably from their originals, that we know anything of the history of book-art in the western Mediterranean region from the sixth to the eighth century: but the little that we do know suggests that we would do well not to apply to it the blanket-word ' Byzantine '. Some centres were clearly capable of innovation and invention. For instance, a presumably Roman artist first included in the decoration of canon-tables representations of the curly columns that stood in front of the tomb of St. Peter (see below, and compare fig. 34).

Material for the history of *wall*-painting in Mediterranean countries in the same period is, by contrast, comparatively full. In Italy, where most of it is to be found, it seems to have had an uninterrupted history although not necessarily in any single centre. Under the impact of immigrants from other parts of the Mediterranean or of local stimuli that cannot even be convincingly guessed at, it might achieve remarkable heights of naturalism in the late Hellenistic tradition, as in the uniquely-beautiful Gospel-scenes at Castelseprio (Lombardy), which most scholars regard as pre-Carolingian; or a hardly less distinguished hieratic dignity, as in the painted figures in what may have been the private chapel of the dukes of Friuli at Cividale: or the pleasing vigour of the scenes from the life of S. Zaccharias (unfortunately very fragmentary) at S. Sofia, Benevento (pls. 24, 25). In lesser hands and other places, however, the wall-paintings of the period achieved at most the crude liveliness of a cartoon, as in the paintings of the tiny church at Naturno

Fig. 33   Extract from a page of one of the few surviving manuscripts of the Bible of Theodulf of Orléans. *London, British Museum* Add. Ms. 24142, fol 5v.

(South Tyrol) (pl. 27)—if these are, in fact, of the eighth century. These dark two centuries were also ones in which the painting of religious images on portable panels really began its long and momentous history: the earliest western examples in Roman churches have emerged in recent years from behind centuries of devotion and repeated re-painting.

In some parts of the Mediterranean area the Antique tradition of small figure sculpture had persisted for many years after the establishment of barbarians in the western regions, in the decoration of objects required for the church's worship, such as diptychs, chalices, etc, or occasionally for use in some rich man's household. The Merovingian Frankish craftsmen who made any attempt to imitate this art eventually reduced the figures and their setting to the abstract patterns which were their more natural form of expression. Their skills, like those of their opposite numbers across the Channel, were seen to best advantage in the jewellery and metal-work worn by members of the magnate class, like the early eighth-century Molsheim brooch (pl. 5) or in the decoration of portable reliquaries (i.e. purses or boxes containing an object that had been hallowed by contact with the tomb of a saint) (pl. 78). One of the finest pieces of church metal-work of the eighth century, the copper-gilt, silver and niello chalice presented to Kremsmünster by duke Tassilo in 781 (pl. 9), was made by Anglo-Saxon craftsmen in Bavaria. Barbarian craftsmen were conspicuously less successful when they tried to cut patterns on stone, although some of their work is by no means lacking in confidence (cf. pl. 6). Free-standing figure sculpture is virtually unknown: the great exception is the group of figures in stucco at Cividale (pl. 7), of impressive simplicity and dignity, which most competent scholars now date to the last years of the independent Lombard kingdom.

There were, then, several artistic currents in western Europe in the years in which Charles began to impose his authority by conquest on his neighbours. How would they react to the new political climate and the new opportunities of patronage? Within little more than a decade from his accession, artists connected with

Fig. 34   Drawing of a reconstruction of the west end of St. Peters, Rome (after J. Ward-Perkins).

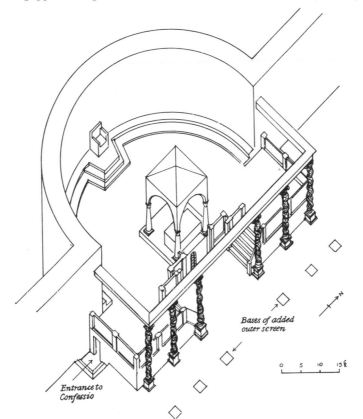

Bases of added
outer screen

Entrance to
Confessio

0   5   10   15 ft

the Frankish royal court—who may or may not be identical with one or other of the scribes of the books in which their work occurs—had begun to create a distinct style from the different elements available to them. The text-pages of the Gospel Lectionary of Godescalc (781-3) (above, p. 99) are preceded by six whole-page illustrations. Four Evangelist portraits are followed by a representation of Christ Blessing (a simplified version of Christ in Majesty) (pl. 38): the detail of the background is different in each picture but all show a similar horizontal division, with

Fig. 35 Fragment of a lost illustrated Gospel-book decorated in the ' court ' style.
London, British Museum, Ada Gospel Fragment.

the middle strip consisting of a simple architectural arrangement, rather like a back-cloth in a child's cut-out theatre; the faces of the figures are high-lighted, the upper parts of the body elongated; the borders use the interlace and trumpet-spiral patterns that had been evolved in Insular centres; the colours are sombre, with a predominance of brown, slate-grey, dull red, dull green. The page facing the first full page of text, however, is something new in surviving manuscript art and strikingly different—the first known representation of the ' Fountain of Life ', a stylized representation of a colonnaded baptistery surrounded by deer, peacocks and other birds (pl. 18). There are reasons for thinking that the Frankish artist did not invent the design but had found it in some manuscript originating in Mediterranean *Romania*: someone at court, however, had recognized the peculiar appropriateness of the iconography to a manuscript commemorating the baptism of a prince in the Lateran baptistery.

A little over two decades later the same or a different artist who was decorating a Gospel-book which was reputedly given by Charles' son Louis and his second wife to the abbey of St. Medard at Soissons, where it remained until the French Revolution, produced a conspicuously superior version of the same theme: his lyrical evocation of an unreal, almost of a magical world, can still arouse the emotions of those from whom its full spiritual sense remains hidden. Combining something of the same sense of mystery with a solemnity and dignity appropriate to its content, is the representation of ' the Adoration of the Lamb ' (back of jacket)—a rare theme in manuscript art although not unknown in mosaic and mural and the subject of one of the high-water marks of European painting. These are among the finest pages of Carolingian book-illustration but they do not make less remarkable the confidence and achievement of the artist responsible for the earlier work.

A Gospel-book now at Abbeville that seems to have been acquired for St. Riquier by its abbot, the ex-courtier Angilbert, and another Gospel-book of

52. West end of St. Peter, Fulda (Germany); minor Carolingian church, c. 822/36.

unknown provenance in the British Museum suggest that between the completion of the Godescalc manuscript and the end of the century the artists responsible for the decoration of these 'Court' manuscripts sought and found new sources of inspiration and ideas. That one of their models was of specifically Roman origin is made almost certain by the appearance of curly vine columns among the decoration of the canon-tables in the British Museum manuscript (pl. 12) and subsequently also in the Soissons Gospels. From manuscripts of Mediterranean origin—whether in Italy or farther east—the artist or artists of the Gospel-books derive the 'impressionistic' modelling of figures and draperies, the perspective drawing of architecture and a skilful if modest interplay of light and shade. All these are shown to advantage in the 'Annunciation to Zacharias' that is one feature in the initial page introducing St. Luke's Gospel in the British Museum manuscript (pl. 23). The treatment of the page as a whole, however, as well as such details as the use of bands and finials of interlace, comes ultimately from Insular art. But from these various elements the artist has again created something that is not a mannerist hodge-podge but is, in fact, a new and coherent style. The representation of the Evangelists in these and later manuscripts of the group is in the same spirit: their postures may be awkward and the attempt to indicate volume half-hearted but the figures have acquired a more spiritual dignity than in the Godescalc manuscript, the background is designed to indicate depth rather than form a rigid back-drop and the colour-scheme, while still subdued in tone, has a greater variety and richness (pl. 20). The likelihood that the lost model or models were used to produce at least one Gospel manuscript with a fuller range of scenes in independent panels is suggested by the fragment, also showing the Annunciation to Zacharias, cut from an unknown manuscript and now also in the British Museum (fig. 35)—a warning against assuming that surviving manuscripts give us anything more than a partial picture of the activity of any particular group of artists or *scriptorium*.

The one Psalter in this, the oldest, group of Carolingian manuscripts—written by Dagulf and others for presentation to Pope Hadrian I—has no illustration. Its decoration is limited to emphasizing the openings of the First, Fifty-first and One Hundred-and-First Psalms with a decorative page using both gold and silver based on the initial letters B, Q, D (fig. 36) which subsequently became standard practice even for quite modest Psalters. The ivory plaques which once formed part of its covers, however, survive and are in the Louvre (pl. 28). On one David is shown choosing the poets of the Psalms in the upper panel and playing his harp surrounded by other musicians in the lower. The other shows St. Jerome with the priest Boniface opening the letter from Pope Damasus in which he is asked to correct and edit the Psalms; and, below, St. Jerome dictates the Psalter to his notary or scribe while other clerics listen. Stylistically this represents an enormous advance over what is generally agreed to be the earliest Carolingian ivory—perhaps roughly contemporary with the Godescalc manuscript, although it could be the later product of a more backward centre. Evidently once the cover of a Gospel-book this shows, on the front, Christ trampling on the lion and the asp and, on the back, the Annunciation to the Virgin Mary and the Meeting of Mary and Elisabeth. The decorative borders of the latter panels come from Insular art; the somewhat rickety architectural backgrounds and other details of the Dagulf panels link them with the eighth-century art of Rome. In both cases, however, the iconography suggests that the artist was using Early Christian, presumably fifth-century, models which the later artist was able to follow with much greater skill.

Another ivory book-cover, in the Bodleian Library (pl. 35), links the themes of

53. Manuscript: *Te Igitur* from the Sacramentary of Archbishop Drogo of Metz: *Paris, Bibliothèque Nationale* Lat. 9428, fol 15v. *Size* 27 × 21 cm.

Fig. 36 'Beatus' page, i.e. beginning of Psalm 1, of the Psalter written by
Dagulf and other court scribes. *Vienna, Österreichische Nationalbibliothek. Lat. 1861, fol 25. (Actual size.)*

the Brussels ivory with the style of the 'Dagulf Psalter' ivory, and exceptionally
allows us to see how the ivory-carvers of the—presumably—Court school at the end
of the eighth century treated their models. The central panel of Christ trampling
on the Lion and the Asp combines a stiff architectural framework with swirling,
indeed restless, draperies that none the less move almost independently of the
human form that they are supposed to cover. Divided from this central panel and
surrounded by borders in which standard Classical ornamental motifs are freely
re-interpreted are smaller panels of scenes from the Gospels. Either the actual
fifth-century models used by the Carolingian artist for six of these panels or a

piece from the same workshop of exactly the same kind is still extant (divided between Paris and Berlin). The composition of the scenes in the earlier ivory is closely followed by the Frankish artist but in his version they are given a greater forcefulness and dramatic power with the draperies more heavily cut and shaded and their outlines more angular.

The final stage in the development of the first style of Carolingian ivory-carving is beautifully exemplified by the one-time covers of another 'Court' manuscript that once formed part of the library of the royal or Imperial monastery of Lorsch: in a ninth-century catalogue it figures as *Evangelium scriptum cum auro pictum habens tabulas eburneas*. The manuscript is now divided and the *tabulae*, certainly the largest and decoratively perhaps the richest of the whole Carolingian period, are respectively in the Victoria and Albert and Vatican Museums (pls. 21, 22). Like the other pieces mentioned they are closely modelled on late Antique ivory panels probably of c. 500 but the artist, whether at the Court itself or at Lorsch (a 'royal monastery' closely linked with the court since 772) or in some other religious community in the area in which the king or Emperor normally resided, has once more imposed his own interpretation on his models: the delineation of both human and angelic figures substitutes pattern for substantial form and their relation to their architectural setting is that of a ghost figure to the physical environment in which it is temporarily manifested.

The nature of the early Carolingian achievement in building and architecture, which to all intents and purposes means church architecture, is much more difficult to define and illustrate. The difficulties created by isolated and chance survival are here enhanced because only one major building of the period still stands in anything like the form in which it was built and our knowledge of most of the others is derived from excavation—which in favourable circumstances produces a reliable plan but can never give us more than an approximate picture of the elevation of a building. A precise or even a closely approximate dating is only possible in a favourable combination of circumstances.

And the problem does not start here. It is virtually impossible to say anything about late Merovingian church-building, for lack of material. Many of the old episcopal sees in Francia had inherited cathedral churches of some size and complexity, and various other buildings associated with them, such as baptisteries, residences, etc, from the fifth and sixth centuries. Where they had to be repaired or rebuilt, this commonly entailed reducing the size of the old buildings with much inferior workmanship: many churches in Italy suffered in the same way in the sixth and seventh centuries. In a few centres in Italy, notably Rome, Ravenna and Milan, and perhaps also in southern Gaul until the eighth-century Frankish invasions, some of the major monuments put up in the first Christian centuries had survived substantially unchanged in their structure. Almost always, however, their internal arrangements had been considerably modified to meet changing needs— notably the growing importance of the cult of saints—and they had been embellished accordingly: the best-documented example is St. Peter's, Rome, where new settings had been devised for the much-visited tomb of the saint (fig. 34); but surviving fragments of *ciboria* (altar-canopies), altar-pieces (cf. pl. 6) and screens are evidence of similar activity elsewhere, on both sides of the Alps.

Very little is known of the original appearance of the innumerable churches, monastic and non-monastic, founded in all parts of Gaul and Italy in the seventh century. A noteworthy exception, if the results of excavations have been correctly identified and interpreted, is the abbey church of St. Denis. These appear to indicate a mid-seventh-century building 57 metres long, with colonnaded nave and aisles and small eastern apse. The dimensions are surprisingly impressive, the supposed capitals of the columns have a crude vigour but the masonry was very poor, consisting for the most part of small stones set in rough lines of coarse, thick mortar. Masonry of a notably superior kind, small blocks of stone set in regular rows, is found in the so-called *Basse Oeuvre* (i.e. pre-Gothic portion) of Beauvais Cathedral which has recently been dated seventh/eighth (instead of fifth) century; and this gains plausibility from the occurrence of similar work in the church of Jarrow, dedicated in 685, in the light of Bede's statement that its sister-church at Wearmouth was built by masons brought from Gaul.

Consisting simply of a hall-nave and a small, square chancel, Jarrow and other churches like it represent one of the most basic forms of church plan, providing the necessary minimum for the celebration of the liturgy and no more; and they may be regarded as the translation into stone of earlier wooden churches of similar design. Wooden and, later, stone churches of the same type, or with wider, shorter naves were built by the Anglo-Saxon missionaries working east of the Rhine in the second and third quarters of the eighth century. Bede described the use of stone in place of wood as building *more Romanorum*. At Rome, thanks to its religious importance and political connections and the constant inflow of men and ideas from other parts of the Mediterranean region, the construction of churches had gone on almost continuously: but those built in the sixth and seventh centuries had little in common with the great colonnaded or arcaded basilicas of the fourth and early fifth century, being more modest in scale and deriving both elevation and plan from types evolved in various provincial centres of the eastern Mediterranean. Similarly, a distinctive type of church plan found in many places in the Eastern Alps (eighth-century Alemannia and Bavaria, modern Switzerland and Italy) from at latest the second quarter of the eighth century, and consisting of a box-nave and three projecting and sometimes horseshoe-shaped apses, seems to have originated farther east.

In the growing communities of the Venetian littoral architectural ideas and styles from distant parts of the Empire combined with techniques that had been evolved elsewhere in Italy, although—as for example in the cathedral of Torcello (pl. 30)—successive rebuildings and modifications were usually within the basic framework of a tri-apsidal and arcaded columnar basilica. In the last three or four decades of its independent existence, the Lombard kingdom and duchies were evidently the scene of a considerable architectural activity, which expressed itself in a wide variety of forms and styles: except perhaps in the simplicity of their exteriors—at the most, simple blind arcades—and the relative exuberance of their internal decoration, there is not much in common between the rectangular nave and chancel of the Cividale chapel, the hall-nave and projecting longitudinal chapels, all with apsidal terminations, of the first church of S. Salvatore, Brescia— a royal foundation—and the centrally-planned arcaded ducal church of S. Sofia at Benevento which, even if it did not originally have the extraordinary star-shape recently claimed for it, was remarkable enough in its treatment of space and volume.

It is probable that towards the end of his life king Pippin had built a small oratory at his villa at Aachen and had deposited there some of the relics of saints hitherto taken around with the itinerant court, whose names, it has been suggested, are partly recoverable from the list of relics he gave to the family-abbey of Prüm. If excavations made just before the First World War are reliable, the oratory was—

54 and 55. Imitations of late-Antique book painting in an early ninth-century Aratus manuscript: *London, British Museum* Harley 647, fol 10v and fol 13v. *Size* 23 × 22 cm.

56. Crypt of St. Michael, Fulda (Germany).

57. Interior of St. Michael, Fulda.

54

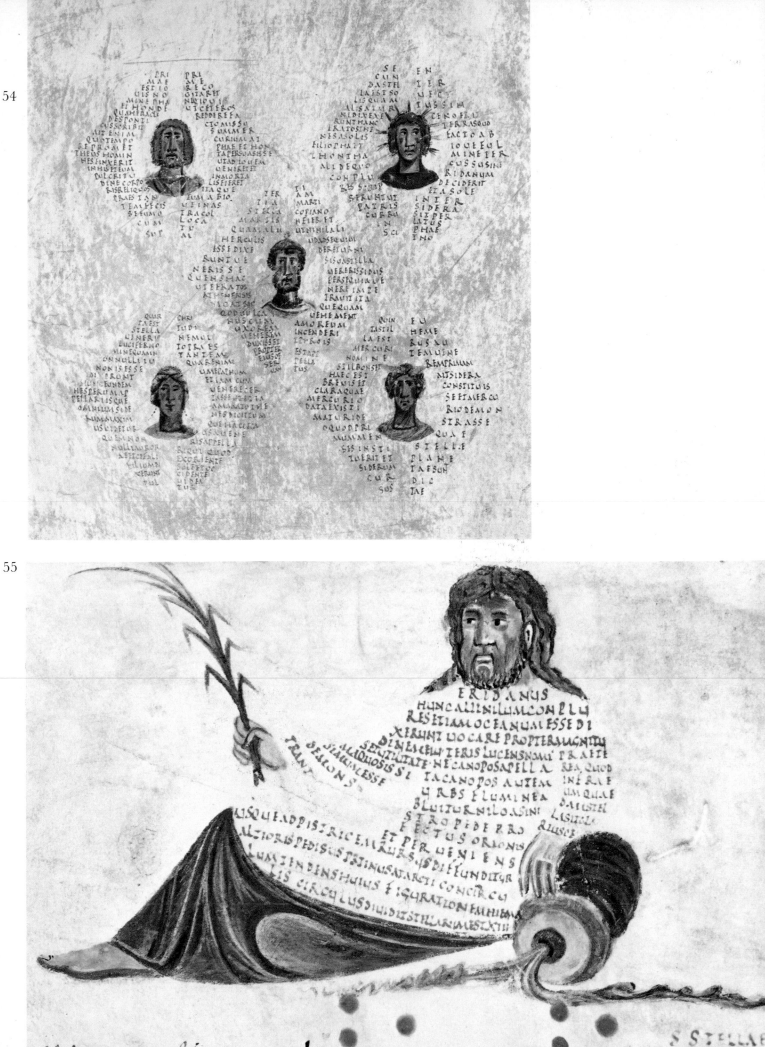

55

in the centuries-old tradition of a *martyrium*—a small round building but nothing is known of its appearance in detail. The first major architectural exercises in Carolingian Francia were the substantial rebuilding of two monastic churches dedicated to saints of particular veneration, St. Denis near Paris and St. Maurice—one of the warrior saints of the Theban legion—at Agaune.

The new St. Denis was begun by abbot Fulrad before Pippin's death, continued under the ostensible patronage of the new king and consecrated in his presence in

A   East Choir Crypt (1st stage)
B   West Choir Crypt (2nd stage)
C   Galleries of the lower entrance
D   Corridors of the Eastern Crypt
E   Corridors of the Western Crypt

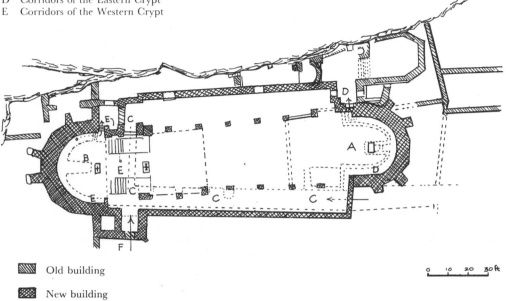

  Old building

  New building

0 10 20 30 ft

Fig. 37   Ground plan of the church of Agaune (after Louis Blondel).

775. There is no means of telling whether the whole church or only part of it was complete at this date. Charles' claim at the time of consecration that 'we have built' the new church could reasonably be accounted for by the archaeological evidence of an early change of plan, designed to provide a setting for the tomb of Pippin that was originally outside the church to the west. The new church was only slightly longer than its predecessor and, like it, an arcaded basilica: but its masonry was markedly superior, consisting of relatively large and well-worked blocks, it was wider (c. 20.4 metres) and it had surprisingly slender columns resting on heavily-decorated bases. More important, its plan incorporated several novel features. Under the apse, which was polygonal externally and round internally, and giving access to the saint's tomb, was a crypt of annular form—an arrangement first created for St. Peter's in the second quarter of the seventh century and then imitated in other Roman churches. In front of the apse was a transept, 28 metres from north to south and therefore projecting only a short distance beyond the aisles: unlike the transept at St. Peter's (and St. Paul's) at Rome it was not open and continuous—the later 'canonical' type in Romanesque and Gothic architecture—but divided from the central bay by arcades. At the west end there may at first have been a second choir and apse but as a result of a (? second) change of plan the apse was opened up to provide a vestibule, the choir was moved upstairs and flanking towers probably erected north and south. There

58. Manuscript; Labours of the Months: *Vienna, Österreichische Nationalbibliothek* Cod 387, fol 90v; 809/21 (?818). *Size 32 × 25 cm.*

may also have been a wooden tower at the crossing. The new St. Maurice was begun by its abbot Willichar, ex-bishop of Vienne and future bishop of Sion, probably in the 760s, and reputedly completed by his successor in the 780s. It too had an externally-polygonal apse, following the design of a sixth-century predecessor but on a larger scale, and underneath it was an annular crypt. As a result apparently of a change of plan while work was in progress, a second polygonal-and-round apse, also with annular crypt, was built at the west end.

The remarkable features common to the two churches can hardly be the result of coincidence: but whereas the crypt and possibly St. Denis' transept followed Roman models, both the western choir and the so-called ' West-work ' that apparently quickly superseded it at St. Denis are—so far as we know—original features. There are obvious objections to supposing that either church was the immediate inspiration of the other, and—particularly in the light of a possible link between Fulrad and Willichar—it is tempting to conclude that the similarities reflect a mutual influence during the course of construction. The final results—if the excavations have been correctly interpreted—establish new concepts and introduce a new aesthetic into the main-stream of western Christian architecture. Particular architectural emphasis is given to the tombs and relics of martyrs and other saints in a church which is the setting for the ordinary liturgical worship of a religious community: and whereas the great early Roman basilicas were, and are, characterized by an uninterrupted forward movement from porch to apse and an insistent rhythm of repeated motifs, the Frankish buildings treat space as something to be blocked off into separate functional parts and—especially at St. Denis—further emphasize these already distinct units by introducing marked vertical accents in the towers or a high porch and raised choir.

In the last decade of the century another church was built, on the initiative of a prominent courtier, which has many of the same features and the same aesthetic notions as St. Denis and St. Maurice, but an even greater boldness in design and scale. This was the new monastery church at Centula—St. Riquier, begun very shortly after Angilbert had received the abbey from the king in 789 and consecrated on 1st January 798, but obviously not complete by that date. Angilbert was inordinately proud of his building, not because of its architectural originality but because it enabled him to display one of the most staggering collections of relics hitherto assembled in one place, brought with the co-operation of Popes, king and Emperor from all parts of the Christian world.

The professional suppliers of relics in Rome and elsewhere—a highly-organized and far from scrupulous group at this period when the demand for relics rose rapidly—had clearly been hard at work; if the support of the saints in Heaven was needed to secure the success of the Carolingian ruler of the Franks, Angilbert and the monks of St. Riquier, celebrating an elaborate liturgy at innumerable altars, were doing their best to make their invocations effective. Almost every site and episode connected with Our Lord's life was recalled by some item and the total of martyrs, confessors and virgins represented in the church was very nearly one hundred. We know all this, and much besides, from an account written by Angilbert himself early in the ninth century. And although the church he built has completely disappeared, its external appearance and layout were carefully described by Hariulf, a monk of the abbey at the end of the eleventh century who also depicted it in an illustration that is now only known from two seventeenth-century copies (fig. 37).

The precise dimensions are not now recoverable but the church can none the less be reconstructed in considerable detail (fig. 38). The nave and aisles were of a mere six bays, squashed between west and east transepts; these projected only a short distance beyond the aisles but rose well above the level of choir and nave and were then topped by open-work turrets, while small additional round towers were placed in the angles formed with the rectangular choir. In front of the west transept was a three-storey porch flanked by circular towers, the whole complex—transept and porch—being a much more weighty version of the west end of St. Denis. The

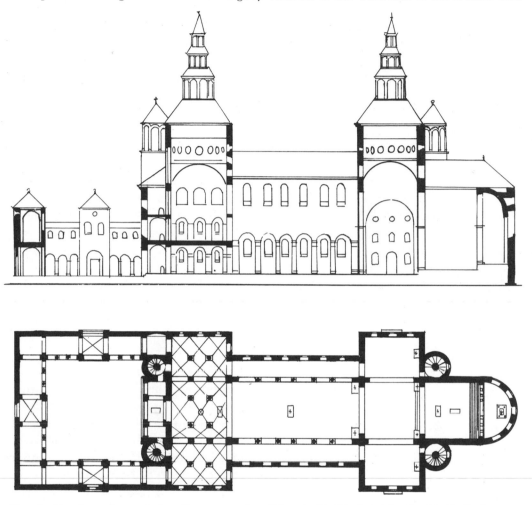

Fig. 38   Drawing and ground plan of a reconstruction of Centula (St. Riquier) (after Frankl, *Handbuch*).

porch and towers formed one side of a square porticoed atrium, each of the three free sides of which was interrupted by a tower gateway with its own chapel dedicated to St. Michael and other angels; here Angilbert asked to be buried. The west gallery had an altar dedicated to the Saviour at which mass was celebrated, in certain circumstances, for laity as well as members of the community. The high altar in the east choir was dedicated to St. Peter and in the apse were the tomb and altar of St. Riquier; in this respect the church was somewhat old-fashioned. The marble columns and wall-facings, and presumably also the marble pavement in the eastern part of the church, had been acquired from Italy with the assistance of the king. At the west end of the church was the inscription, composed by Angilbert, invoking God's blessing on king Charles ' through whose goodness (*virtus*) I have carried this through '.

Hariulf's description and miniature remind us that this church was in fact only one element in a group of monastic buildings, including other subsidiary churches or chapels, within a walled precinct or *claustrum*: but it is evident that we must not at this date envisage the regular layout which is a feature of most medieval monasteries and which was hopefully anticipated by the monastic reformer who, two decades or so after the consecration of the rebuilt St. Riquier, drew up—as a guide to the needs of a well-organized and properly regulated monastic community— the St. Gall plan. It is perhaps unreasonable to ask that Angilbert, as well as building his remarkable monastery church, should also have laid out the ideal monastery—which was in any case not something that exercised Charles as it exercised his son.

The earliest churches in Saxony were apparently more modest in scale and less original in design. Even more conservative in plan was the monastic church of St. Johann at Münster (Müstair) in Graubunden which was reputedly a foundation of Charles himself. Built in the last years of the eighth century, it differs from the other Alpine churches with a hall-nave and three apses, two of them horseshoe-shaped, only by its grander scale, both in plan and elevation, and by its elaborate decoration (below p. 156), which is the most powerful argument for believing that the tradition of royal origin may not be false. The plan with three niches or apses in a square east-end wall occurs again in the modest church of S. Benedetto at Malles (Italy) (pls. 51, 68) which on very flimsy evidence is usually claimed as a one-time dependent church of St. Johann and dated on not very much better grounds to c. 805 or 805/881; it is certainly early Carolingian. A similar plan is found also on the far side of the Alps in the church that the ex-bishop of Verona, Egino, built for himself at Niederzell on the island of Reichenau (Lake Constance) and therefore in the years immediately after 799: here, however, the apses are preceded by a five-bay nave and aisles leading into a choir entered now and perhaps originally by a low flight of steps.

This particular combination suggests that Egino may have found inspiration for his church plan outside the Alpine region, whether at Verona or elsewhere. A striking, although not an exact, analogy is provided by the Roman church of S. Maria in Cosmedin, as radically rebuilt by Pope Hadrian I: it, too, combined three apses in a square east wall with an arcaded nave and a slightly-raised choir, but the latter is not architecturally distinct, as apparently at Niederzell, and the proportions are very different. S. Maria has, however, an additional interest since it is a very early example—in southern Europe probably the earliest example— of a colonnaded crypt (of four bays) which, unlike the church mentioned above, introduces a transept before the apse.

Either just before or just after the end of the century Pope Leo III completed the process of reviving the basic basilican plan used in early Christian Rome by rebuilding the church of S. Anastasia as a columnar-aisled basilica with a projecting single apse and a transept that did not project beyond the aisle walls. Even those scholars most reluctant—and rightly—to see in every artistic revival of older styles and motifs a conscious political programme or deep purpose may be willing to see here a deliberate symbolism: the plan chosen for the church accords well with the evidence provided by contemporary texts for a new interest in Rome's Constantinian past in the second half of the eighth century, and for the efforts of its bishops to demonstrate that the destinies of the Imperial and Petrine city had been 'translated' to them. No one can have any doubt about the programmatic significance of the new assembly hall erected by Pope Leo in his Lateran residence

Fig. 39 Pope Leo, King Charles and St. Peter in the mosaic of the Lateran Triclinium arch, Rome, as restored in the eighteenth century.

and its choice of decoration. Colonnaded and richly decorated, it must have closely resembled similar rooms in Imperial palaces: over one of the apses was a mosaic (of which we unfortunately have only an eighteenth-century restoration and some earlier water-colour copies) (fig. 39) on which was depicted St. Peter handing a *pallium* to Pope Leo and the banner (*vexillum*) of the city to a kneeling king Charles.

While Roman masons and artists were at work on Leo III's *triclinium*, Frankish

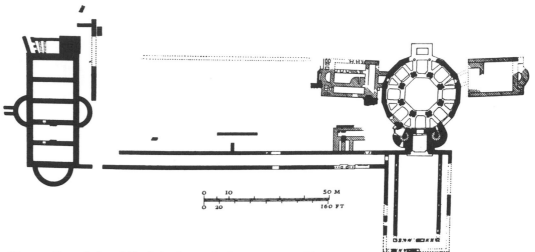

Fig. 40 Ground plan of Charles' palace at Aachen, as recovered by excavation (after Conant).

masons and artists, and possibly some Italians too, were creating Charles' own Lateran north of the Alps at Aachen. Probably in the early 790s (there is no means of determining the exact year), work began on the construction of a new and distinctive *palatium* running north from the site of Pippin's small round chapel and to the west of the natural warm baths so beloved of Charles (as we know from Alcuin as well as Einhard) where also some new building seems to have been done. A poem written in 799 (below, ch. 6) shows that the palace and other buildings were then well on the way to completion. The evidence of texts and of excavation shows (fig. 44) that an apsidal throne-room with a small projecting gallery on one long side and residential quarters below, a building called by Einhard the *regia*, was linked on the south side with a chapel—architecturally the most conspicuous unit—and its associated structures by a galleried *porticus* of considerable length; half-way along its length was a tower gateway, the upper room of which was later used for courts of justice. Palace, baths and miscellaneous buildings—doubtless mostly of wood—were surrounded by a precinct wall, the course of which can still be approximately traced on the street-plan of Aachen. To many scholars it has seemed natural to suppose that the idea of a fixed royal residence, which was also an architectural symbol both of the king's pre-eminence over his subjects and fellow monarchs and of the Divine favour that he enjoyed, came from Constantinople. There are reasons for thinking, however, that the immediate inspiration was within Charles' own dominions (cf. further, p. 166). The subordinate kingdom of Italy was already administered from the palace of Pavia, built by Theodoric and, like his other palace at Ravenna, displaying a representation of himself on the facade. In 801 Charles brought back from Ravenna a horsed statue that was believed to be that of Theodoric to put in front of his own palace. The tall, deep

149

niche in the facade of the Aachen palace chapel (pl. 11) has been plausibly compared with the so-called ' Palace of the Exarchs ' or ' Palace of Theodoric ' at Ravenna. The plan of the chapel, with its central octagon, sixteen exterior walls and circular towers flanking the west porch has been derived from Ravenna's San Vitale; and provided we recognize that in the Middle Ages derivation from a model had little to do with making an exact architectural copy—any more than Wren's Sheldonian Theatre immediately evokes the Theatre of Marcellus which was *his* model—this is far more plausible than the supposed derivation from buildings in Syria, Armenia or even Constantinople which are more closely parallel in form.

Aesthetically, the Aachen chapel is much closer to St. Denis and St. Riquier than to San Vitale. The spaciousness and airiness of the latter is completely lost in this solid little building. Externally and internally at ground floor level, where there are no columns to lighten the effect of the angular piers, and where the low ambulatory is covered by heavy interpenetrating triangular and quadripartite groin vaults, the main impression is of heaviness. Technically, however, it is very accomplished. The masonry is well-cut and laid with great regularity (pl. 2). The ambulatory holds up a loftier gallery whose own vaults buttress the vault of the octagon and which is opened up to the central space by two tiers of marble columns in pairs, each with Corinthian capitals. It is in the detailing and decoration of the chapel that the extraordinary qualities of some of the artists summoned to work on the royal building are most clearly seen. If the capitals (pl. 3) are to be faulted, it is because of their over-refinement, but their quality is such that if they were not of local stone one would have been tempted to assume that they had been brought from some demolished building in Italy. Original too, and apparently made on the spot, are the bronze grilles that form the balustrade of the gallery (pl. 15). The design in each bay is different, varying from the simplest geometrical shapes to more complex patterns. The miniature capitals and frames, on the other hand, display the characteristic features of first- and second-century ornament without any of the deadness which is commonly found in an accurate copy; and the technical skill of the casting fully realizes the creative ideas of the artists. The visual magnificence of the upper parts of the chapel culminated in the mosaic covering of the vault, an exotic or Antique technique of decoration here revived with unexpected skill to represent Christ with the Elders and Beasts of the Apocalypse (although what we see now is only a nineteenth-century imitation based on copies made while the Carolingian original was still substantially intact). The choice of subject—a fully-developed version of the *Maiestas* which has already been seen in more summary form in the decoration of ' Court ' manuscripts—is significant: it symbolizes the Divine government of the Universe of which the earthly rule of kings and Emperors is but a reflection. In the internal arrangements as well as in the decoration of the chapel the honour due to the Divine ruler is inextricably linked to that also due to his representative among the Franks. It has even been suggested (but cf. below) that the aesthetic contrast between the lower and upper portions of the church is part of the same idea: ' From the ground floor the servants and the common people looked up at all this splendour while they themselves stood among plain pillars of ordinary stone ' (H. Fichtenau). On great occasions they looked up to the enthroned king or, later, Emperor surrounded by his magnates. The upper storey of the *porticus* leads directly to a vaulted ante-chamber—which still substantially survives—adjacent to the west gallery of the octagon and thence to the gallery itself: here, raised on steps, was a simple royal throne originally of wood and subsequently encased in marble (pl. 10). The grille

59. East end of St. Johann, Münstair in Grisons (Switzerland), showing the statue of Charles. *Height of statue* 1.90 m.

59

in front of the throne was hinged to open and the monarch could look up to the mosaic in the cupola, across to the altar of the Saviour in the east gallery—we unfortunately do not know if this suggested or was suggested by the arrangement at St. Riquier—and down to the altar of the Virgin Mary and the relics associated with it which stood in front of and later in the tiny choir that preceded the existing Gothic one (fig. 41). Moreover, if it is true, as various indications suggest, that there was an *ambo* (pulpit) directly in front of the altar, possibly with an arrangement of veils or curtains on either side similar to that represented on some ivories of the period, then the intended focus of *popular* attention when ceremonies took place in the chapel is even more clear.

Only a few of the relics and their rich and elaborate settings that originally linked this royal church with the saints in Heaven have survived the disasters of centuries. The last remaining reliquary cross that was partly of Carolingian date was destroyed in the Second World War. The purse-reliquary of St. Stephen, now in Vienna, was only lost to Aachen when its treasures were taken to Paderborn to

Fig. 41 Drawing of the view from the throne in the Octagon, Aachen Cathedral (after Felix Kreusch).

60. Symbolic representation of 'law giving' or 'dispensing justice' in an early ninth-century legal manuscript. *St. Paul in Carinthia* (Austria) Cod XXV 4.8, fol 1v.

escape the revolutionary armies in 1794; although it has some stylistic links with the similar reliquary from Enger (Saxony) (pl. 78), reputedly given by king Charles to Widukind on the occasion of his baptism in 785, it is more likely to be of the mid-ninth century. Almost certainly of Charles' own time, however, is his so-called Talisman, a gold and jewelled setting of a relic of the True Cross, perhaps originally set in crystal (pl. 42) which is said to have been found around Charles' neck when his tomb was opened and whose technical links with, for example, the Molsheim brooch justify the dating to Charles' own time. Typically, it is now at Rheims (France's royal city) because it was given to the Empress Josephine as a thank-offering for the return of most of the treasures from Paderborn in 1804.

These few survivals of a once infinitely greater number of treasures make it difficult to appreciate the effect that the original chapel and its contents must have had on people unfamiliar with such concentrated magnificence, even although the losses are partly compensated for by the objects introduced into the building at a later date—such as the great candelabra symbolizing the Heavenly Jerusalem given by the Emperor Frederick I (pl. 79)—and often made by re-using the raw materials of the treasures on which the metal-workers of an earlier age had lavished their skill. Some idea of the almost fabulous wealth of precious metals, jewels and fabrics displayed in a major Carolingian church can be gathered from Angilbert's and Hariulf's accounts of St. Riquier. As a result of gifts by the king and his family and by ordinary magnates of the realm and others, each of the main altars had at least a frontal of gold and silver and each was covered by a *ciborium* from which hung a crown; in front of the altar of St. Riquier were six columns of bronze supporting a cross-beam on which other richly-decorated objects were placed. Most of the several score vessels and other objects used in the celebration of the liturgy were of gold or silver or both and often jewelled; only a few were of ivory. Vestments numbered several hundred. The equal splendour of the churches of Rome is shown by the *Liber Pontificalis'* long list of gifts made by each Pope and the less frequent references to the presents sent by kings and Emperors. Of all this magnificence, in large measure an indirect consequence of Charles' successes in war, virtually nothing survives that can be dated with confidence to his own time and not much more that belongs to the next half-century. There are a few chalices, none as splendid as Tassilo's gift to Kremsmünster (pl. 9), one or two patens and a number of liturgical objects in ivory. The fragments of a silver-gilt altar at Conques (pl. 47) and the superb gold altar made by a certain Volvinio (whose name suggests that he may have been a Frank in the strictest sense) for Sant'Ambrogio, Milan, in the second quarter of the ninth century (pls. 48, 49) are the only surviving examples of their kind from two centuries and the reconstructed *ciborium*, also at S. Ambrogio, is one of the few anywhere of which any significant part is of Carolingian manufacture. We have to advance well into the ninth century to find a substantially-intact gold or silver book-cover (pl. 67), although we know that many religious communities had one or more of them quite early in the century. Paschal I's enamel reliquary-cross and its silver case (pl. 61) are among the very few objects of early Carolingian date that once enriched the churches of Rome. There is no complete vestment of this period and not many fragments (cf. pl. 75). Our picture of Carolingian art and the wealth of the churches of the period is based on chance survivals that do not add up to the total furnishings once to be found in a major church.

No less serious is the almost total disappearance of the one-time decoration of the interior surfaces of palaces and churches. The nineteenth-century ' liquorice '

Fig. 42 Ivory liturgical comb, ninth century. *Nancy, Cathedral Treasury.* (*Height* 21 cm. *width* 12 cm.)

marble covering of the pillars and arches of the Aachen chapel may conceivably give a reasonable general impression of how they looked in Charles' time. But it is far more likely that this marble has replaced an earlier scheme of paintings, stuccoes and terracotta or a combination of these. The way in which the different techniques were combined and the general effect they achieved can still be gathered from the—iconographically untypical and damaged—decoration of the east wall of S. Benedetto at Malles (pl. 51) of the ?early ninth century. The high quality of

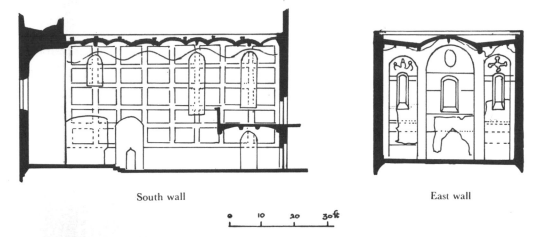

South wall   East wall

0   10   20   30 ft

Fig. 43 Plan showing the layout of the original Carolingian frescoes on the south and east walls of St. Johann in Münstair (after Linus Birchler).

Carolingian stucco ornament, in which artists of the period were evidently as much at home as in metal-work, is even better shown in the early ninth-century monastery church of S. Salvatore (S. Giulia) at Brescia, as a result of recent discoveries and the skilful removal of later accretions: here the under-surfaces of arches, niches and much else besides were encrusted with beautifully 'classicizing' designs that are very different from those used on the Aachen bronze balustrade but breathe the same spirit (pl. 29). If the lifesize statue of St. Johann at Münster (pl. 59) is indeed of this period, rather than of the twelfth century, then some Carolingian stuccoists also boasted a skill of a different kind. Most of the surviving examples of Carolingian stucco decoration are in the Alpine region or in north Italy from where, on the evidence of Cividale, the technique may have been disseminated in the late eighth century. It was none the less used north of the Alps, where climatic conditions are less favourable to its survival. Angilbert's St. Riquier included a stucco of the Nativity and when bishop Theodulf of Orleans built his church of Germigny-des-Prés he gave it an elaborate stucco decoration (figs. 1, 2, 12), closely related to the ornament of the canon-tables in his Bible manuscripts, of which regrettably only damaged fragments survive.

A characteristic activity of the Court poets and their successors in the first half of the ninth century was the production of verse *tituli*, which in some cases perhaps represented ideal schemes like the St. Gall plan rather than inscriptions to accompany actual works of art, for sequences of narrative painting. The secular examples which once decorated the walls of royal palaces and other residences have completely disappeared. A number of churches on both sides of the Alps contain bits of painting that seem to belong to the Carolingian period and to have formed part of a once elaborate scheme, although their fragmentary nature makes them difficult to interpret and impossible to date with any confidence. In two churches, however, S. Salvatore at Brescia and St. Johann at Münster, it is possible to get an impression of the overall character of such schemes; and at Münster nearly eighty panels on the north and south walls and part of the painting on the west wall can still be discerned (fig. 43) although all are faded, many are damaged and some are beyond certain recognition. The depiction of the Last Judgement at the west end is the earliest known example of the—later very popular—subject in this position. The two side walls have five tiers of paintings of scenes from the Old Testament and the Gospels. Estimates of their artistic quality have varied widely: they are perhaps dully impressive rather than moving and are probably an inferior expression of earlier traditions of painting in north Italy, represented by the paintings at Cividale and possibly in the unparalleled paintings at Castelseprio.

Mr. Beckwith has recently stressed that the style of the Münster and Malles frescoes (he unfortunately does not discuss the stuccoes) ' is not Carolingian in the sense of issue or influence from the court workshops or their dependencies '. As a purely stylistic judgement this is perhaps acceptable, although the propriety of the qualifying words, in the absence of any surviving specimens of wall-paintings produced by these court workshops, is questionable. The influence of the Carolingian court, and ultimately therefore of the personality of the monarch, may have made itself felt in ways other than style. Is it mere coincidence that St. Johann is reputedly a foundation of Charles himself and S. Benedetto a supposed dependency; that S. Salvatore is a Lombard royal foundation which, in the ninth century, was always an appendage and often a residence of a queen or Empress or some other female member of the ruler's family? With so many unknown factors it would be foolish to do more than pose the question. Both Charles and his public activities created the milieu in which artists could flourish, provided them with patronage and inspired certain specific works of art. With so little surviving, however, and with so few securely-dated examples, it is impossible to say to what extent the court was responsible for the creation of forms and styles that subsequently determined the course of artistic development in other centres of the kingdom and Empire: the history of architecture, at least, suggests that the influence may have been two-way.

The continuing existence of art-styles probably or certainly independent of the court is shown not only by wall-paintings in north Italy and the Alpine regions but also in manuscript-illustration like that of the Kremsmünster *Codex Millenarius* (pl. 26). It is none the less in manuscripts that it is occasionally possible to trace unequivocally a translation of the style and iconography of court art to other places and at the same time to see evidence of the dissemination of manuscripts of which not a fragment survives. The ' Egino Homiliary ' from Verona contains four full-page illustrations of the Fathers in the act of composing or delivering their sermons (pl. 33). Except for the St. Jerome ivory, these are much the earliest examples of their particular subjects. The style is recognizably that of the second group of Evangelist pictures in the court manuscripts, whether the artist had actually come from the court or was simply basing his work on another manuscript that originated there. In view of the existence of supplemented Gregorian sacramentaries of the ninth century, and later with ' author-portraits ' of the Pope Gregory, and the unlikelihood on non-artistic grounds that such a subject would have been included in much older manuscripts, it is tempting to conclude that the iconography of the Egino manuscript represents the invention of court artists a few years previously. About the same time an artist working in some Irish or western Scottish centre—

61. ' Teca d'Argento ': the silver case for the Paschal I Cross; *Museo Sacro, Rome.*

CXLVIII ALLELUIA
CANTATEDNO
CANTICUMNOUUM·LAUS
EIUSINECCLESIASCORUM·
LAETETURISRAHELINEOQUI
FECITEUM·ETFILIISIONEX
SULTENTINREGESUO·
LAUDENTNOMENEIUSIN
CHORO·INTYMPANO
ETPSALTERIOPSALLANTEI·
QUIABENEPLACITUMEST

ALLELUIA
DNOINPOPULOSUO·ETEX
ALTABITMANSUETOSIN
SALUTE·
EXSULTABUNTSCIINGLORI
A·LAETABUNTURINCUBI
LIBUSSUIS·
EXSULTATIONESDIINGUT
TUREEORUM·ETGLADII
ANCIPITESINMANIB:EOR·
ADFACIENDAMUINDICIA

INNATIONIBUS·INCRE
PATIONESINPOPULIS·
ADALLIGANDOSREGESEORU
INCOMPEDIBUS·ETNO
BILESEORUMINMANICIS
FERREIS·
UTFACIANTINEISIUDICIU
CONSCRIPTUM·GLORIA
HAECESTOMNIBUSSCIS
EIUS·

Iona is the favourite candidate but the principal argument for this attribution has recently been demolished—based the decorative scheme of his canon-tables, which incorporated representations of the beasts symbolizing the Evangelists in the spandrels of the arcades, on an apparently incomplete set in a manuscript from the Carolingian court (pl. 41).

It is in manuscripts, too, that we find the clearest visual counterpart to the intellectual endeavours made in the last years of the eighth century to express in new terms the authority exercised by the Frankish king over so much of the Latin Christian world. About the time that Aachen became the normal residence of the king and his court, it welcomed new artists or new models or most probably both. The result was the luxurious ' Coronation Gospels '—so-called because the medieval German Emperors made their coronation oath on them—now at Vienna to which city they came from Aachen via Paderborn in 1801. The columns and arches of the canon-tables cast their shadows behind them. The four whole-page representations of the Evangelists are the most Classical portraits in medieval art, with their serene loosely-robed sensitive figures, detached from the world of the spectator, in a setting in which colour is used to indicate space and depth with whites, greys, soft blues and purples. Who the extraordinarily gifted artist or artists were is not known and it is only a plausible guess that they were refugees from the Byzantine East who had settled in Italy. No model for their portraits that is at all close has been discovered unless, as indeed may be the case, the rubbed and possibly incomplete picture of an Evangelist inserted into another Gospel Book produced at the palace (pl. 34) is regarded not as another example of these strangers' work but as a unique survival of an earlier phase of Christian art from which they drew their inspiration. The artists of the other decorated pages in this second Gospel Book (formerly at Xanten, now at Brussels) and in two others, and also probably of the immediate model of an astronomical and computistic manuscript formerly at Prüm and now at Madrid, seem to be their pupils. One of the Gospel Books is still at Aachen. The columns of its canon-tables (which unfortunately it has proved impossible to reproduce) represent different Antique marbles—many of them found in the columns of the palace chapel—with such accuracy that they can be identified without difficulty. On the only other illustrated page, uniquely, all four Evangelists —toga-ed Classical scholars like the Evangelists of the ' Coronation Gospels ' and the Xanten leaf—are represented in miniature together with their symbols, set in a strange rocky landscape (pl. 37). In the original, of which the lapis-lazuli blue is exaggerated and the opalescent pinks (which hardly recur in art again until Turner) are coarsened in reproduction, this page has every claim to be considered as one of the supreme moments of Carolingian book-painting.

For a north European court dominated by the personality of its king and speculating on his and its destinies shortly before the fateful year 800, a Mediterranean artist inspired by a remoter Classical past in Christian guise had created an ideal art: one that offered the court a link between the forms of ordinary existence and that Other World for which the earthly life was but a preparation and a foreshadowing.

62. Detail of a page from the Utrecht Psalter. *Bibliotheek der Rijksuniversiteit te Utrecht* Ms. 32, fol 83. *Size* 33 × 25 cm.

From Rex Francorum to Imperator

In 787 a poet at Charles' court, the *Hibernicus exul* whom some scholars identify with Dungal, wrote a poem that combined praise of the Muses with a commemoration of the king's success over duke Tassilo of Bavaria. Twelve years later the same poet, as it seems, wrote a much more elaborate account of the journey made to Francia by the then Pope, Leo III, and his dealings with the king when they met at Paderborn (Saxony). The later poem is, as we would expect, conspicuously superior to the earlier in Latinity, versification and literary achievement. The picture they give of the Frankish king and his court at the two dates is even more different. In 787 he is still the barbarian leader of a warrior band, a receiver and giver of gold and jewels, a victor in battle, a punisher of breach of faith—although he is also the man who has subjected the people of the Franks to impartial laws. In 799 king Charles is head of the world, a man to be acclaimed as the crowning glory of Europe, father of the continent, Augustus; a sovereign with his own capital, a ' second Rome ', worthily provided with buildings; superior to all other rulers in goodness and as a dispenser of justice; the monarch to whom the chief bishop of the world turns for protection and help.

Charles' enhanced reputation and standing in the eyes of both his educated courtiers and of the other rulers of western Europe had not, of course, developed quite as abruptly as this contrast suggests. Charles inherited from his father and grandfather a reputation that extended beyond the frontiers of his kingdom and at the time of his accession he was already, in the eyes of the Pope, ' patrician of the Romans ' and protector of the holy city, the ancient *caput orbis*. In 773 king Alchred of Northumbria—the king who had raised Alcuin's teacher Aelbert to the see of York and approved the missionary Willehad's departure for Germany—sent legates to king Charles and a letter, with a request for prayers, and gifts (twelve cloaks and a gold ring) to bishop Lul of Mainz: the legates were to secure *pax et amicitia* between the two kings. In the ensuing decades annalists in northern and southern England regularly took note of Charles' successes: several of their entries were incorporated in the *Anglo-Saxon Chronicle* at the end of the ninth century. The English kingdom with which closest relations were established, however, was that of Mercia, whose king Offa had imposed his authority over neighbouring territories and tried to make it secure by methods not very different from those used by Charles himself. In the late 760s or early 770s moneyers in Kent began to mint silver coins (pennies) in his name that were more regular in weight than previous English coins. A year or two before 792 the Mercian-controlled Kentish mints started producing coins that were manifest imitations of current Frankish *denarii* in both appearance and weight: the equation of ' 240 pennies = 1 pound ' established by this change persisted in Britain until 1971 although with a much altered significance. Trade between the two kingdoms is unlikely to have been the only or even the main reason for this conscious imitation; but trade across the Channel there certainly was and it seemed of sufficient importance for Charles to put a stop to it as a form of political blackmail. The occasion, in 790, was Offa's reply to the request that his daughter should be sent as a bride for Charles' eldest son, Charles: he asked that the king's daughter Bertha—future lover of Angilbert and mother of the chronicler Nithard—should be given in marriage to his own son, a request that the Frankish king found totally unacceptable. Six years later Charles was again in touch with Offa about goods and merchants that passed between the two countries. If Einhard is to be believed, even ' kings of the Scots ' came to give their allegiance to Charles: perhaps there is confusion here with his relations with the kingdom of Northumbria in the last years of the eighth century and the early years of the next when deposition or death was the fate of a succession of monarchs.

The declared and usually the genuine purpose of such contacts between the monarchs of the Christian Latin west was the establishment of ' peace and friendship ': and they supplemented and strengthened the links between ecclesiastics that kept distant parts of Europe in some sort of contact with one another and served as a constant reminder that unity under God and His earthly Vicar had not been destroyed by political fragmentation and linguistic divergence. Charles' relations with the Emperor in Constantinople, on the other hand, provided a constant reminder of the existence of one major political, cultural and spiritual division. The annexation of the Lombard kingdom and the duchy of Spoleto brought the Franks for the first time in centuries to the borders of Imperial territory and the Emperor, whose control of the Venetian littoral and the bay of Naples was in fact very weak, had promptly bestowed the dignity of patrician on the son of the deposed Lombard king. When the premature death of the Emperor Leo IV left the Empire to a minor for whom Empress Irene acted—for the first time in Byzantine history—as Regent, negotiations were opened for a future marriage between the

Fig. 44 Reconstruction of Charles' palace at Aachen. *Mainz, Römisch-Germanisches Zentralmuseum.*

boy-Emperor and the king's daughter Rotrud. (A century and a half later Constantine Porphyrogenitus still felt obliged to justify excepting ' the Franks alone ' from the general disapproval of Imperial marriages with aliens ' for they alone were excepted by that great man, the holy Constantine, because he himself drew his origin from those parts '.) A formal betrothal actually took place in 781 and Rotrud was put to learn Greek, not from anyone who was already at the court but from a certain Zacharias who was probably of Greek birth. The gifts that would certainly have passed between the courts at this time may well have included works of art that subsequently provided models and inspiration to Frankish artists. Characteristically, the Royal Annals do not mention this episode: for seven years later the betrothal was broken off, leaving Rotrud to become a correspondent of Alcuin and the mistress of count Rorgo of Le Mans (to whom she bore a future abbot of St. Denis).

The immediate occasion of the breach was apparently the recognition of Charles' sovereignty by the heir to Benevento, at a time when his widowed mother was in negotiation with the Imperial court. It is difficult to believe that the king described by the ' Irish Exile ' was himself offended by the summoning of the Council of Nicaea to consider the problem of images and by the references in the acts of the Council to the achievements of ' a new Constantine and a new Helena ' by whom peace had been restored to the church: the Pope was prepared to employ similar flatteries and recognized the council as oecumenical. By the end of the decade, however, the learned clerical element at the Frankish court was clearly in a position to influence the king's views about the nature and scope of his authority, even to the point of encouraging disagreement with the Pope. In the ' Caroline Books ', Charles' ecclesiastical counsellors insist that it is the responsibility of the Roman church and its incumbents to maintain the unity and orthodoxy of the church's faith, and then proceed to show that Pope Hadrian has allowed himself to be diverted from the *via regia*, the ' king's highway ' of the Old Testament Prophets and the only way to salvation, by the arrogance and vain-glory of the Greek clergy and their rulers assembled at Nicaea. This may be compared with the statement in the preface to the collection of papal correspondence with Charles and his predecessors, made at the Frankish court in 791, that it was right that a king who exceeded all others in prudence and wisdom should be able to pass on to posterity a worthy monument to his work.

When the leading Frankish laity and clergy came to Frankfort in considerable numbers in the early summer of 794, still under the shadow of the disasters of the preceding two years and of the continuing threat of disunity within the universal church, it was clear that ideas about the king's authority had evolved even further. The bishops and their subordinates met separately from the lay magnates in ' the great hall ' of the palace. The king presided in spite of the presence of two papal legates: he personally ordered Elipand's statement of his doctrinal position to be read out and then, rising from his throne and standing on the top of the steps on which it had been put, he indicated to those present how their deliberations should proceed and reserved to himself the final decision in matters on which they were unable to make up their minds. The results of these deliberations having been approved by the king, he incorporated them in a single capitulary with the orders and decisions on secular matters that had been agreed with the magnates: they were to derive their authority, even when it was a matter of doctrine, from the will of the king. Moreover, the synodal resolutions against Adoptionism for which Alcuin was largely responsible (above, p. 112) make it clear that in their author's

63. Manuscript; Genesis scenes from the Moutier-Grandval Bible: *London, British Museum* Add. Ms. 10546, fol 5v; Tours c. 840. *Size* 51 × 36 cm.

tates uide. principio amico filium restituerit tibi generum firmum. & si
inuenies uirum; CHR quid istic. si ita istuc animum induxti esse utile. nolo
lum commodum in me claudier; SYM merito te semper maxumi feci chre
R sed quid agis; SYM quid; CHR qui sciseos nunc discordare inter se. SYM ip
dauus. qui intumus est eorum consilus dixit. & is mihi suadet nuptias; qu
quem ut maturem; num censes facere t filium nisi sciret eadem haec uell
adeo. iam eius audies uerba; heus euocate huc dauum; at q; eccum uideo f

DAUUS **SIMO** **CHREMES**
SERUUS EIDEM

Lostq; simo pcepsus
ut uocare dauus
quo manifestare
uoluntate filii
de nuptiis in
ueniens eu
dixit

64   65   49.

& sicut mutus non aperiens os suum;

t factus sum sicut homo non audiens

view the Frankish king, acting here as the divinely-commanded leader of the church within his dominions, had presided as *rector populi christiani* over a synod which could properly be called ' universal ' because—although it was of limited geographical scope in its membership—it had re-asserted and defended the true doctrines of a universal church.

At the end of the resolution against Adoptionism by the Italian bishops present at Frankfort, Charles is acclaimed with a wide range of epithets including ' king and priest ', *rex et sacerdos*. The same phrase occasionally occurs elsewhere. But no one therefore supposed that the king had the power that belonged to the humblest of priests, that of bestowing the sacraments on the faithful. Paulinus, the author of the resolution, had previously defined the responsibilities of the king as the subjugation of barbarians, the defence of the Church, the securing of priests in their sacred ministry and in their appropriate law, while the wielding of spiritual weapons was the task of the bishops. This is very much the point of view expressed in the letter sent in Charles' name to Pope Leo III in 796. The king owed his ' priestly ' character to the fact that he was anointed of God, *christus Domini*. In the absence of anything not addressed to or written for him by one or other of his advisers, it is rash to look for an expression that seems to symbolize the king's own view of the nature of his authority. But there is much to be said for the suggestion—recently renewed by several scholars approaching the problem from different directions—that this is to be found in the notion of ' a new David ', of the Frankish king as the true successor of the kings of the Old Testament who had led God's Chosen People by His command and slain His and their enemies.

David as a by-name or epithet of the king is frequent in the letters of Alcuin, Paulinus and others at all periods of the reign from which they survive. It is, however, apparently only in 797 that references begin to appear in Alcuin's letters to Charles' *imperium*, both in an abstract sense (' rule ', and particularly rule of a superior kind) and in a territorial one: the newly-conquered territory in the Danube valley is an extension of the *imperium Christianum;* Charles has *imperium* over men in a territory of enormous extent and his friendship is sought by others. Consequently Alcuin came increasingly to think of the *populus Christianus* as those Christians who acknowledged Charles as *rex Francorum et Langobardorum et patricius Romanorum*. It is therefore pointless to try to decide how far Alcuin's conception of a ' Christian empire ' was a spiritual one, that of people bound together by their unity in Christ, and how far it was a this-worldly one, of men acknowledging a single political authority. By the end of the century these were two co-terminous ideas, two facets or perhaps two visions of a single Divine creation. Christian orthodoxy ended where the rule of the Frankish king ended and where the rule of the Emperor in Constantinople began. Alcuin could look forward to the Frankish king's embodying in himself Augustine's ideal emperor who uses his power to spread the worship of God and acts—in Augustine's words—' not out of vain-glory but out of love for everlasting bliss '.

Perhaps in these same years, rather than after 800, Alcuin was writing his ' Dialogue on rhetoric and the virtues ' in an effort to guide Charles along the *via regia* which was the path of the true Christian ruler. It is by no means safe to assume, however, that the views expressed by Alcuin, who was no longer at court, were precisely those also of the king: there was at least one issue in these years—a serious judicial dispute—in which the king rejected arguments of both an historical and a legal nature put forward by the abbot and accepted the arguments of his opponents. Equally, and unlike many recent writers on the origins of the Carolingian Empire,

64. Detail of a page from an illustrated Terence manuscript showing a comedy scene: *Rome, Biblioteca Apostolica Vaticana* Vat. Lat. 3868, fol 12. *Size* 32 × 29 cm.

65. Psalter illustration: *Stuttgart, Würtembergische Landesbibliothek* Ms. Fol. 23, fol 49; second quarter of the ninth century.

Fig. 45 Stucco work on the east
wall of S. Benedetto, Malles.

I do not feel confident that either Charles or his close advisers had developed a clear and consistent attitude to the Empire in the east, whether before or after 794. Much stress has been laid on the building of the palace at Aachen, with the chapel a prominent feature of it, which, it has been argued (notably by Professor Fichtenau) ' can hardly have been undertaken simply out of a desire for rest ' but must have been ' imitating the customs of the eastern empire '; and support has been claimed for this view in the adoption of the expression *sacrum palatium* for the new royal residence. It seems to have been overlooked that when this expression occurs in Frankish texts for the first time—at Frankfort in 794—it is applied, first (in the resolution of the Italian bishops), to the royal residence at Frankfort itself and, secondly, to the still-itinerant royal court. Moreover, contrary to what has been confidently asserted, this phrase was used of the palace at Pavia more than once, in the days of the independent Lombard kings; and it is not absolutely excluded that it was also used of a papal residence in Rome in the early years of the eighth century. The evident architectural and other links with palace and church buildings in Ravenna and Pavia, the transporting of a statue of Theodoric from Ravenna to Aachen in 801, and perhaps also an awareness of the existence of a palace-complex that incorporated a centrally-planned building (S. Sofia: above, p. 140) at Benevento, which the reviser of the Royal Annals correctly described as *caput illius* [sc. *Beneventani*] *terrae* when describing the negotiations of 787 between the king and the Franks and its prince, all these suggest, in my view, more likely sources of immediate inspiration for the Aachen palace and chapel than analogies with the *chrysotriklinos* (cupola-roofed throne-room) in the vastly different palace at Constantinople.

To doubt whether Aachen was envisaged from the start as a deliberate demonstration of the Frankish king's ' equality ' with the supposedly unorthodox ruler in Constantinople is not, however, to deny that the new royal residence and its centrally-planned chapel with the royal throne in an upper gallery looking down on the main altar (above, ch. 5 and fig. 41) and its relics was in all probability designed with a symbolic as well as a practical purpose. If the ' Epic of Charles and Leo ' quoted at the beginning of this chapter is taken at its face-value—and there is good reason for doing so, particularly if we accept the view that it was written before the coronation at Rome—it is evident that there was one element at the Frankish court that was vigorously canvassing the claims of Aachen to be regarded as a ' second Rome ', the proper capital for a Frankish monarch who was ' head of the world ', who was to the new age of the victory of Christian arms what Constantine had been to the first age of Christian triumph; and the lack of any reference to that other ' new Rome ', Constantinople, as the city which Frankish Aachen— with its magnificent buildings, precious relics and splendid court—was now ready to supersede and replace cannot—in a context in which any use of words that has possible symbolic significance is made out to be pregnant with meaning—be entirely overlooked. This is not to say that there was, in 798/9, an element at the Frankish court that had the clearly-formulated intention of persuading the ruler of the western *imperium Christianum* to become Emperor by a formal constitutive act and make once-lowly Aachen the imperial capital. This, like the supposition that the palace that had begun under other inspiration was coming to be regarded as the counterpart of its grander counterpart in the Greek east, is certainly possible; but it is not proved.

In the first years of its existence, the last years of the eighth century—a period which is so vividly if incompletely recorded in the writings of the men whom

Charles had attracted to his court many years previously that it has often coloured the picture of the whole reign—the palace at Aachen was the setting for many notable displays and colourful legations, some of which were still remembered a century later. Early in 796 the immense treasure captured when armies from Italy broke into the Avar ' ring ' or camp—the product of centuries as the semi-official annalist says—was brought there. Shortly afterwards legates arrived from the new Pope, Leo III, with ' keys from the tomb of St. Peter ' and ' the banner of the city of Rome '. ' A large part ' of the treasure was sent with Angilbert to the Pope, who doubtless distributed it among the churches of the Holy City, while the rest was given to the Frankish magnates, clergy and churches. Later that year one of the leaders of the Avars came with a group of his people to receive Christian baptism and they in turn departed laden with gifts. Finally, towards the end of the year king Pippin brought more treasure won from the Pannonian Avars who were still pagan. In 797 the court at Aachen was host successively to the Arab governor of Barcelona come to surrender his city once again to the Frankish king; to a claimant to the Emirate of Cordova seeking help against the son and heir of the brother who had ousted him nine years previously; and to a messenger from the governor of Imperial Sicily. In 797 or 798, three legates were dispatched to the court of Caliph Harun al-Rashid—he of the Thousand-and-one-Nights: two died on the journey and the third eventually returned to Europe with an elephant ' whose name was Abul Abaz '. At the beginning of 798, for the first time so far as we know, a legate came from the king of Asturias—the Christian kingdom in north-west Spain from which the centuries-long ' Reconquest ' had already been launched—bringing the usual precious gifts. Charles' reputation and prestige among his neighbours had clearly not diminished as advancing years forced him to leave the command of armies in battle to others.

In the spring of 798 a far more important mission reached the court when, for the first time for more than a decade, legates came bearing a letter from the Imperial court. There is no reason to doubt the statement of the Royal Annalist that it contained—in addition, of course, to the usual courtesies—simply a request for ' peace ', that is to say the settlement of border-disputes and other causes of political friction in Italy. For in the previous year the Empress Irene had, as the Annalist learnt and recorded, deposed and blinded her son and now claimed to be an Empress ruling in her own right; and in the circumstances she needed as little trouble on her frontiers as possible if she was to secure her shaky position on the throne. Her extreme position on images would in any case have made the opening of negotiations on this subject with the west quite pointless even if—which is improbable—she would have felt it to be appropriate.

We do not know the point at which Irene's conduct and unparalleled personal rule began to seem important to influential men at the Frankish court, or indeed if such a feeling existed before the date of Charles' own coronation as Emperor. The recognition that the so-called ' Annals of Lorsch ' are a contemporary record for the years just before and just after 800 means that the much-discussed statement that the Frankish king was put forward for the higher dignity ' because the name of emperor [*nomen imperatoris*, a phrase that had then a much more powerful content than the literal translation conveys] had now ceased to exist in the land of the Greeks and because they had a woman as emperor ' cannot be dismissed as of no account. But since these annals were certainly written in Alemannia and there is no good reason for associating this portion in any way with the abbot of Lorsch, Ricbod, who was also bishop of Trier and a close connection of the court;

Fig. 46 Capital from the south-west corner of St. Justin, Höchst.

and since this particular entry was not written until after the end of 801, the passage is not good evidence of what either the king or the Pope or their respective courts thought in 799 or 800. What crystallized the ideas circulating in various quarters—among the abbot of Tours and his correspondents, in the papal curia at Rome, in the Frankish court and not improbably in Charles' own mind although (I repeat) we cannot prove this—and led to the Imperial Coronation of 25th December 800, although they were not the reason for it, were events in the city of Rome affecting the Pope himself.

The constitutional position of the Frankish king in the former Imperial territories that stretched diagonally across Italy from the mouths of the Tiber and Marta to the deltas of the Po and Adige had been ambiguous ever since 774. In that year the king ostensibly renewed the concession previously made by his father which 'conveyed' temporal authority over the greater part of northern and central Italy; and after some delay he certainly allowed the Pope to exercise this authority over the 'duchies' of Rome and Perugia and over the ex-Imperial territory beyond the Appenines that had been conceded to him by the last Lombard kings. It is probable that writers throughout the 'patrimony of St. Peter' dated their documents thereafter by the pontifical year of the ruling Pope. It is certain that in those territories which the king added to the 'patrimony' in the 780s, the Pope's name and year replaced the king's name and year in local documents; and that coins minted at Rome in this period bore only the name of the Pope. When in 796 the new Pope sent to the king the banner which was reputedly the symbol of secular authority over the city of Rome and its inhabitants and when, before 800, the Pope and his representatives treated the king of the Franks in other ways that had previously been the prerogative of the emperor—in the liturgy, for example—this still did not amount to a final recognition of a temporal sovereignty identical with that previously held by the Emperor. On the other hand, coins that bore Charles' name were minted at Ravenna; there is some slight evidence that he made grants of property that lay within the patrimony; and, less significant of course, there are traces of Frankish judicial and other institutions in papal territory at an early date. The situation is the more complicated in that some religious communities in areas transferred by the king to papal sovereignty—notably, the great and influential abbey of Farfa in the Sabina—continued to look to him for protection, privileges and grants of land lying within his *regnum* proper. Beyond question, however, the Frankish king was not only the defender of the Christian church in general but of the see of Rome in particular: and its bishop, whose unique authority now rested on the Donation of Constantine as well as on Christ's commission to St. Peter, had begun to accord him those honours which pertained to the highest representative of the Emperor, and other prerogatives without actually 'translating' the Imperial dignity itself.

Charles was showing no disinclination to evade this responsibility. At the end of 797 he dispatched a legation to Rome led by Fardulf, a Lombard and probably one-time hostage who had been given the abbacy of St. Denis for his part in revealing the plans for rebellion in 792. Its purpose was to ask the Pope to bestow the *pallium* on bishop Arno of Salzburg so that he could exercise metropolitan (archiepiscopal) authority over the bishoprics of the south-east and particularly over Passau, which like his own diocese was engaged in considerable missionary activity. The request—which is an interesting reminder that the Frankish king still recognized certain limitations on his power to determine the organization of the church within his dominions—was granted. Arno went to Rome to receive the

66. Ivory plaque showing Christ in Majesty from the *Fitzwilliam Museum, Cambridge. Size* 15 × 15 cm.

66

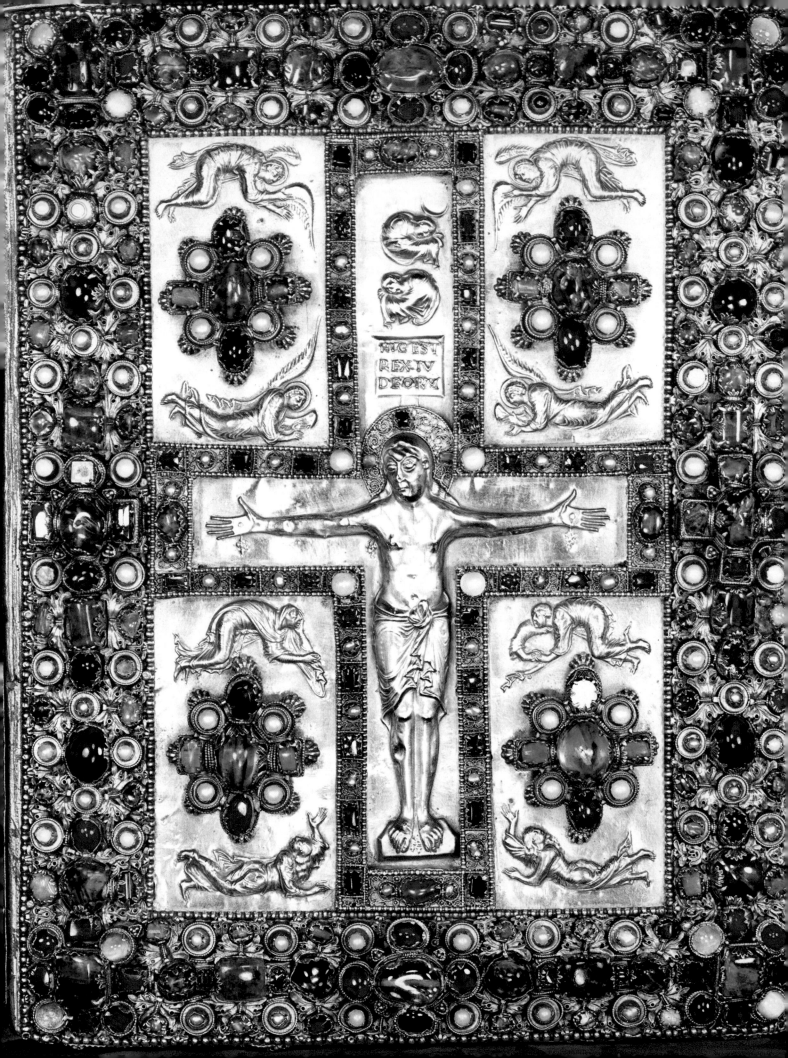

pallium in person and warm congratulations (and some suitable advice) from Alcuin. He apparently found time to help other royal representatives who were travelling round Tuscany trying to settle outstanding disputes and dispense justice and then started back northwards, sending and bringing news of the serious difficulties that the Pope was facing in his city and apparently making by no means favourable comments on the Pope's own conduct.

The cause and significance of the latest troubles are, as in the case of all similar episodes in early medieval Rome, singularly obscure—because we know only the papal side of the story and because there is almost no documentary evidence to provide a background. The leading protagonists in the final critical episode in the spring of 799, however, were leading papal officials who were relatives of the late Pope Hadrian I. Leo, whatever his other faults may have been, was a man who had made his way in the church on the strength of his own abilities and there is at least a suspicion that the persistent rivalries among Roman families for office, and for the wealth it brought with it, had been exacerbated by the election of a Pope of humble and not ' noble ' background. Charles' answer was to send the abbot of Stablo to join with the duke of Spoleto in keeping a close watch on developments in the city. It proved of no avail. On 25th April 799 while Leo was approaching the church of San Lorenzo in Lucina—another of the churches substantially rebuilt by his predecessor—to begin the procession of the Greater Litany, and therefore in the presence of a great crowd of citizens, one of his officials who was not properly dressed for the occasion came up to him with a false excuse; he was then savagely attacked and imprisoned successively in two monasteries, both—interestingly—communities of Greek monks. After a few days, however, he escaped and found safety with the royal legates who had arrived at St. Peter's with troops from the duchy of Spoleto. His supporters claimed that he had been blinded and had his tongue cut out—a false claim but making possible a ' miraculous ' recovery.

The Frankish king's representatives conducted the Pope and his entourage across the Appennines and the Alps, then down the Rhine and across southern Saxony to Paderborn, where a month previously Charles had established his summer camp preparatory to an expedition across the lower Elbe. The choice of meeting-place seemed not inappropriate both to the poet who commemorated the encounter and to Alcuin. The Saxon town, previously the scene of two great demonstrations of Charles' power in 777 and 785, already boasted a royal palace and great church; and the existence of a royal ' seat ' in what less than quarter of a century previously had been a land of militant paganism, was a striking illustration of the Frankish king's ' enlargement of the Christian Empire ', *dilatatio imperii christiani*. The Pope remained at the royal court for more than two months and it is apparent that a decision on what was to be done about the situation in Rome came to take precedence over all other problems. To introduce a further complication, letters arrived from Leo's enemies in Rome accusing him of various offences, notably of the fashionable medieval ones of perjury and adultery.

When Leo left Paderborn in October, accompanied by the archbishops of Cologne (who was also arch-chaplain) and Salzburg, no less than five other bishops and three counts, it is highly probable that the king had decided to initiate some judicial process at Rome in which the Pope would be called on to clear himself of the charges made against him and that Leo knew this. Passages in Alcuin's letters in which he makes it clear that he disapproves of any proposals to ' judge ' the Pope or expose him to proceedings that might end in his deposition are difficult to interpret in any other way; and this reading of the evidence gains plausibility

67. Front cover of the Lindau Gospels, in silver and jewels; *Pierpont Morgan Library, New York.* *Size* 36 × 27 cm.

from the names of those who went with him from the Frankish court. (In view of the claims currently made by one group of scholars for the particular influence and importance of an ' Imperial aristocracy ', drawn from a limited number of families, it is interesting to note that none of the three counts who went to Rome on this crucial occasion can be linked with any of these families, although one of them had accompanied Leo *from* Italy and another is later found as both a judicial *missus* and an Imperial courtier in the narrow sense.) It is no less evident that a king who, only a year or two later, showed no inclination to accept Alcuin's interpretation of the (ecclesiastical) law of sanctuary and no sympathy with his protests about the application of secular law to the detriment of the community at Tours is unlikely to have assented automatically to the same adviser's views on the limits of his authority with regard to the bishop of Rome.

The last months of 799 saw Frankish arms celebrating new successes—as well as lamenting one defeat, in which the duke of Friuli and the count of the Bavarian March were both killed in an ambush along the Dalmatian coast—and the Frankish king enjoying an even wider fame. The still nominally Imperial Balearic Isles transferred their allegiance to Charles in return for help against Arab attacks and Frankish ships succeeded in capturing the raiders' banners and presenting them to the king; the count of the Breton March carried out a successful invasion of the Breton peninsula; the governor of another Spanish Arab town surrendered it to the Franks; and a monk who had been sent by the patriarch of Jerusalem arrived with relics from the Holy Sepulchre. When the latter started home again in the early part of 800, he was accompanied by one of the king's chaplains, bearing suitable gifts in exchange. One new problem had to be faced before the king could turn his whole-hearted attention to the position of the Pope—if that indeed was his plan. The North Sea coast was ' infested with pirates '. Seven years previously ships from Norway had plundered Lindisfarne, to the horror of Alcuin, who rightly observed that ' it was not thought that such an inroad from the sea could be made '; and the Norse warriors who had perhaps only recently built ships designed for long open-sea voyages had subsequently extended the range of their raiding activities. Notker of St. Gall later told a tale of an ageing Charles weeping as he saw the ships of the Northmen and foresaw what they would do to his land. His actions at the time were of a more practical and less defeatist kind, namely, organizing coastal defences and creating a fleet, the latter presumably from among the Frisians who were now finally incorporated in the Frankish kingdom. Having celebrated Easter among the saintly splendours of Centula-St. Riquier, the king proceeded to Tours—according to the Royal Annalist and another contemporary text—to pray at the tomb of St. Martin. Here he was unexpectedly detained by the illness and death of his fourth and last wife. He had ample time to talk with Alcuin and doubtless did so but it is surely rash to conclude, as has often been done, that these encounters finally determined the course of events in the next few months. It is very striking that Alcuin's letters made no allusion to these supposedly crucial conversations; and although those written at this particular time when he was journeying with the king back to Aachen contain many references to contemporary events at court and elsewhere, it is evident that his main pre-occupation was with the Adoptionist heresy and the renewed activity of its exponents and supporters. At Aachen in June Alcuin persuaded bishop Felix to make a formal retraction: amid the general confidence that orthodoxy had finally triumphed, legates who were known to be well-qualified for the task were sent to the Pyrenees to extirpate the last consequences of the ' pernicious doctrine '. Once more, Charles had apparently vindicated his claim to be the one true defender of the church, the supreme 'orthodox ruler' of the Christian West.

The general assembly that met at Mainz in August was an exceptionally large one and, when Charles had assured himself that peace prevailed throughout his kingdom, he set out for Rome with a splendid following. In Italy a full week was spent at Ravenna, one-time residence of the Imperial exarch and a city still full of reminiscences of Theodoric. From here king Pippin was ordered to lead an expedi-

Fig. 47 Phases of the sun and moon; Signs of the Zodiac; Salzburg, second decade of ninth century: *Vienna, Österreichische Nationalbibliothek* Cod 387, fol 165v.

tion against Benevento. Charles went with him as far as Ancona, a journey that would have taken him under or past at least three Roman triumphal arches, and then left the coast to cross the Apennines by the old Via Salaria, finally approaching Rome along the already little-used Via Nomentana. On 23rd November, the day after his arrival at Mentana, he was met by the Pope. For the latter to come in person to the twelfth milestone from the city was an extraordinary honour. On the occasion of the last Imperial visit to Rome, in the later seventh century, Pope Vitalian had come out a mere six miles: although Charles was still only king and patrician, he was being treated like an emperor. Having feasted, Pope and Emperor entered the city together; and on the next day with the full panoply of ceremonial of which the city was capable, Charles was formally received at St. Peter's.

Almost a year previously the high ecclesiastics and counts who had accompanied Leo back to Rome had met in the Lateran *Triclinium* to conduct a preliminary inquiry into the charges made against the Pope: using a procedure that was to become well-established in ninth-century Francia, although used in very different circumstances, they seem to have sought evidence of fact in support of the accusations and when this was not forthcoming they arrested the conspirators and sent them to Francia. The decision on the charges and counter-charges (i.e. conspiracy and assault) was, however, left to another tribunal—evidently one in which the king would take part, in whatever capacity. A week after Charles' arrival in Rome, by his command, king and Pope, archbishops, bishops and abbots (who, as befitted their dignity, remained seated), together with priests, Frankish magnates and Roman notables or ' senate ' (who stood) assembled in St. Peter's to hear the preferring of the charges against the Pope. According to the Royal Annalist, no one was prepared to sustain an accusation; according to the ' Popes' Book ', at some point in the protracted proceedings, the higher ecclesiastics declared that they should not be asked to judge the apostolic see—the view long maintained by Alcuin; according to the south German writer of the ' Lorsch ' Annals, when the king saw that the accusations had been made out of spite and not on the basis of law, he invited the Pope formally to declare his innocence and thus avoid the necessity of passing judgement; according to the papalist account, the Pope offered of his own accord to make a declaration of innocence and this was accepted. On 23rd December the Pope formally made known his ' ignorance ' of the offences with which he was charged.

On the same day that Leo's innocence was admitted, legates arrived from Jerusalem bringing to Charles symbols of authority over that city similar to those which he had been sent from Rome more than four years previously. On the next day, if we believe the south German annalist, Charles, as the man who controlled the city of Rome ' where emperors were accustomed to reside ' and the other ' seats ' in Italy, Gaul and Germany, was offered the (supposedly-vacant) Imperial dignity which he was graciously pleased to accept.

On 25th December, at the end of the third mass of Christmas, which the Pope celebrated at St. Peter's, the king was kneeling in prayer before the tomb of the saint. In accordance with normal practice he would have taken off the crown he wore on special occasions, together with his weapons and other insignia. As he rose the Pope placed the crown upon his head and an obviously well-rehearsed section of the congregation chanted three times a novel version of an acclamation with a long history behind it: ' To Charles, the most pious Augustus, crowned by God, the great and peace-giving Emperor, life and victory '. ' And after the

68. Fresco from S. Benedetto, Malles (Italian Tyrol), showing a martyrdom scene.

69. The nave arcade of St. Justin, Höchst (Germany).

70. Capital in St. Justin, Höchst.

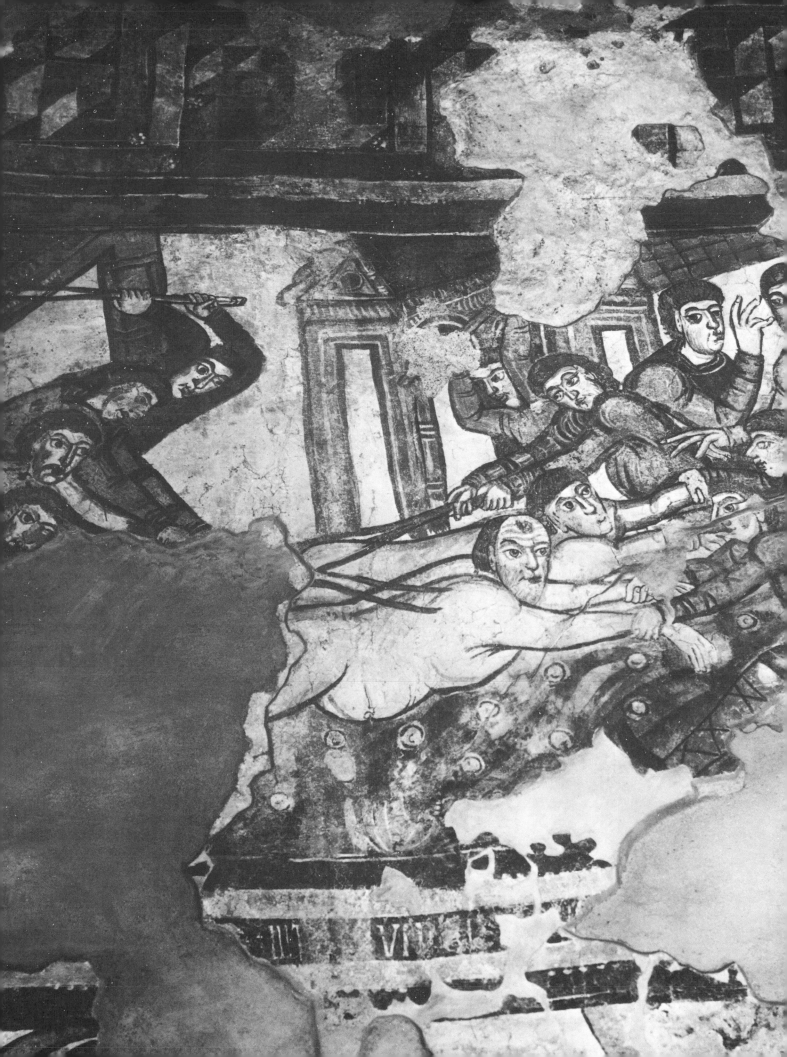

74

ET SYRIAM SOBAL · ET CONVERTIT
IOAB · ET PERCYSSIT EDOM INVAL
LE SALINARVM · XII MILIA

[liturgical] praises ', says the Royal Annalist, ' he was adored by the Pope in the manner due to princes of old; and his dignity of patrician being taken away, he was called Emperor and Augustus '. The account of the ceremony in the ' Pope's Book '—from which the version of the acclamation just quoted is taken—adds that Leo anointed Charles and a chronicler at Constantinople, who wished to ridicule the whole proceeding, declared that Charles was anointed from head to toe (i.e. received what would later be called in the west ' extreme unction '!). Most scholars suppose that this particular episode is a later invention, either because an Emperor-making ceremony already seemed incomplete without consecration or because it served to emphasize still further the crucial part played by the Pope. To the Frankish courtiers and magnates present in St. Peter's it is probable that the crowning seemed the constitutive act; later usage gave the name of ' coronation ' to a whole complex of acts of which the crowning was (and is) only one. In the eyes of the Romans, and therefore in a certain sense constitutionally, it must have been the acclamation that created the Emperor. Few even among the Franks, however, could have been in any doubt about what had happened, even though it was some months before the *nomen imperatoris* was introduced into Frankish official and other documents. A few days later the conspirators against Leo were brought before Charles to be tried for their *crimen majestatis*, i.e. committing an offence against the Imperial person or someone or something in his special ' sacred ' protection. Subsequently, the name of the Emperor appeared before that of the Pope in the dating-clauses of papal privileges and of documents written within the Patrimony of St. Peter; and for the first time Charles' name appeared on papal coins.

It is in the light of these facts and contradictions that we have to interpret Einhard's claim that Charles' ' affirmed that, even though it was an important feast day, he would not have entered the church if he had known in advance the plan of the Pope '. The ceremony was not sudden and spontaneous: parts of it were clearly well-rehearsed and, as we have seen, it had been elaborately prepared for. It has ingeniously been suggested that, whether Charles actually said this or Einhard invented it, the claim was to show the king and Emperor's modesty and humility, like the reluctance shown by Mr. Speaker in the British House of Commons when he is conducted to be installed in his official chair. It is equally possible that Charles was conscious of the unfavourable reaction that would follow at the old Imperial court or—particularly if we accept the evidence that Charles had been offered and accepted the Imperial title on the previous day—that his objection was to the Pope's part in the ' translation ' of the dignity. Charles, in this case, had presumably intended to place the crown on his own head,[1] the congregation would have acclaimed him and the Pope's part would have been limited to the act of ' adoration ' or prostration—a conscious imitation of the practice in the older Imperial court—with which in fact the ceremony ended. These ambiguities and contradictions are but one element in a continuing debate, for the ceremony introduced new factors into western European polity. It revived the Imperial title in the west; it gave specific content to the Frankish link with Rome and the papacy; it gave a new dimension and richness to the symbolism associated with the making and authority of rulers; it provided a model for future ceremonies in a wider context; and it gave the monarchs of future generations an aspiration and a lure. At the time, it appeared to set the seal on the life and endeavours of one monarch, the Frankish Charles.

[1] As Napoleon did, one thousand years later in the presence of the Pope.

71. Frescoes from S. Benedetto, Malles, east end interior.

72. South aisle of St. Philibert-de-Grandlieu (France); c. 820.

73. Nave of the parish church of S. Zeno, Bardolino (Italy); c. 860/70.

74. Manuscript; the St. Gall Psalter, showing Carolingian soldiers: *St. Gallen, Stiftsbibliothek* Ms. 22, o. 140; 890-920.

A Frankish Emperor and his Empire
The End of the Reign

To the overwhelming majority of scholars, the brief ceremony in St. Peter's on 25th December 800 has seemed and seems the most important event in Charles' long reign. And so in a sense it was. Whatever those present thought they were taking part in, whatever Charles may have felt as he left the church, no highly-placed cleric or layman could have been unaware for very long that the acts of acclamation and coronation had revived the Imperial office in the Latin west by bestowing it on a man of barbarian origin and speech, the centre of whose active world was five hundred miles from the Mediterranean. To some scholars this has not seemed enough. For them the ' Coronation of 800 ' has become not only the central but the uniquely important moment in Charles' reign—an event for which all other episodes and aspects of the reign are merely the preparation and from which (for not a few of them) the subsequent history of Europe is almost a prolonged act of derogation, the triumph of particularism and selfish ambition; yet an event at the same time that provides a constant and powerful stimulus to particular as well as universal political and cultural aspirations. The inadequacy of such a point of view should surely be evident. Although the Imperial title in one respect reflects Charles' hegemony in western Europe, it had commonly been achieved by force and the apparent unity was only superficial and even deceitful. Because the coronation involved the Vicar of St. Peter and through him Christ, as well as the highest form of secular authority to which men could be subject, it at once posed the problem of the relation of spiritual and secular powers in a sinful world. This problem had then to be resolved in the context of political organizations, whose roots lay in the period when the ancestors of the Carolingians were only one landed family among many, and which owed their later characteristics in large measure to the actions taken by the Carolingian royal dynasty before 800.

There has been much talk in recent years of ' the two-Emperor problem ' but it is doubtful if either party ever saw it in this light and, in the sense in which, say, there has been a ' problem of two Germanies ' since the Second World War, there never was one. To Byzantium the Roman ceremony was a challenge and an insult, whether or not we should suppose that Charles foresaw this, and the problem of the eastern court was: how can the unlawfulness of the claim of the king of the Franks to be Emperor be asserted without increasing the Empire's already considerable external difficulties? When before the end of May, the Emperor passed through Ravenna on his way back to Aachen, the Frankish writing-office had already adopted the new style of ' Charles, the most serene Augustus, crowned by God, the great pacific Emperor, governing the Roman empire ' and also the seal-legend, *Renovatio Romani imperii*. With their adoption as a consequence of the coronation the central questions in the west were: what content should be given to the new title or, alternatively, how did it affect the authority of the former king over his subjects and how were the future relationships of Emperor and Pope, Rome and Aachen to be decided?

The Frankish court in the last thirteen years of Charles' reign was no longer a

*A Frankish Emperor
and his Empire.
The End of the Reign*

court of scholars in the sense in which that phrase can be used of the 780s and 790s and no literary panegyric worth the name acclaims the new Emperor. But in the generation since Pippin's burial at the entrance to the abbey-church of St. Denis, the imagination of patrons and the skills of craftsmen had given buildings and their decoration the power to express complex ideas, whether architectural, artistic or symbolic. In the opening decades of the ninth century a number of clerics closely connected with the court or formerly belonging to it revealed their view of the new Empire and its head through the forms and details of the buildings they commissioned. A striking example is the charming and intriguing ' tower-gateway ' that still stands some distance to the west of the monastery-church of St. Nazarius, Lorsch (pls. 39, 44, fig. 48). No text throws any light on its date of construction or original purpose; but the relationship of the singularly beautiful composite capitals —which again one might have thought to be imports had they not been in local stone—on the one hand to those in the gallery of the Aachen Octagon and, on the other, to the capitals of the church of St. Michael at Fulda, consecrated in 822, which were re-used when the church was rebuilt in the tenth century (pl. 57), as well as the character of the masonry suggest that it belongs to the early years of the ninth century. It was presumably built, therefore, by abbot Ricbod, bishop of Trier, who died in 804, or by abbot Adalung who succeeded at the beginning of 805. The pointed blind-arcading—although of Ionic pilasters—the masonry patterns and the overall proportions owe little or nothing to a remoter past, and the Classical details at first sight only emphasize the unclassical nature of the building; the inspiration or, in the context of the period, the model is none the less clearly the Arch of Constantine in Rome. The Frankish Empire, too, was to have its triumphal arches —but in a Christian setting.

Constantinian Rome similarly provided the model for what has come to be recognized within the last quarter of a century as the Carolingian building with the

Fig. 48   Lorsch ' tower-gateway '; reconstruction of original appearance. *Mainz, Römisch-Germanisches Zentralmuseum*

A Frankish Emperor
and his Empire.
The End of the Reign

greatest influence on the subsequent development of western European architecture. In 790 or shortly afterwards abbot Baugulf of Fulda began to rebuild Sturmi's simple hall-nave and apse church on a grander scale, with a nave and two aisles over fifty metres long leading to a wide eastern apse in which was placed the main altar dedicated to the Saviour; the relics of St. Boniface were in a second altar in the centre of the nave. The next abbot, Ratger, who took office in 802, had far more grandiose ideas: one of the many complaints made against him in a petition presented to the Emperor by the monks of Fulda in 812 was that he was responsible for 'immense and superfluous buildings and other useless works' as a result of which 'the brothers are worn out beyond measure and the dependants utterly perish'. The most notable feature of these 'immense buildings' was, as we learn from the life of Ratger's successor Eigil who completed the work and had it consecrated in 819, a second apse to the west which was preceded by a huge transept, as a more fitting setting for the tomb of St. Boniface, placed there *Romano more*. There can be no doubt that Ratger's lay-out was consciously modelled on St. Peter's where, alone among the Roman basilicas, several of its distinctive features are to be found. The nave, in which large columns with composite capitals seem to have supported an architrave, was nearly sixty-four metres long—vast by the standards of recent church-building north of the Alps, although still small in comparison with St. Peter's itself—opening into apses fifteen metres wide. The measurements and proportions of the transept, of which the ends were closed off by a colonnade exactly as at St. Peter's, with a span of seventy-seven metres and a width of fifteen were almost precisely those of the 'model'. Other more recent Roman sources provided other features of the monastery church and its associated structures. Hall-crypts were introduced under both west and east apses and when after 822 a new cloister was planned it was agreed that it should not be to the south but to the west, *Romano more*, to be near to the martyred Boniface.

The unique importance of an architectural scheme that associated large continuous transept, apse, crypt and long-aisled nave was not apparent for many years to come. There were other competing forms of symbolism and more than one way of emphasizing that Imperial glories and the Imperial title had been revived by and for the ruler of the Franks. The circular arcaded ambulatory plan adopted for the small funerary chapel of St. Michael at Fulda, consecrated in 822 and not seriously modified in the tenth century rebuilding (pl. 57), seems to have been a conscious imitation of the church of the Holy Sepulchre at Jerusalem which would have been known to the community from Adomnan's or Bede's *De locis sanctis*; but it embodied other symbolic ideas, such as the single crypt column (pl. 56) that represented Christ or the eight columns that stood for the Eight Beatitudes. A striking phenomenon was the building of private or estate churches that were grander than most city or monastery churches existing only one or two generations previously. In the early years of the ninth century bishop Theodulf of Orleans, in his capacity as abbot of Fleury, built an oratory at Germigny-des-Prés. According to a later writer at another house with which Theodulf was associated, his *basilica* was 'on the model of that established at Aachen'. Yet, except that it had a central and not a longitudinal plan and was richly decorated, the similarity between the two is not very obvious. Notable features of its decoration were the stucco ornament (figs. 1, 2. 12), removed in a ruthless and destructive nineteenth century 'restoration', and the drastically 'restored' apse mosaic representing the Ark of the Covenant (pl. 76) which has a more strongly Byzantine character than any other work of art of the period. With its round west porch, north and south apses and triple horseshoe-

75. Fragment of Byzantine silk in Charles' tomb, Aachen. *Height* 66 cm.

76. Mosaic in the apse of Germigny-des-Prés; much restored.

75

76

*A Frankish Emperor
and his Empire.
The End of the Reign*

shaped apses projecting from a square central area of nine vaulted bays, its affinities are with buildings in Theodulf's own Spain and ultimately with others in the eastern Mediterranean. The charming but sadly mutilated church at Steinbach (pl. 45), built by Einhard to serve one of his estates a year or two after Charles' death, was originally of considerable architectural complexity, combining a tower-porch west end, dwarf transepts with small eastern apses and an elaborately developed cross-corridor crypt. (Einhard's second estate church, at Seligenstadt, adopted the Roman plan of an apsidal basilica with continuous transept.) Not surprisingly the designers of cathedral and monastery churches in the same period laid out buildings that were on a far grander scale than anything hitherto known north of the Alps. When the arch-chaplain and arch bishop Hildebold began the reconstruction of the cathedral of Cologne shortly before or shortly after Charles' death, he adopted a plan that seems to have had features in common with both the St. Denis/St. Maurice type and with the new ' Roman ' plan—an east apse and square choir preceded by a short projecting transept probably but not certainly of the ' continuous ' plan and a larger western apse with annular crypt; but it had the staggering length of one hundred metres, approximately that of the papal church of St. John Lateran and exceeded in the west only by the great basilicas of St. Peter's and St. Paul's.

The desire in educated circles to possess or re-create the artistic monuments of a Christian Roman past—which Charles' coronation did not create but certainly greatly stimulated and extended—is clearly reflected in several striking and justly-famous manuscripts of the opening decades of the ninth century. Except for Terence, none of the great Classical poets or prose-writers had been transmitted in texts accompanied by illustrations that provided models for Carolingian artists (pl. 64). A number of collections of astronomical and chronological works, however, have illustrations of the Heavens, the zodiacal signs, constellations (pls. 50, 54, 55) and of other themes such as the Cardinal Virtues and Labours of the Months (pls. 36, 58) that in many cases are obviously very accurate copies of fourth to sixth century originals; and from a variety of Antique models other more enterprising artists occasionally succeeded in creating a style of book-illustration that was at once Classicizing and original, exemplified most beautifully in the slightly later ' Utrecht Psalter ' from Rheims (pl. 62). Some of the rediscovered Antique themes were transferred to the walls and furnishings of secular as well as ecclesiastical buildings. The residential quarters of the *villa* of Germigny apparently had frescoes representing the Seven Liberal Arts and the Four Seasons as well as a map of the world. A miniature triumphal arch in silver, given by Einhard to the monastery of St. Servais at Maastricht of which he was lay abbot and perhaps made by him—as a young man at court he had a reputation as a worker in precious metals—as a stand for a cross, showed Christ and the Apostles and the Evangelists on the upper two rows of decoration but figures from Antiquity, warriors and two horsed (?) Emperors, below. The treasures of the palace at Aachen at Charles' death included three silver tables bearing designs that had evidently been adapted from manuscript illustrations. The more elaborate of two round ones had three concentric circles containing tiny figures to represent the Universe, very much as in the two Salzburg book-illustrations shown in plate 50 and figure 47; the second represented Rome, presumably along the lines of the schematic circular maps that are thought to have accompanied some manuscripts of the ' pilgrims' guides' to the city that circulated at this time. The third table was a square one showing a map of Constantinople.

77. Reliquary of Charles' arm, showing Louis the Pious in Imperial insignia, *Paris, Louvre.*

78. Reliquary from Enger (Germany); *Staatliche Museen, Berlin;* end eighth century. *Size at base* 16 × 14.5 cm.

*A Frankish Emperor
and his Empire.
The End of the Reign*

The unmistakeable symbolism of these last objects, in the context of a court that had been transformed from a Frankish royal to a western Imperial one, needs no emphasizing. They may be compared with Charles' taking the supposed statue of Theodoric the Ostrogoth from Ravenna to set up outside his palace at Aachen in 801; and with—if a recent ingenious suggestion is correct—the creation of a truly Imperial throne in the octagon gallery there by covering the existing wooden royal throne with slabs of Italian marble. Even though, to an extent that is difficult to appreciate today, visual symbols of power and dignity directly reinforced attempts to give effect to assertions of authority, they could not themselves provide the content of that authority or enforce it in ordinary practical terms; but their presence in the palace was a constant reminder of the greater responsibilities that the Frankish monarch had accepted at his coronation. The task of translating idea into action still remained.

Arriving back at Aachen in the summer of 801 Charles remained there until after Easter 803, except for hunting-trips to the Vosges and the Ardennes in the second half of 802. It was at Aachen therefore that the magnates of the Empire assembled in March 802 to hear the Emperor's word. According to the well-informed ' Annals of Lorsch ', the Emperor was disturbed at the situation of the *pauperes* of his dominions who could not get the justice that was due to them. The action that he took is briefly described by the annalist in a passage that has no parallel elsewhere in the annalistic records of the reign and is illustrated in considerable detail in a remarkable group of capitularies that were promulgated on this occasion. The Empire was divided into *missatica* to each of which was sent as *missi* a highly-placed ecclesiastic and a layman whose word would carry greater weight than the vassals who had been *missi* on previous occasions, even if this meant that a count exercised the higher authority in the area of his own comital jurisdiction: thus a large area of northern France centring on Paris was entrusted to abbot Fardulf of St. Denis and count Stephen of Paris. Each of them may have had a written list of the extensive range of matters into which they were to inquire; but their instructions and the spirit that dominated the Aachen assembly can only be understood in the light of another text—already quoted in the Introduction—that covers the same matters in considerably greater detail and often expresses itself in an unusual way. This more elaborate document promulgated in the Aachen assembly is in effect a programme of Imperial rule rather than a set of instructions to Imperial officials. And at times the austere formal wording of the normal capitulary takes on a new emotional tone with strongly worded comments or injunctions in the first person, which suggests that here, uniquely, we have the record of additions made at Charles' insistence to a text drawn up by members of his court and in his view insufficiently forceful or categoric.

As Charles was now Emperor, a new oath of fidelity was required from his subjects: but the notion of fidelity was here defined in detail to show the positive obligations of all men towards the person and property of the Emperor, the church and those weaker than themselves; and the oath itself was re-phrased to give it a more clearly religious character. This was the counterpart to the Emperor's recognition of his own enhanced obligations before God. In practical terms this meant, in the first place, enforcing more strictly the rules governing the life of canons, monks and parish clergy and still further strengthening the powers of those who held the highest offices in the this-worldly hierarchy of the church. In the second place, there was a greater insistence on the strict enforcement of the established laws, in accordance with their accepted written versions and not in the

*A Frankish Emperor
and his Empire.
The End of the Reign*

arbitrary interpretation of the judges, and, accompanying this, the application in some instances of more severe punishments and the reservation of certain types of case to a court held in the Imperial presence. But the *missi* were not only to act on their specific instructions to punish wrong-doing, eliminate abuse and do justice to all men in the spirit of the new Imperial commands: they were also to expound the new programme to the Emperor's subjects.

When the lay and ecclesiastical magnates assembled again at Aachen in the

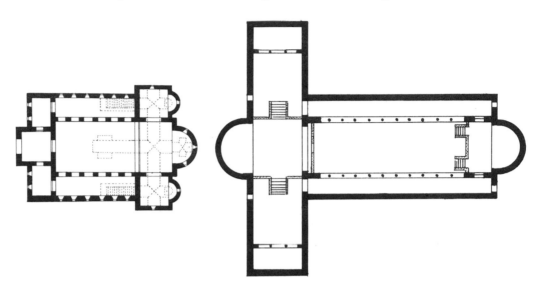

Fig. 49 Ground plan of St. Michael's Church, Steinbach in Odenwald (after Edgar Lehman).

Fig. 50 Ground plan of the Abbey Church at Fulda (after Edgar Lehman).

autumn of 802 the injunctions and undertakings put before them were clearly determined in large measure by the reports brought back by the *missi*. One problem in particular had clearly emerged—the deficiencies and uncertainties of the written law. Existing codes of 'tribal' or 'national' law were accordingly corrected and supplemented and subsequently circulated in the amended versions and one or two others were written down for the first time. Perhaps at the same time professional judgement-finders were established at Aachen—comparable to others who seem to have existed earlier at Pavia—as permanent members of the palace tribunal. All this was something more than the re-assertion in firmer language of an old-established royal authority; and it suggests that the sixty-year-old Emperor still possessed abundant vigour and had lost nothing of the gift demonstrated in earlier years of tackling a new or more difficult situation with new and bolder ideas. Violence, usurpation, neglect of churches and all the other problems dealt with in 802 or 789 or 779 are a recurrent theme of the unusually numerous instructions to *missi* that survive from the last eleven years of Charles' reign. Some scholars, in understandable reaction against the notion that the Emperor left behind him a realm in which all was orderly and peaceful and justice everywhere prevailed which his successor then allowed utterly to be destroyed, have concluded that after 802 Charles suffered a check which was a prelude to the beginnings of political disintegration in his own lifetime. It is legitimate to ask whether the existence of these instructions, and the regular activity of *missi* which they presuppose, is not good evidence that the ultimately insoluble problems of medieval society were being tackled with at least as much vigour as—and conceivably with no less effect than—earlier in the reign.

More difficult to determine is the significance of the surprisingly frequent references to the difficulties of the ' free poor ' and the pressures to which they were subject. It is possible to regard these as no more than specific examples of the deeper responsibilities that in Charles' view followed from his God-given Imperial authority. It has been suggested, however, that he was trying to check the process by which the ordinary free peasant, a man with a piece of land by which he and his family were maintained and for which he owed neither rents nor services, a man moreover who still had his place in the Imperial host, was becoming the servile tenant of a man who lived by the labours of others. If this is true it suggests a remarkable percipience on the part of the monarch or of some anonymous adviser and it implies also the favouring of a policy that would probably have made more difficult the maintenance of public order and the exercise of Imperial authority. Attractive although the notion is, it is better to remain sceptical.

There is even less warrant for the theory that attributes to Charles in his last years as king and in his thirteen years as Emperor an ' economic policy ' directed at the encouragement of agricultural production and of trade. It was entirely natural for an energetic monarch and other great landlords to wish to draw the maximum benefit from the lands whose cultivators they controlled; and some of their stewards and agents may well have looked for new ways of increasing crop-yields. It is certainly striking that the new Germanic names for the months that Charles sought to introduce suggest that important changes were taking place in the cycle of the agrarian year in parts of his Empire: the Salzburg ' Labours of the Months ' (pl. 58) already seem to reflect northern modification of a Mediterranean cycle. It is quite another matter to conclude from this and from the supposedly supporting evidence of the capitulary *De villis* that agriculture and the new agrarian cycle ' loomed large in Charles' thinking ' (L. T. White), and that he can claim some personal credit for the widespread adoption of a three-field instead of a two-field rotation of crops, especially in villages between the Loire and the Rhine but also elsewhere in his Empire. Similarly, there is ample evidence (ample, that is, in relation to the total body of documentation for the period) of the activity of merchants, of the buying and selling of a variety of commodities and of the readiness of the Emperor to take financial and other advantage of this activity. In the late eighth and early ninth century the products of Rhineland potteries of a non-luxury type were exported to England and elsewhere in northern Europe; so apparently were querns (mill-stones) quarried in the Moselle region. Frankish glass, also produced near the middle Rhine, was evidently in demand in southern Scandinavia and the Baltic in the period before the great Viking raids. The port of Quentovic was a flourishing centre of cross-Channel and coastal trade, which was reflected in the high standing of the resident representative of the Imperial authority. In 805 a capitulary listed the points along the eastern frontier—among them Magdeburg, mentioned for the first time—at which alone merchants should cross into Slav or Avar territory; and it also prohibited trade in weapons and breast-plates. Trade along the Po, particularly of salt, increased sufficiently in the first half of the ninth century for men of Cremona to acquire their own boats for the purpose. If these isolated facts are taken as evidence that the Carolingian Empire before the Viking invasions enjoyed a degree of prosperity unknown earlier, then this is better regarded as a not unimportant but certainly indirect result of the relative peace and order that Charles had imposed, of the degree of political unity

79. The candelabra in the Octagon, Aachen Cathedral, put up by Frederick I on the occasion of the canonization of Charles.

80

81

A Frankish Emperor
and his Empire.
The End of the Reign

he had created and of the friendly relations he had established with other powers, rather than the product of a carefully thought-out *dirigiste* policy.

The record of the Emperor Charles' contacts with his neighbours, whether peaceful or warlike, does not entirely justify the view of his last years as ones of comparative failure—any more than does the record of his administrative measures. Apart from the completion of the overthrow of the Avars, which should not be dismissed as unimportant, organized wars of conquest were certainly a thing of the past; and local campaigns or raids, whether against Danes or Slavs or Beneventans or the subjects of the Emperor in the east, were as likely to end in defeat as success— they always are. But the record is not one of consistent failure. Pressure was steadily kept up in the area beyond the river Saale that subsequently became the Sorbian Mark and in the second half of 805 a Frankish army even penetrated Bohemia. In 806, the Emperor's eldest son Charles led one of two armies that simultaneously attacked across the Elbe-Saale frontier: and later in the year Pippin sent a fleet against the Saracens who were once again active in the western Mediterranean, while king Louis received the submission of territories at the western end of the ' Spanish March '. The complex of post-Saxon forts along the north-eastern frontier belongs in part to this period and seems to have been designed with an offensive as much as a defensive purpose. Further north, king Godfred of southern Denmark was so worried by the continuing threat to his southern, Saxon, frontier that in 808 he initiated what was, except for Offa's Dyke, the most massive of all the defensive earthworks built in the eighth or early ninth century, the so-called ' Danework ' extending across the peninsula from the Schlei to the Eider; and when he learnt that the Emperor had taken exception to his attack on the Abodrite Slavs which had resulted in the destruction of the Baltic port of Reric, he readily opened negotiations in 809. In 810, however, a Danish fleet made a devastating attack on Frisia. Charles was sufficiently disturbed to issue a general summons to the host and himself to travel to Saxony with his court—including the elephant Abul Abaz who died there—and, although he was forestalled by the murder of the Danish king, while he was waiting there Wilzite Slavs crossed the Elbe and captured the march-count of the east Saxon frontier. A year later, however, representatives of the new Danish king agreed to peace terms with his representatives; armies were sent against the Wilzites into the unconquered parts of Pannonia and into Brittany; and new and enterprising measures were taken to secure the North Sea and Channel coasts against further attacks, including bringing the Roman lighthouse at Boulogne back into use. Moreover, throughout these years a steady pressure was maintained, mostly by armies from north Italy working in conjunction with the church of Aquileia (whose patriarch was in fact resident in the comital or ducal town of Cividale), on the Slovenes and Croats who lived between the river Drau and the Adriatic coast; and in spite of the failure of the Emperor to secure more than the temporary allegiance of Byzantine Dalmatia (below), when he died the Frankish Empire and its church were the dominating political and cultural influences in an area which Constantinople had long regarded as falling within its own sphere of influence.

Even in his relations with the Imperial court at Constantinople and with the territories in the west that were gradually emancipating themselves from Greek rule, Charles by 812 could boast of more success than failure. If a contemporary Byzantine chronicler was correct in his assertion that in 801 the recently widowed Frankish monarch sought the hand of the Empress Irene, then we must admit that a few months after his coronation Charles was not entirely free of ' universalist '

80. ' The "A" of Charlemagne ';
St. Foi, Conques. Height 43 cm.
Length 40 cm.

81. Charles' shrine, Aachen; completed in 1215.

*A Frankish Emperor
and his Empire.
The End of the Reign*

ambitions. But this extraordinary marriage proposal was never raised again. When a Greek legate arrived at Aachen early in 802 it was ' for the establishing of peace ', and the Frankish legates sent to Constantinople in return had a similar commission. There were indeed ample causes of tension between the two powers, independently of the coronation, in the several areas where they shared a frontier. By the time the legates reached Constantinople, Irene had been overthrown and it was from the new emperor Nicephorus that a further legation arrived, at a court that had abandoned Aachen because of earthquakes, with a projected treaty in writing. These negotiations, too, were taken no further. By 804 a ' palace revolution ' among the ruling class of the communities from which Venice was to grow—arising from family rivalries which are as obscure as the similar ones in Rome—had brought pro-Frankish elements to power; and a year later the duke (Doge) seems to have persuaded the *archon* of Byzantine Dalmatia and the city officials of this fragmented coastal province to transfer their allegiance to the Emperor in the west. For about twelve months in 805-6, Charles' Empire stretched from Schleswig nearly to Durazzo.

Nicephorus, however, was a ruler who had already realised the importance of an effective fleet if the Empire based on Constantinople was to survive and before the end of 806 Venetia and Dalmatia had been persuaded to revert to their original sovereign: but in the long run Dalmatia's Latin culture and ecclesiastical links with Rome were more effective than fleets in determining its political allegiances. In 809 an East Roman fleet again appeared in the northern Adriatic and attacked Comacchio in the Po delta—at this time the main supplier of salt to north Italy and today one of the few places where medieval techniques of sea salt production can still be studied—although unsuccessfully. A year later king Pippin of Italy had his revenge on the treacherous Venetians: he occupied the narrow strip of mainland vital to the islanders—as we learn later—for the grazing of horses and pigs and as the source of wood for building houses and ships, and then moved his troops over to the islands. The use by the Franks of a fleet for both local transport and for a demonstration against Dalmatia is a further reminder that the common picture of Frankish neglect of shipping and coastal defence is not borne out by the evidence of Charles' later years.

When Pippin died in July 810, Venetia was once again a part of the Western Empire. By this time the Byzantine court was evidently ready for a definite settlement even if it meant a major concession on the subject of Charles' usurpation of the Imperial dignity. Although the exchange of written texts (felt to be necessary to secure a *foedus firmissimum*) of the treaty agreed between the two Emperors was not completed until after Charles' death, final settlement had effectively been reached in ceremonies at Aachen in April 812. The draft treaty that was handed over to the Greek legates in the palace chapel evidently abandoned Frankish claims to Venetia and Dalmatia in return for which the Greeks seem to have recognized Frankish supremacy over the Croats. Clauses that defined the rights of traders, and others that laid down the rights of the Venetian island communities on parts of the *terra firma* became, it has been plausibly suggested, the basis of the Western Imperial treaties with Venice in and after 840—which, if correct, gives the reconstructed earlier treaty a surprisingly modern flavour. The legates of the Byzantine Emperor concluded proceedings by chanting in Greek the *laudes* or acclamations used on great ceremonial court occasions: the Frankish monarch was hailed by men from Constantinople as ' *imperator* and *basileus* '. It does not matter if, as is likely, the legates and those who had instructed them thought of the western Emperor as one

*A Frankish Emperor
and his Empire.
The End of the Reign*

who was thereby admitted to the dignity of ' brother of the Emperor ' rather than one who now shared his office as an equal, nor that the concession was personal to Charles—although in fact the *Basileus* in the east subsequently added the qualification ' of the Romans ' to his own title. The heirs of Augustus and Constantine had acknowledged that the barbarian who, forty-three years previously had inherited a modest-sized kingdom that nowhere approached the Mediterranean, was worthy of the highest secular dignity that existed under God.

Charles, too, had at first regarded the Imperial dignity as something personal to himself; and when, at the beginning of 806, he began to make arrangements for the disposition of the Empire after his death, his main concern was to obviate conflicts between the three lawful claimants to the succession, which he not unreasonably feared. At Aachen in February 806 he revealed his plans to an assembly of magnates, shortly before he dispatched his eldest son on an expedition against the Sorbs and sent his other sons back to the kingdoms for whose order and security they were responsible. Pippin was to receive Bavaria and the newly conquered territories to the east of it, part of Swabia and Rhaetia as well as his Italian kingdom; Louis was to have substantial parts of southern Gaul as far as the Alps added to his existing kingdom of Aquitaine; Charles was to receive the rest. The three kings were not to interfere in each other's kingdom nor to allow hostages or exiles held in their territory to return home without the appropriate ruler's consent. Free men who had acknowledged them or anyone else as their ' lord ' were not to abandon their superior in his life-time but might choose whom they would at his death. Provision was made for the settlement of boundary disputes by due process of law. All three kings were severally responsible for the churches and their property within their respective kingdoms and jointly for the protection and support of the see of St. Peter. Peace and a fraternal spirit were to prevail everywhere. Clearly, older Frankish notions that treated a kingdom as a patrimony to be divided between all surviving sons had not been ousted by the development of a newer concept of *imperium*. But we should not therefore assume that this had no place in Charles' ideas. As the prologue of the ' Division ' makes clear, all three sons were to succeed as equals and the unity was to be that of the Trinity, not that of the Godhead. The Imperial dignity and title, however, was to die with Charles.

In 810 king Pippin died suddenly while Charles was in Saxony. Provision had been made for such a contingency in the official text of the *Divisio:* the other two brothers were each to receive a part of the dead man's share with the proviso that a son might be chosen by the subjects of his father's former kingdom to rule in that territory as a subordinate king. Pippin had certainly left at least one son but he was probably still a minor and Charles sent his relative, abbot Adalhard of Corbie, to act as a viceroy or regent in Italy; subsequently in 812 he also sent the abbot's brother, count Wala, to take charge of the defence of the kingdom against Saracen attack. At the beginning of December 811, however, the young Charles too had died. The arrangements proposed in 806 could no longer be put into effect.

No contemporary source throws any satisfactory light on who counselled Charles at this time or by what steps he arrived at the decision to pass on the Imperial dignity to his one surviving son. Probably this is not very important. The artistic evidence suggests that the magic of the Imperial idea had not lost its power either at court or among the great ecclesiastics since 800; and it must surely have been strengthened by the ceremonies that took place at Aachen in 812. Charles for his part was increasingly concerned with the problems of the church over which it was his duty, he said, to watch ' with his whole mind '; and it may be

Fig. 51 Charlemagne presents relics to Aachen. Scene from the ' Charlemagne ' window in Chartres Cathedral.

Fig. 52 Charlemagne gives orders to soldiers who build a church. Chartres Cathedral.

A Frankish Emperor
and his Empire.
The End of the Reign

that he had come to see a direct link between making this responsibility effective and the Imperial dignity. Some months before his eldest son's death he had arranged for the distribution of the treasures and silver, including the decorated tables, among the twenty-one metropolitan churches that now existed in his empire and also of his other possessions to other beneficiaries as alms for the good of his soul. At the March assembly of 813, church councils were ordered to be held in five metropolitan cities. The records of their proceedings, which provide a link between Charles' reign and the great series of 'reform councils' that took place in Francia in the time of his son, were brought to the palace in September when Charles summoned to his capital 'the whole army, the bishops, dukes, counts and their deputies'. The main purpose of this gathering is vividly described by Louis' biographer Thegan. The Emperor had been compelled to abandon a hunting expedition because of illness: now accordingly he exhorted the gathering 'to show fidelity to his son and asked them all, from the greatest to the least, whether it pleased them that he should pass on his Imperial name to his son Louis; they all replied with enthusiasm that it was God's suggestion. On the next Sunday after this [11th September 813] Charles put on the royal garb and a crown on his head; then he entered the [Palace Chapel] on the altar of which he had placed a crown of gold, different from the one he wore'; after Louis had promised to serve his subjects well, 'his father ordered him to take in his own hands the crown that lay on the altar and to put it on his head to remind him of all that his father had exhorted him to do: this he did; they heard mass together and went into the palace'. New circumstances had demanded new measures. Charles had transmitted the Imperial title to his son at Aachen without the intervention of the Pope.

When father and son parted for the last time 'they embraced and kissed each other and out of joy for their love began to weep'. Charles himself was reputed to have spent his remaining months in prayer and alms-giving and 'correcting books', including the texts of the Gospels from Greek and Syriac. Einhard preferred to believe that he had again gone hunting. On 21st January 814 he had an attack of fever when he emerged from the warm springs where he regularly bathed. Seven days later, having received communion at the hands of his arch-chaplain, he died. On the same day he was buried at Aachen in the chapel. Over his tomb was placed a portrait and an inscription with the words: 'Beneath this tomb lies the body of Charles, the great and orthodox Emperor, who nobly increased the kingdom of the Franks and reigned prosperously for forty-seven years. He died in his seventies in the year of the Lord 814 in the seventh indiction, on the fifth of the Kalends of February'.

82. Reliquary 'of Pippin' from Conques; c. 1000 but crucifix is of ?early ninth century. *Height* 185 cm. *Length* 186 cm.

83. The so-called horn of Roland (Auch) from Toulouse (France).

82

83

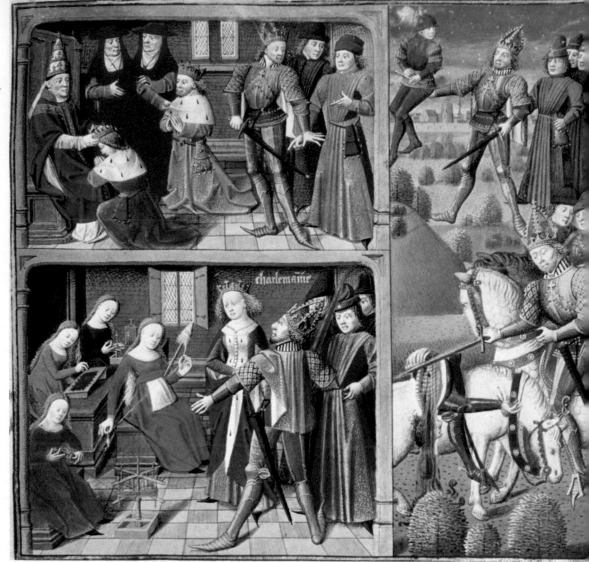

84

85

Epilogue.
The heritage of Charlemagne:
legend and reality

Some time during the reign of the Emperor Louis—known to posterity as ' the Pious '—a monk of Bobbio, where Irish traditions died hard, wrote a Lament for the dead Charles. *A solis ortu usque ad occidua Littora maris planctus pulsat pectora; Heu mihi misero* ' From the rising of the sun to the shores of the sea where the sun sets breasts are beaten in lamentation; Woe is me ', he began. ' Franks, Romans and all Christian folk are plunged into mourning and overwhelmed with sorrow '; ' he was the common father of all orphans, pilgrims, widows and virgins '; ' Francia which has suffered such dread misfortunes, has never borne a sorrow so great as when it committed the august eloquent Charles to earth at Aachen '; ' receive the pious Charles, O Christ, into thy holy seat with thine apostles '. The idea of a Carolingian Golden Age was already formed.

When Einhard wrote his ' Life of Charles ' against whom his successors were being measured and found wanting, this age seemed long past. The quarrels within the Carolingian family had taken a serious turn; the Frankish episcopacy no longer met under the leadership and guidance of the monarch but had achieved independence of action and coherence in opposition to him; magnate families had identified their local and personal rivalries with the cause of one or other claimant to Imperial or royal dignity. The Emperor was failing to display either the *prudentia* or the *virtus* of his father; *inconstantia* had succeeded to *constantia* and *infidelitas* was taking the place of *fidelitas*. A few years later Nithard, the son of Angilbert and Bertha, recorded the tragic history of the quarrels between Louis' three sons that culminated in the terrible ' judgement of God ' at the battle of Fontenoy (841). In 843 the once-united Empire was partitioned—irrevocably if not with finality (the struggle over the allegiance of the lands from the Ardennes to the Vosges seems only now to be ending): the re-unification under the west Frankish Charles ' the Bald ', shortly before his abdication and death in 887/8, was as short-lived as it was unreal.

The legend of Charlemagne and the idea of Empire long outlived the reality and took possession of their ghosts. Charles' contacts with Jerusalem and the Caliph of Baghdad were transformed into a journey in person to receive the surrender of the Holy Places. The disaster of Roncesvalles became a noble moment in a series of wars against the Infidels in Spain. ' Rise up and remember the manly deeds of your ancestors, the prowess and greatness of Charlemagne ' declaimed Pope Urban at Clermont in 1095 when he called on men to liberate the Holy Land from its defilers; and about the same time the portrait of the patriarchal Emperor who was the doughty champion of Christendom received its canonical form in the *Chanson de Roland*. Churches on the pilgrim routes to Spain that were ' remembered ' as those once taken by Charles' armies were proud to display treasures which were believed to have been given them by the Emperor or a member of his family, like the ' *Chasse* of Pippin ' (pl. 82) which is partly Carolingian in date or the strange reliquary known as ' the "A" of Charlemagne ' which is two centuries younger (pl. 80.) In the next generation a place was found in southern French churches for

84. Charles and his warriors, from the *Miroir Historial; Musée Condé, Chantilly.*

85. Scenes from the life of Charles in the *Chroniques de St. Denis; Bibliothèque Sainte Geneviève.*

relics of Roland and his companions who died at Roncesvalles (pl. 83); and in the twelfth and thirteenth centuries the widely disseminated literary legend provided those responsible for the decoration of churches with a rich and novel source of visual imagery (figs. 51, 52). The new public for literature in the vernacular was supplied with innumerable accounts of the 'Doings' of the great Emperor. Most of them are tedious today: but they inspired many polished or lively examples of manuscript art in the fourteenth and fifteenth centuries (pls. 84 and 85) as wealthy laymen too came to regard books as part of the essential furniture of living.

There was a constant interaction between Charlemagne as the universal hero, the monarch who became one of the Nine Worthies along with Abraham and Caesar, and the efforts of particular places and dynasties to claim him for themselves. Each shift of the political spectrum, each adjustment of the mechanism of secular and ecclesiastical government produced its crop of expanded chronicles and falsified or forged diplomas. To the noble and royal dynasties that emerged out of the wreck of the Carolingian Empire there was eventually, however, no finer asset than a lineage that began with the Carolingians themselves. When the Capetians replaced the descendants of Charles on the west Frankish throne in 987, the new king and his supporters and successors insisted that they were merely continuing or renewing the work that had been left undone at his death. It was none the less as much by accident as by design that nearly all the early Capetian kings took wives who had some Carolingian in their ancestry. But by the twelfth century, when—whatever Holinshead and Shakespeare may have believed—women were held capable of transmitting kingdoms, this could be turned into a positive political asset. Both Louis VII and his queen Adela had more than one Carolingian ancestor: when, therefore, their son Philip succeeded in 1180 it was a *reditus regni Francorum ad stirpem Karoli.*

Philip's biographer dubbed him *Augustus.* Another century was to elapse before the courtiers of a French king were to declare him 'Emperor in his own kingdom'. The Imperial dignity was still felt to be superior to that of ordinary kingship and unique: and its possession was for many centuries, like Aachen itself, a priceless asset of the rulers of the eastern or German half of the Frankish Empire. Otto III, grandson of the monarch of Saxon lineage who had revived the Imperial office in the west in 962, demonstrated the source and bias of his own universalist ideas by his actions in the year 1000: returning from Gnesen, where he had tried to create a satellite kingdom of Poland, he proceeded to Aachen to what was believed—probably justifiably, in spite of the uncertainty introduced by Viking destruction in the late ninth century—to be the tomb of the great Frankish Emperor Charles. The ghostly figure of Charles loomed large in the propaganda war over the respective rights of lay rulers and the head of the church in the later eleventh and early twelfth century. When the Emperor Frederick I renewed the struggle later in the century, it was as another Charlemagne—perhaps for the first time the analogy was made specific—destined to triumph over the enemies of the Empire. It was because it seemed to be a symbolic weapon of unique power that at Aachen on 29th December 1165 Frederick and his ecclesiastical supporters proceeded to the proclamation of a new saint, St. Charles.

To justify the cult an appropriate new 'Life of Charles' was prepared. From it were taken the scenes which, with the figures of those who had received Imperial coronation at Aachen, formed the decoration of the splendid reliquary that was to provide a worthy setting for the bones of one in whom the this-worldly and other-worldly heroic virtues were uniquely combined (pl. 81): in July 1215, following his

Fig. 53 Early sixteenth-century representation of Charles the Great made as part of the preliminary work for the Emperor Maximilian's tomb at Innsbruck; pen and wash, by ?J. Kölderer. *Innsbruck, Sammlungen Schloss-Ambras.*

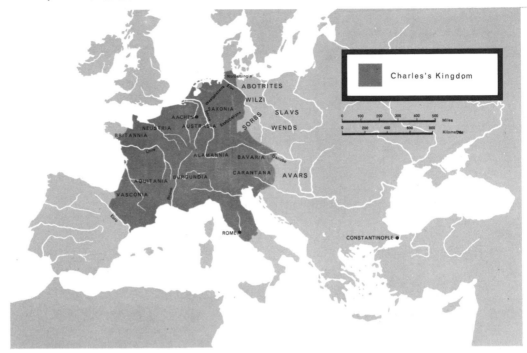

own coronation, the first Frederick's grandson, another Frederick, fittingly completed the process that his grandfather had begun by personally knocking in the last nails that closed the shrine. Yet it proved to be a gesture of honour to a figure of the past rather than a gesture of political significance for the present and the future. Charles the warrior, Charles the leader of European chivalry (pl. 84), even Charles the lawgiver (pl. 87) was taking over from Charles the German Emperor. When, in the early sixteenth century, the Emperor Maximilian I planned an elaborate funerary monument to himself in the Court chapel at Innsbruck, Charlemagne (fig. 53) stood not among his forebears and ancestors but with Arthur and the other Worthies. Charlemagne as the pattern of supreme political authority, as the apostle of universal dominion, was only to re-emerge in another and radically-transformed Europe.

Was it then Charles' greatest achievement to leave a legend and were the accomplishments of his life-time brought to naught in the unhappy years that followed his death? By no means. Many of the churches that were being built in the early years of the Emperor Louis, although on the grander scale that the activities of his father had encouraged, were in a style that could legitimately be called old-fashioned (cf. pl. 72): in many areas the new architectural ideas established themselves only slowly. At the same time, there was a steady evolution of the decorative details used in buildings of every variety of plan and elevation, and minor as well as major buildings displayed a confidence and technical competence that would have been unthinkable only a few decades earlier (pls. 45, 73). The earliest illustrated Tours Bible and the gold altar of Milan were produced in the very years in which the political troubles of the Empire were at their worst. The middle decades of the century likewise saw some of the most outstanding intellectual and literary achievements that we think of as characteristically Carolingian—and rightly so, because their ultimate inspiration and the resources they exploit stem from the activities of Charles' own life-time. The bishops who opposed, criticized and ultimately also supported Charles' son and grandsons did so in the light of the broader vision, stricter organization and higher standards that his reign had revealed or created.

The impact of the methods and measures of Charles' reign on the rest of the ninth century and beyond are no less evident in the history of secular institutions and of monarchy itself. Itinerant *missi* did not cease to function in 814; the most elaborate set of regulations for the royal control of coinage belongs to the later years of the reign of the Emperor's youngest grandson; the use of a body of men to declare on oath what they knew about a matter in dispute, of which the first tentative beginnings are to be seen in the last years of the eighth century, was enormously extended in the half-century after Charles' death. Even when effective authority shifted away from the person and court of the king or Emperor to local magnates acting without serious restraint, the scope and nature of this authority and the techniques they used to impose it bore the stamp of the changes that had taken place between 768 and 814. The magnate class of western Europe in 850 was not just a mirror-image of its predecessor in 750: and if, as is probably true, one effect of Charles' methods of government had ultimately been to strengthen magnate dominance over other elements in the society of the day, powers had been placed in the hands of monarchs that no subsequent weakness could finally destroy. Not least important, the visual symbols of royal and Imperial authority had been permanently enriched by Charles' endeavours, just as new levels of skill had been reached in giving them material form. Soon no court in western Europe, even when beyond the limits of Carolingian military success, was complete without its palace buildings, ornamental throne and royal insignia and no public occasion possible without its appropriate ceremonial display that corresponded to a functional need. And no ruler who combined energy, a sense of purpose and a measure of luck could fail to draw advantage from these precious assets.

What was the relation of the person of Charles to all this? We do no service either to the man or to the understanding of history by weaving from the legends of the past another legend more appropriate to our own time, nor by creating the image of a super-human being, civilized, far-sighted, in control of his own destinies and of the humblest of his subjects. The harshness and uncertainty of life were not suspended for half a century nor the insuperable problems of communication and the chain of command overcome. For all but a few of the ordinary people in the Frankish kingdom and Empire the period of Charles' rule probably seemed much like any other. The recently reported words of Chinese peasant farmers asked about the dramatic events of the past fifty-five years in their country could surely be put with only slight alteration and without incongruity into the mouths of ninth-century European peasants: ' I have no idea when the dynasty went [a reference to 1911]; we never noticed anything in our village of these revolutions '; ' various armies were fighting each other, bringing misfortune over the land; and landlords plundered and hit and swore and took people for forced labour, and one army was worse than the next; that was all we farmers knew '. In some areas the worst disorders and violence were temporarily checked—thus far the legend may be accepted. Some communities clearly felt the impact of agricultural innovation. Few men, however, can have appreciated the changes that were taking place in the languages they spoke although, where the educational reforms made themselves felt on the ordinary clergy, their parishioners must have been very conscious that the words of the liturgy had become even less intelligible to them.

Charles was a man recognizably of his own period, trained in a hard school; a

man of passions, lustful, crucl, ready in his earlier years to exploit any situation that seemed to offer a potential advantage, observant of the externals of the Christian religion but hardly concerned with its deeper implications. What set him apart from other men and other rulers were his extraordinary vigour, both physical and mental; an ability to respond to checks and disasters by even more vigorous efforts and the devising of new measures to overcome recurrent problems; a notable curiosity and a readiness to learn; a perception, however vague, that the human spirit could aspire to something more than carnal pleasure and the thrill of fear; an ability to recognize the latent gifts of others; above all, the quality of impressing them with the strength of his own personality and inspiring them to rise to unanticipated heights. An apparently sudden rise to new levels of human achievement in war or in government, in art or in literature is usually in fact the culmination of a period in which ideas and skills have been slowly maturing: but the quickening of pace, the change from tentativeness to confidence, the acceptance by many of standards that have hitherto seemed beyond the reach even of a few demand the catalytic effect of an event or of a person. It is because he acted as this catalyst that we can properly talk of ' the Age ' of Charlemagne. The greatest of its achievements and the noblest of its aspirations, created and proclaimed in a far harsher environment than that of Europe today, still speak to us across more than eleven centuries. For this reason, if for no other, it is an age worth studying.

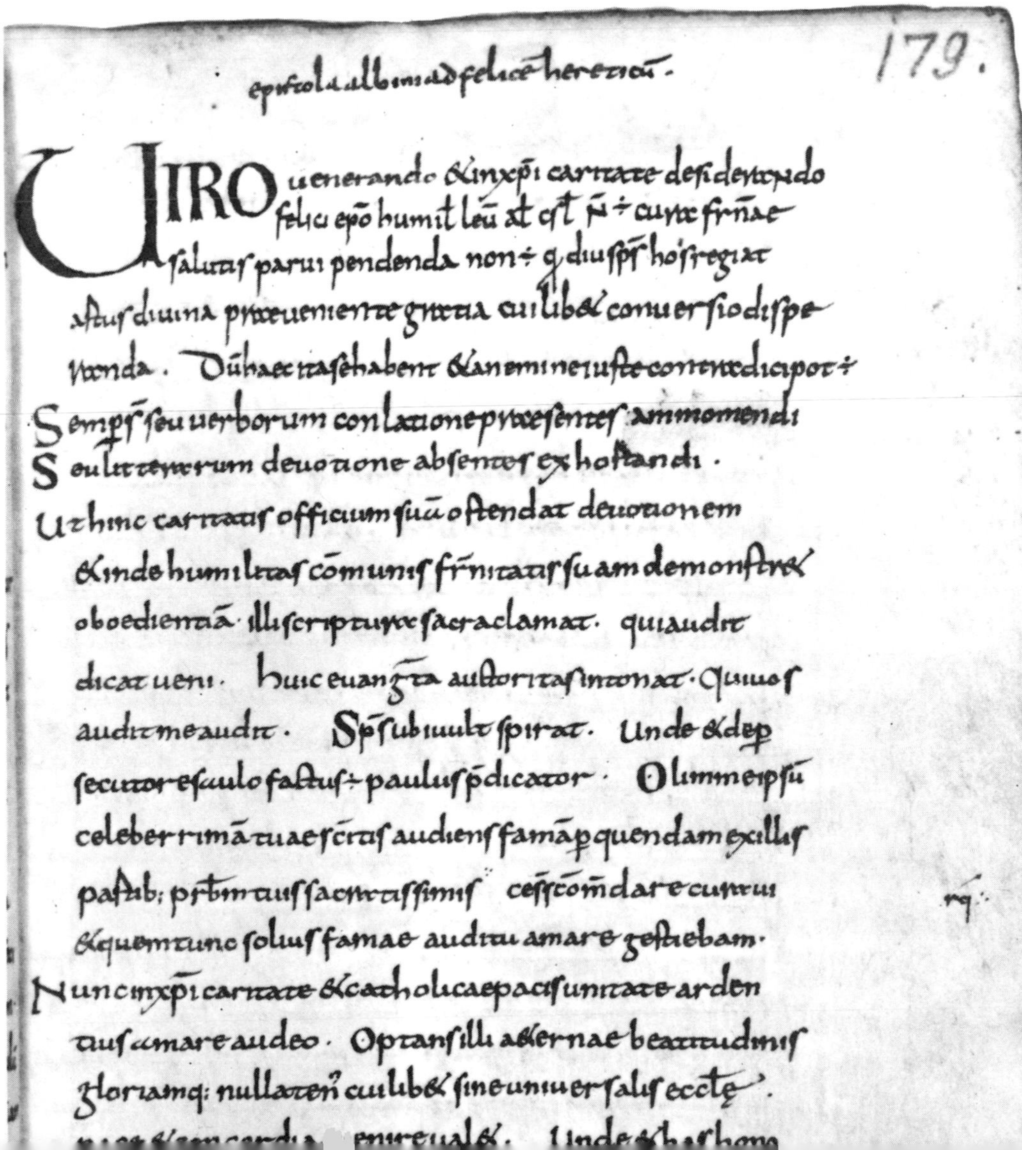

Fig. 54   Part of a page of the earliest manuscript of Alcuin's letters, written by Salzburg clergy, 798/9; *Vienna, Österreichische Nationalbibliothek* Cod 795 fol 179. (*Actual size.*)

87. Detail of the head of Charles from *Retable du Parliament de Paris.*

Bibliography and Notes

General and Introductory

For the European setting of Charles life and reign see F. Lot, C. Pfister, F. L. Ganshof, *Les Destinées de l'Empire en Occident de 395 à 888* (2 vols., Paris, 1940); M. Deanesly, *A History of Early Medieval Europe, 476-911* (London, 1956). The fullest account of the reign is still S. Abel and B. Simson, *Jahrbücher des fränkischen Reiches unter Karl dem Grossen* (2nd ed., 2 vols., Leipzig, 1883-88): their chronology and references are partly corrected and supplemented by J. F. Böhmer and E. Mühlbacher, *Regesten des Kaiserreichs unter den Karolingern* (2nd ed., Innsbruck, 1908) and—for the Saxon wars—by L. Halphen, *Études critiques sur l'histoire de Charlemagne* (Paris, 1921). The most helpful modern accounts are A. Kleincausz, *Charlemagne* (Paris, 1934) and L. Halphen, *Charlemagne et l'Empire Carolingien* (Paris, 1947), 57 ff. H. Fichtenau, *The Carolingian Empire* (Oxford, 1957) is an 'interpretation' of the reign. The non-documentary sources for the reign are surveyed and critically examined in Wattenbach-Levison, *Deutschlands Geschichtsquellen im Mittelalter: Vorzeit u. Karolinger*, ii (b, W. Levison and H. Löwe), iii (by H. Löwe), *Beiheft* (by R. Büchner) (Weimar, 1953-7); for the capitularies see also F. L. Ganshof, *Recherches sur les Capitulaires* (Paris, 1958), *Was waren die Kapitularien?* (Weimar, 1961).

The institutional and legal history of the period are comprehensively surveyed in H. Brunner, *Deutsche Rechtsgeschichte*, ii, ed. C. von Schwerin (Munich-Leipzig, 1928); a comprehensive and critical bibliography has been prepared by F. L. Ganshof and R. C. van Caenegem for the *Introduction bibliographique à l'histoire du droit et à l'ethnologie juridique*, ed. J. Gilissen (Brussels, 1964). The standard account of the literary history of the period is M. Manitius, *Geschichte der lateinischen Literatur des Mittelalters*, i (Munich, 1911); an excellent survey in English is M. L. W. Laistner, *Thought and Letters in Western Europe, 500-900* (2nd ed., London, 1957), 189 ff. All extant pre-800 manuscripts are catalogued, with facsimiles the size of the original, in E. A. Lowe, *Codices Latini Antiquiores* (Oxford, 1934 ff.) (*CLA*). A good concise account of Carolingian art and architecture is J. Beckwith, *Early Medieval Art* (London, 1964), 11 ff.

The history of the church in this period is admirably surveyed in H. Jedin (ed.), *Handbook of Church History*, iii/1, by F. Kempf, H.-G. Beck, E. Ewig, J. A. Jungmann (London, 1969). For the Eastern Empire (Byzantium) see G. Ostrogorsky, *A History of the Byzantine State*, transl. J. Hussey (London, 1956).

Most of the main sources for the reign have been published in one of the several series of the *Monumenta Germaniae Historica* (MGH): (diplomas) *Diplomatum Karolinorum*, i (Hannover, 1906) (*DK*); (capitularies) *Capitularia Francorum*, i (Hannover, 1883) (MGH *Cap*); (letters) *Epistolarum*, iii [*Codex Carolinus*, etc.], iv [Alcuin, etc.], v [Einhard] (Hannover, 1892-98) (MGH *Epist*); (poetry) *Poetarum*, i, ii (Berlin, 1881-4) (MGH *Poet*); (church councils) *Concilia*, ii (Hannover-Leipzig, 1906) (MGH *Conc*).

Nearly all the narrative sources have been published in the folio-series of *Scriptores* (MGH SS). The most important have been re-edited for the *Scriptores rerum Germanicarum*: e.g. *Annales regni Francorum* and their revision, ed. F. Kurze (Hannover, 1895) (*Ann. reg.*; *Ann. reg. (rev.)*); *Annales Bertiniani*, ed. G. Waitz (Hannover-Leipzig, 1883) (*Ann. Bert.*); *Notkeri Gesta Karoli Magni Imperatoris*, ed. H. F. Haefele (Berlin, 1959) (Notker). The best editions of Einhard, *Vita Karoli* (*Vita Kar.*) and of Nithard, *Historiarum Libri IIII* (Nithard) are respectively by L. Halphen (Paris, 1947) and P. Lauer (Paris, 1926) [with French translations]. The best editions of the *Vitae* of Louis the Pious (Astron, *Vita*; Thegan, *Vita*) are in *Quellen zur karolingischen Reichsgeschichte*, i, ed. R. Rau (Berlin, 1955), 213 ff. [with German translation].

The *Liber Pontificalis* was magnificently edited and annotated by L. Duchesne (2 vols., Paris, 1886-92; re-issued with a supplementary volume, 1955-57).

There is no comprehensive edition of the *notitiae iudicati*, except for Italy: C. Manaresi, *I Placiti del ' Regnum Italiae '*, i (Rome, 1955). The most important collections of private charters are: *Urkundenbuch der Abtei Sanct Gallen*, i, ed. H. Wartmann (Zürich, 1863); *Codex Laureshamensis*, ed. K. Glöckner (3 vols., Darmstadt, 1929); *Memorie e Documenti per servire all'istoria . . . di Lucca*, iv, v, ed. D. Barsocchini (Lucca, 1818-41).

Many substantial contributions to the history and art-history of the period, henceforward indispensable to any serious study of it, will be found in *Karl der Grosse: Lebenswerk und Nachleben*, ed. W. Braunfels et al. (4 vols. and index-volume; Düsseldorf, 1965-7) (*Karl der Grosse* in subsequent references). I have attempted to evaluate some of these contributions and other recent publications on the period in *Engl. Hist. Rev.*, lxxxv (1970), 59-105.

Chapter I

Imperial ceremonial: Constantine Porphyrogenitus, *De ceremoniis*, ed. and transl. A. Vogt (Paris, 1949 et seq.), the quotation from the Preface (1). Vendetta: J. M. Wallace-Hadrill, *The Long-haired Kings* (London, 1962), 121-47. Forests: Eigil, *Vita Sturmi* c. 8, MGH SS. ii, 369; Richer, *Historia*, ed. and transl. R. Latouche, iv, 50. Germanic terminology for king and lord: D. H. Green, *The Carolingian Lord* (Cambridge, 1965), esp. 500 ff. Merovingian kingship: Wallace-Hadrill, cit., 163 ff. Alien origin of ' independent ' dukes: S. Hellmann in *Festgabe für K. Th. Heigel* (Munich, 1903); E. Zöllner in *Mitt. des Instituts für Österr. Geschichtsforschung.* lix (1951), 245 ff. Internal colonisation: C. Verlinden, *Les origines de la frontière linguistique en Belgique* (Brussels, 1955), 112-29; A. Bergengruen, *Adel u. Grundherrschaft im Merowingerreich* (Wiesbaden, 1958), 104-40. Charles ' Martel ': see esp. the *Continuatio Fredegarii* in Wallace-Hadrill (ed.), *The Fourth Book of the Chronicle of Fredegar* (London-Edinburgh, 1960), 87-97. Bede: *Historia Ecclesiastica* v, 23, ed. Plummer (Oxford, 1896), i, 349; *contra*, D. H. Wright in *Anglia* lxxxii (1964), 114. Poitiers: *cont. Fred.* c. 13 (90-1); *cont. Isidorii Hispanica* cc. 104-6, MGH. *Auct. antiquiss.* xi (Mommsen), 361-2. Echternach: C. Wampach, *Gesch. der Grundherrschaft Echternach*, i/2 (Luxemburg, 1930), n. 27. Missionaries: W. Levison, *England and the Continent in the Eighth Century*, (Oxford, 1946), chs. 3, 4; T. Schieffer, *Winfrid-Bonifatius u. die christl. Grundlagen Europas* (Freiburg, 1954). Thuringia: E. Lehmann, *Der frühe Deutsche Kirchenbau*, i (Berlin, 1949), 129; cf. Wampach, nn. 7, 26. Synods: MGH *Concilia* ii, nn. 1, 2, 6; T. Schieffer, *Angelsachsen u. Franken* (Mainz, 1951), 1446-71 [dating the first two councils 743 and 744]. Attacks on images: E. Caspar in *Zeitschr. f. Kirchengesch.* lii (1933), 29 ff.; G. B. Ladner in *Medieval Studies*, ii (1940), 127 ff.; Ostrogorsky, *Byzantine State*, 142 ff. Papal reply and Pippin's consecration: *Ann reg.* s.a. 749 (from an unknown source), 750; *cont. Fred.* c. 33 (102); cf. *De civ. Dei* xix, 13 and H. Büttner in *Das Königtum* (*Vorträge* v. Forschungen), iii; Lindau, 1956), 155 ff. Madonna (now kept in the Lateran *Sancta Sanctorum*): *Lib. Pontif.* i, 443; C. Cecchelli in *Dedalo*, vii/2 (1926/7), 295 ff.: recent restoration has confirmed that it is VI/VII cent. Papal journey: *Lib. Pont.* i, 446 ff.; *Cod. Carol.* no. 7 (ed. cit., 491); *Ann. Mettenses priores* s.a. 753, ed. Simson (Hannover, 1905), 45. Donation: (convenient text) C. Mirbt, *Quellen zur Gesch. des Papsttums* (Tübingen, 1924); (transl.) N. F. Cantor, *The Medieval World* (New York, 1963), 126-33; (interpretation) W. Ullmann, *The Growth of Papal Government* (London, 1955), 57 ff. *Vassus* and *beneficium*: F. L. Ganshof in *Études dédiées à la mémoire de H. Pirenne* (Brussels, 1937), 173-89; ibid., *Feudalism* (London, 1952), pt. 1. ' Discovery ' of stirrup: L. T. White, *Medieval Technology and Social Change* (Oxford, 1962) ch. 1; and the criticisms and new material provided by Bullough in *Engl. Hist. Rev.*, lxxxv, 85-90 and by B. S. Bachrach in *Studies in Medieval and Renaissance History*, vii (1970), 49-75. Raadanite Jews: R. S. Lopez, I. W. Raymond, *Medieval Trade in the Mediterranean World* (Oxford, 1955), 31-33. Legations and movement of ecclesiastics: F. L. Ganshof in *Annali di Storia del Diritto*, v/vi (1964), 1 ff.; D. A. Bullough in *Deutsches Archiv*, xviii (1962), 223-30. Liturgy: G. Tellenbach, *Römischer u. Christlicher Reichsgedanke in der Liturgie* (Heidelberg, 1934). *Lex Salica*: *Lex Salica* ed. Eckhardt, 3 vols. (Weimar, 1953-56), i, 82 ff.

Chapter II

Pippin's burial: *Oeuvres complètes de Suger* ed. Lecoy de la Marche (Paris, 1867), 187. Charles' mother: *Annales Bertiniani* ed. Waitz (Hannover, 1883), 1; DK. no. 16 of 762. Stars: MGH *Epist*. iv 238 ff., 250 ff. Münster statue: C. Beutler, *Bildwerke zwischen Antike u. Mittelalter* (Düsseldorf, 1964), 117 ff. Papal protest, 770: *Cod. Carol.* no. 45 (ed. cit., 561). Hildegard: *Vita Karol.* c. 18; Thegan c. 2. Uncle: Rotbert, see *UB St. Gallen*, i, no. 57. Herstal and Jupille: J. Brassine in *Bull. Soc. Art et Hist. dioc. de Liège*, xii (1900), 270 ff. Buraburg and roads: R. v. Uslar, *Stud. z. frühgesch. Befestigungen* (Cologne-Graz, 1960), 38 ff.; W. Görich in *Gesch. Atlas v. Hessen* (Marburg, 1960 ff.), 7. Irminsûl: H. Löwe in *Deutsches Archiv*, v (1941), 1-22. Hadrian's reply: *Lib. Pont.*, i, 487 f. Chiusa wall: *Monumenta Novaliciensia* ii, ed. C. Cipolla (Rome, 1901), 175 and n. Lombard hostages: *Cod. Carol.* no. 50 (569 f.); *Mem. e Doc. di Lucca*, v/2 (Lucca, 1837), no. 189; DK no. 208. Cathwulf: MGH *Epist* iv, 502 ff. Breton march: M. Lipp, *Das Fränkische Grenzsystem* (Breslau, 1892), 11 ff. Hohensyburg: v. Uslar, 34 ff. Baptismal vow: W. Braune, K. Helm, *Althochdeutsche Lesebuch* (Halle, 1949), no. 3. Fulda as mission-centre: *Vita Sturmi*, cc. 22 ff., MGH SS ii, 376-7; *contra*, Halphen, *Études critiques*, 212 ff. Saxon society: G. Baaken in *Vorträge u. Forschungen*, vi (Konstanz-Stuttgart, 1961), 35 ff. Spanish campaign and the 'Chanson': R. Menéndez Pidal, *La Chanson de Roland et la tradition épique des Francs* (1960); Engl. transls. of the 'Chanson' by C. S. Scott-Moncrieff (1919) and Dorothy Sayers (1957). Rebellion of 778: *Ann. reg.* and *Ann. reg. (rev.)* s.a.; *Vita Sturmi* c.23 (SS ii, 376). Private armies, etc.: MGH *Cap* i, no. 20. Thanksgiving in 785: *Cod. Carol.* no. 76 (*Epist.*, iii, 607). Gerona: *Chron. Moissacense*, SS i, 297. Privileges of *Gothia*: DK no. 217; *Cap* i, no. 132; R. d'Abadal in *Rev. Historique*, ccxxv (1961), 320 ff. Benevento expedition: R. Poupardin in *Le Moyen Age*, 1906, 256 ff. Recognition by Grimoald: Erchempert c. 4, MGH *SS rer. Lang.*, 236; W. Wroth, [Brit. Mus.] *Catalogue of the coins of the ... Lombards* (London, 1911), 170 f. Perils of Italy: *Epist* iv, 367 f., 418 f. Tassilo's Bavaria: articles by E. Zöllner and F. Prinz in K. Bosl (ed.), *Zur Gesch. der Bayern* (Darmstadt, 1965); H. Fichtenau in *Mitt. Inst. Österr. Geschichtsforsch.*, lxxi (1963), 1 ff.; for Arbeo see also W. Levison in Wattenbach-Levison, *Deutschlands Geschichtsquellen*, i (Weimar, 1952), 144 ff. Avars: G. László in *Archeologica Hungarica*, n.s. xxxiv (1955); Zöllner in *Mitt. Inst. Österr. Gesch.*, lviii (1950), 244 ff. Bavarian march and its commander: E. Klebel in *Wege der Forsch.*, i: *Die Entstehung des deutschen Reiches* (Darmstadt, 1956), 56 ff.; M. Mitterauer, *Karolingische Markgrafen im Südosten* (*Archiv f. österreichische Gesche.*, 123; Vienna, 1963), 1-25. Canal: *Ann. reg.* s.a. 793; H. H. Hofmann in *Karl der Grosse*, i, 437 ff. Aachen: *ad palatium quod Aquis vocatur, Ann. reg.* s.a. 794, cf. *in Aquis villa*, ibid., s.a. 765, etc.; (springs and Roman remains) H. Christ in *Germania*, xxxvi (1958), 119 ff.; W. Kämmerer in *Karl der Grosse*, i, 322 ff.

Chapter III

Charles's administrative methods and reforms: F. L. Ganshof, *Frankish Institutions under Charlemagne* (Providence, R.I., 1968): Aquitaine: Astron. *Vita Hlud.* c. 3; Ganshof in *Mélanges Ch. Gilliard* (Lausanne, 1944), 133 ff. Pavia: D. A. Bullough in *Engl. Hist. Rev.*, lxxvii (1962), 627 ff. Royal domain: W. Metz, *Das Karolingische Reichsgut* (Berlin, 1960). Coinage: P. Grierson in *Karl der Grosse*, i, 501 ff. *Palatia*: Metz, 119 ff.; [Max-Planck Inst. f. Gesch.] *Deutsche Königspfalzen*, i (Göttingen, 1963); (Frankfort) *Germania*, xxxiii (1955), 391 ff. *Comitatus* for 'court': *Vita Karoli* c. 14; Notker I 5, etc. Eating and drinking: *Vita* c. 24; *Poet.* i, 246; *Epist.* iv, 183. *Participes*: Nithard, I 2. Proceedings before the king: E. Kaufman, *Aequitatis iudicium* (Frankfort, 1959). *Vassi*: C. Odegaard, *Vassi and Fideles in the Carolingian Empire* (Cambridge, Mass., 1945); Bullough in *Le Moyen Age*, lxvii (1961), 221 ff. Wibod: *Poet.* i, 487 ff. Einhard: ibid., i, 245, 248, 487. *Capella*: J. Fleckenstein, *Die Hofkapelle der deutschen Könige*, i (Stuttgart, 1959). Arch-chaplains at court: MGH *Conc.* ii, no. 19 c. 55. Transport of produce: MGH *Epist* v, 111, 113. Purchase of land by vassal: *Mem. e Doc. di Lucca* v/2, nos. 344, 347, 355. Nature and extent of counties: Metz, 162 ff.; M. Chaume, *Les Origines du duché de Bourgogne*, ii/3 (Dijon, 1931); Bullough in *Papers of the Brit. Sch. at Rome*, xxiii (1955), 148 ff. Count William: J. Calmette in *Ann. du Midi*, xviii (1906), 145 ff. Comital families generally: for a rather different view from that stated in the text, see G. Tellenbach (ed.), *Stud. u. Vorarb. zur Gesch. des grossfränkischen u. frühdeutschen Adels* (Freiburg i. Br., 1957). *Scabini*: R. H. Bautier in *École des Chartes. Positions des thèses, 1943*, 9 ff.; Ganshof, *Frankish Institutions*, 77-83. Alcuin: MGH *Epist*. iv, 411. Theodulf: MGH *Poet*, i,

495 ff.; G. Monod in *Rev. Hist*, xxv (1887), 1 ff. *Missi*: Bautier, 17 f. Immunities: Ganshof in *Les Liens de Vassalité* (*Soc. J. Bodin*; ed. 2, Brussels, 1958), 171 ff. *Admonitio generalis*: MGH *Cap* i, no. 22. Parish priests: *Cap* i, no. 36 c. 14, no. 81 cc. 5, 12. Tithes: G. Constable, *Monastic Tithes* (Cambridge, 1964), 24 ff. Pavia bishopric: Bullough in *Engl. Hist. Rev.* lxxvii, 626 ff. Letter to Leo III: MGH *Epist* iv, 137 ff. Saxon capitularies: MGH *Cap*, i, nos. 26 (785), 27 (797); cf. Halphen in *Études critiques*, 171 ff. Alcuin: MGH *Epist* iv, 153 ff., 156 ff. Rebels' oaths: *Ann. Nazariani* s.a. 786, MGH SS i, 42. General oaths of fidelity: MGH *Cap* i, nos. 23, 25; Ganshof in *Mélanges Louis Halphen* (Paris, 1951), 259 ff. Intercession and penitence: MGH *Cap*, i, no. 21; Ganshof in *Misc. L. van der Essen*, i (Brussels, 1947), 123 ff. Frankfort: MGH *Conc*, ii, no. 19; Ganshof in *Misc. Historica A. de Meyer*, i (Louvain, 1946), 306 ff.

Chapter IV

Godescalc lectionary: Paris B.N. nouv. acq. 1203; *CLA* vi, 681. Dagulf psalter: Vienna Nat. bibl. lat. 1861; *CLA* x, 1504. Grammatical collection: Brussels, Bib. roy. 11-2572; *CLA* x, 1553. Verses and catalogue: Berlin Staatsbibl. Diez B. 66; *CLA* viii, 1044. Corbie and St. Amand minuscules: Lowe, *CLA* vi, xxiii f.; x, xii ff. Bavaria, glossary: H. Löwe in *Mainzer Abhandlungen, Geistes- u. Sozialwiss. Kl.*, 1951, 909 ff.; J. K. Bostock, *Old High German Literature* (Oxford, 1955), 82 ff. Paulinus: *DK* no. 112. Notker: *Gesta*, I, 1. Abbot Adam: Wattenbach-Levison, ii, 194. Alcuin: E. S. Duckett, *Alcuin, Friend of Charlemagne* (N.Y., 1951); L. Wallach, *Alcuin and Charlemagne* (Cornell U.P., 1959); (prophecy) MGH *Epist* iv, 332. Paul: Wattenbach-Levison, ii, 203 ff.; (petition) *Gedichte des Paulus Diac.* ed. K. Neff (Munich, 1908) no. 18. Cadac: B. Bischoff in *Hist. Jahrb*, lxxiv (1955), 72 ff. Notker's letter: *Formelbuch des Bischofs Salomo*, ed. Dümmler (1857), 72. Alcuin's riddles: Duckett, 115 ff. Porfyrius: D. Schaller in *Medium Aevum Vivum: Festschr. f. W. Bulst* (Heidelberg, 1960), 22 ff. *Hadrianum*, etc.: C. Vogel in *Le Chiese nei regni dell'Europa occidentale* (*Centro di Studi sull'Alto Medioevo*; Spoleto, 1960), i, 275 ff. *Dionysio-Hadrianum*: Büchner in Wattenbach-Levison, iv. 69. Text of Benedictine Rule: St. Gall cod. 914; J. McCann, *St. Benedict* (N.Y., 1958), 91 ff.; P. Meyvaert in *Scriptorium*, xvii (1963), 83 ff. *Libri Carolini*: ed. H. Bastgen, MGH *Conc.* ii/Suppl. (1924); (authorship) Ann Freeman in *Speculum*, xl, 203 ff. Papal letter to Spanish bishops: *Codex Carolinus* no. 95. Creed: Wallach, 154 f. Alcuin's marginalia: Bischoff in *Medievalia et Humanistica*, xiv (1962), 34 ff. Mandate on education: Wallach, 198 ff. Vernacular religious texts: Bostock, chs. 6-9. Month- and wind-names: *Vita Kar*. c. 29; and note that none of these has survived in mod. standard German, although dialects preserve (or preserved) some of them. Songs and Louis: Thegan, *Vita*, c. 19. Hinield: MGH *Epist*. iv, 183. Lay of Hildebrand: convenient text with transl. in *Penguin Book of German Verse* ed. L. Forster (1957). *Orationale* at Verona: bibl. capit. LXXXIX; *CLA* iv, 515. Egino Homiliary: Berlin Staatsbibl. Phillips 1676; *CLA* viii, 1057. 'Rule': (Verona-Swabia) St. Gall 110; *CLA* vii 907; (Freising) Munich Clm. 6330; (Reichenau) St. Gall 916; (Verona) Verona LII; *CLA* iv 505. Tours manual at Verona: Munich clm. 6407; *CLA* ix, 1242. Salzburg mss.: Lowe, *CLA* x, viii ff. *De cursu*: Vienna Nat. bibl. Ser. N. 37; *CLA* x, 1510. St. Martin's, Tours: Bischoff in *Med. et Hum.*, xiv, 31 ff.; E. K. Rand, *A Survey of the manuscripts of Tours* (Cambridge, Mass., 1929). Bible: F. L. Ganshof in *Bibl. d'Hum. et Renaiss*, ix (1947), 7 ff.; B. Fischer in *Karl der Grosse*, ii, 156-216. *Codex Millenarius*: W. Neumüller and K. Holter, *Der Cod. Mill.* (Linz, 1959). Chelles: Bischoff in *Forsch. zur Kunstgesch*, iii (Wiesbaden, 1957), 395 ff. Commentary: Vienna Nat. bibl. Lat. 743; *CLA* x, 1488. Dedication verses: MGH *Poet*. i, 89 f. For the whole chapter see B. Bischoff in *Karl der Grosse*, ii, 42 ff., 233 f.

Chapter V

Gregory's letter: *Libri Carolini*, ed. cit., 82. Antique illustration: K. Weitzmann, *Ancient Book Illumination* (Cambridge, Mass., 1959); F. Wormald, *The Utrecht Psalter* (Utrecht, 1953). Autun: ms. Bib. Mun. 3; F. van der Meer, *Maiestas Domini* (Vatican City, 1938), 321 ff. Curly columns: E. Rosenbaum in *Journ. Warburg and Courtauld Insts*, xviii (1955), 1 ff. Tassilo chalice: G. Haseloff, *Der Tassilo-Kelch* (Munich, 1951). 'Court' artists: F. Mütherich in *Karl der Grosse*, iii, 1 ff. Fountain of Life: P. Underwood in *Dumbarton Oaks Papers*, v (1950), 43 ff. St. Peter's:

J. M. C. Toynbee and J. B. Ward Perkins, *The Shrine of St. Peter and the Vatican Excavations* (London, 1956), 195 ff. St. Denis: S. McK. Crosby, *L'Abbaye royale de St. Denis* (Paris, 1953), 12. Beauvais: K. J. Conant, *Carolingian and Romanesque Architecture* (London, 1959), 17 f. 'Box' churches: R. Krautheimer in *Art Bulletin*, xxiv (1942), 4 f.; articles by E. Poeschel and L. Birchler in *Akten zum III Internationale Kongress f. Frühmittelalterlicheforsch.* (Olten-Lausanne, 1954), 119 ff and 167 ff. Brescia: G. Panazza in *Atti del 8° Congresso di studi sull'arte dell'Altomedioevo* (Milan, 1962), ii, 9 ff. Benevento: H. Belting in *Dumbarton Oak Papers*, xvi (1962), 175 ff. St. Denis: Crosby, 10, 13 f., 68-9; *DK* no. 92. Agaune: L. Blondel in *Akten z. III Int. Kongr*, 271 ff. Centula: W. Effmann, *Centula-St. Riquier* (Münster, 1912); I. Achter in *Zeitschr. f. Kunstgesch*, xix (1956), 133 f. East-Frankish churches: W. Boeckelmann in *Wallraf-Richartz-Jahrb*, xviii (1956), 27 ff. Münster: Birchler in *Akten* cit., 167 ff. S. Maria in Cosmedin: Krautheimer, *Corpus Basilicarum Romanarum*, ii/3 (Vatican, 1962), 277 ff. S. Anastasia: Krautheimer in *Art Bulletin*, xxiv, 16 f. Aachen: H. Beenken in *Jahrb. des Rhein. Vereins f. Denkmalpflege*, 1951, 67 ff.; W. Boeckelmann in *Wallraf-Richartz Jahrb.*, xix (1957), 9 ff.; articles by Bandmann, Kreusch and Hugot in *Karl der Grosse*, iii. Mosaic: *contra*, H. Schnitzler in *Aachener Kunstblätter*, xxix (1964), 1 ff. Talisman: *Les Trésors des Eglises de France* [exhib. cat.] (Paris, 1965), no. 131. St. Riquier: *Hariulf—chronique de St. Riquier*, ed. F. Lot (Paris, 1894), 66 ff., 87 ff. Volvinio altar: V. H. Elbern in *Relationes: Festschr. Mgr. H. Krey* (Milan, 1961), 1 ff. Stuccoes: *Atti del 8° Congresso*, cit., i, passim. Egino homiliary: E. Arslan, *La pittura e la scultura veronese* (Milan, 1943), 27 ff.; *contra*, H. Belting in *Frühmittelalterliche Studien*, i (1967), 125 ff. Kells: A. M. Friend in *Medieval Studies in memory of A. K. Porter* (1939), ii, 611 ff.; P. McGurk in *Scriptorium*, ix (1955), 105 ff. 'Palace school' mss.: Mütherich, cit., 45 ff.

Chapter VI

Poems: MGH *Poet*, i, 396 ff.; 366 ff.; H. Beumann in *Erste Jahrtausend*, i, 296 ff. Letter of Alchred: *Bonifatii et Lulli Epist.* ed. M. Tangl (Berlin, 1916), no. 121. Coins: C. E. Blunt in *Anglo-Saxon Coins*, ed. R. H. M. Dolley (London, 1961), 39 ff. Constantine Porph.: *De Administrando imperii* c. 13; ed. G. Moravscik (Budapest, 1949), 71. Rotrud: in the 'minor' annals s.a. 781, MGH SS, xvi, 497 (rev.), s.a. 788; *Vita Kar.* c. 19; *Ann. reg.* (*rev.*), s.a. 788; and in the Greek chronicle of Theophanes. Charles at Frankfort: Wallach, *Alcuin and Charlemagne*, 147 ff. Alcuin and *imperium*: F. L. Ganshof, *The Imperial Coronation of Charlemagne* (Glasgow, 1949), esp. 13 f., 22 f.; W. Ullmann, *The Growth of Papal Government* (London, 1955), 103 ff. Alcuin's 'Dialogue on Rhetoric': Wallach, 29 ff. *Chrysotriklinos*: H. Fichtenau in *Mitt. Inst. Österr. Gesch. forsch*, lix (1951), 1 ff. Annals of Lorsch: (text) MGH SS, i, 38 f.; (ms.) Vienna Nat. bibl. Lat. 515; *CLA* x, 1482; (Ricbod) Fichtenau in *Mitt.*, lxi (1953), 287 ff. Charles' authority in papal patrimony: P. E. Schramm, *Die Anerkennung Karls des Grossen* (Munich, 1952), 8 ff.—with a different interpretation. Events in Rome: *Liber Pontificalis*, ii, 4 ff. Paderborn meeting: above, under 'Poems'. Protection of coast: *Ann. reg.* s.a. 800. Supposed conversations with Alcuin: P. Munz, *The Origin of the Carolingian Empire* (Leicester, 1960), 24. 'Trial' of Leo III: *Lib. Pont*, ii, 7; Wallach in *Harvard Theol. Review*, xlix (1956), 123 ff. Coronation: texts collected and translated in, e.g., R. E. Sullivan, *The Coronation of Charlemagne: what did it signify?* (Boston, 1959), 2 f. and R. Folz, *Le Couronnement impérial de Charlemagne* (Paris, 1964), 273 ff. [*Crimen*] *maiestatis*: F. S. Lear, *Treason in Roman and Germanic Law* (Austin, Texas, 1965).

Chapter VII

'Two-Emperor problem': W. Ohnsorge, *Das Zweikaiserproblem im früh. Mittelalter* (Hildesheim, 1947). Lorsch gateway: Krautheimer in *Art Bulletin*, xxiv, 32 ff.; H. Walbe and W. Meyer-Barkhausen, *Die Torhalle in Lorsch* (Heppenheim, 1953). Sturmi's church: Boeckelmann in *Wallraf-Richartz-Jahrb*, xviii, 42 ff. Petition of 812: *Corpus Consuetudinum Monasticarum*, ed. K. Hallinger (Siegburg, 1963), 324. Ratger's church: *Vita Eigili* cc. 14 f., MGH SS, XV/I, 229 f.; Krautheimer, *Art Bulletin*, xxiv, 8 ff. St. Michael's, Fulda:(symbolism) *Vita Eigili* cc. 17 f. (230 f.). Germigny: Letaldi *Mirac. S. Maximini* in Mabillon, *Acta Sanctorum O.S.B.* i, 601; (architecture) J. Hubert in *Congrès Archéologique*, xciii (1930), 534 ff.; (mosaic) A. Grabar in *Cahiers Arch.*, vii (1954), 171 ff. Steinbach: O. Müller, *Die Einhartsbasilika zu Steinbach* (Seligenstadt, 1937). Cologne: O. Doppelfeld in *Kölner Domblatt* 8/9 (1954), 33 ff. but see W. Weyres in *Karl der Grosse*, iii, 384 ff. and *Burlington Mag.*, cviii (1966), 324. Germigny frescoes: MGH *Poet*, i, 544 ff. St. Servais arch: B. de Montesquiou-Fezensac in *Cah. Arch.*, viii (1955), 147 ff. Tables: *Vita Karoli* c. 33; F. N. Estey in *Speculum*, xviii (1943), 112 ff. in 'Renovatio Imperii' (Faenza, 1963), 63 ff. Autumn assembly: *Capit* i, nos. 36, 37; Ganshof, art. cit., 91 ff. Aachen judgement-finders: Bautier, 17. 'Décomposition': Ganshof in *Zeitschr. f. Schweiz. Gesch.*, xxviii (1948), 433 ff. Freemen: E. Müller-Mertens, *Karl der Grosse, Ludwig der Fromme u. die Freien* (Berlin, 1963). Economic change: W. Metz in *Karl der Grosse*, i, 489 ff.; White, *Technology and Social Change*, 69 ff. Glass: H. Arbmann, *Schweden u. das Karol. Reich* (Stockholm, 1937), 26 ff. Frontier trading-points: MGH *Capit*, i, no. 44 c. 7. Forts: P. Grimm, *Burgwälle der Bezirke Halle u. Magdeburg* (Berlin, 1958), 47 ff. and fig. 15. 'Danework': J. Brøndsted, *The Vikings* (London, 1965), 166 ff. Negotiations with Byzantium: Ohnsorge, 25 ff. Venice: H. Kretschmayr, *Gesch. v. Venedig*, i (Gotha, 1905), 53 ff. Comacchio: *Ann. reg.* s.a. 809; (salt) L. M. Hartmann, *Zur Wirtschaftsgesch. Italiens* (Gotha, 1904), 72 ff., 123 f.; M. Merores in *Vierteljahrschr. f. Sozial- u. Wirtschaftsgesch*, xiii (1916), 71 ff. Treaties: R. Cessi, *Le Origini del ducato Veneziano* (Naples, 1952), 175 ff. *Divisio* of 806; *Ann reg.* s.a.; MGH *Capit*, i, no. 45; *contra*, H. Beumann in *Hist. Zeitschr.* clxxxv (1958), 540 ff. Testament: *Vita Kar.* c. 33. Louis' designation and coronation: Thegan, c. 6. Charles' last months: Thegan, c. 7; *Vita Karoli*, c. 30. Epitaph: ibid., c. 31.

Epilogue

Lament: text and transl. in *The Penguin Book of Latin Verse*, ed. F. Brittain (London, 1962), 148 ff.; authorship (?Cadac-Andreas): Bischoff in *Hist. Jahrb*, lxxiv, 97 f. *Iudicium Dei*: Nithard, II 10. Journey to Jerusalem: J. Coulet, *Étude sur le voyage de Charlemagne en Orient* (Paris, 1907). Conques treasures: *Trésors* catalogue, nos. 537, 541. Charles and French monarchy: Folz, *Couronnement impérial*, 243 ff. Charles and Germany: Folz, *Le Souvenir et la Légende de Charlemagne* (Publs. de l'Univ. de Dijon; Paris, 1950). Coinage: MGH *Capit*, ii, no. 273, cc. 8-24. *Inquisitio*: R. C. van Caenegem, *Royal Writs in England* (London, 1959), 51 ff. Chinese peasants: J. Myrdal, *Report from a Chinese Village* (London, 1965).

Index

(abb. *abbot;* archd. *archdeacon;* bp. *bishop;* ct. *count;* d. *daughter;*
dk. *duke;* dy. *duchy;* emp. *emperor;* k. *king;* q. *queen;* s. *son;* sis. *sister*)

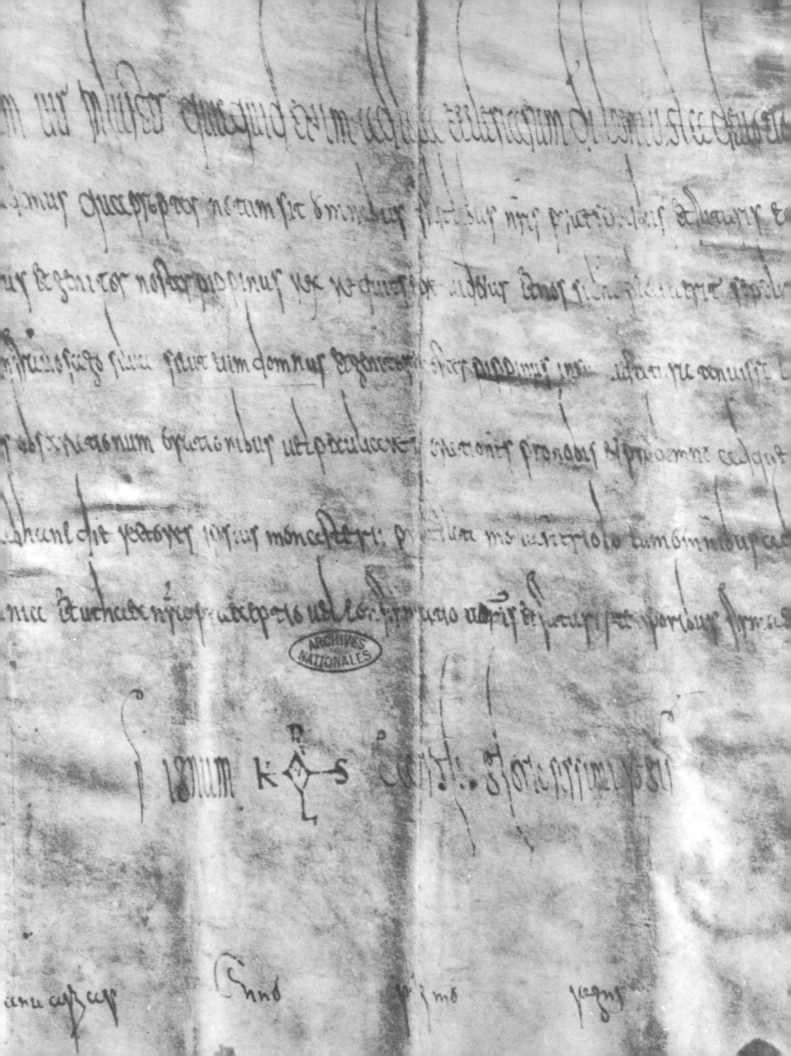